Law and the Media

The Future of an Uneasy Relationship

The College of Law
of England and Wales

LIBRARY & INFORMATION SERVICES

This .... ginal
case .... rplay
betw .... that
peop .... This
prom .... yday.
It arg .... o the
medi .... ks to
make .... ndly,
claim .... ends
in au .... well as .... The
book .... isers.
This .... legal
self-l .... stitu-
tions .... xam-
ines .... l in a
furth .... vhich
judg ....

Dr I .... main
resea .... nt of
med .... as a
form

Birmingham • Chester • Guildford • London • York

Law and the Media

The Future of an Uneasy Relationship

Lieve Gies

Routledge·Cavendish
Taylor & Francis Group
a GlassHouse book

First published 2008
by Routledge-Cavendish
2 Park Square, Milton Park, Abingdon, Oxon OX14 4RN

Simultaneously published in the USA and Canada
by Routledge-Cavendish
270 Madison Ave, New York, NY 10016

A GlassHouse book
Routledge-Cavendish is an imprint of the Taylor & Francis Group, an Informa business

Typeset in Times by
RefineCatch Limited, Bungay, Suffolk
Printed and bound in Great Britain by
Antony Rowe, Chippenham, Wiltshire

British Library Cataloguing in Publication Data
A catalogue record for this book is available from the British Library

Library of Congress Cataloging-in-Publication Data
Gies, Lieve.
Law and the media: the future of an uneasy relationship / Lieve Gies.
        p.   cm.
Includes bibliographical references and index.
ISBN-13: 978-1-84568-101-2 (hbk)
ISBN-10: 1-84568-101-0 (hbk)
ISBN-13: 978-1-904385-33-2 (pbk)
ISBN-10: 1-904385-33-8 (pbk)
    1. Justice, Administration of—Great Britain.   2. Mass media and criminal justice—Great
Britain.   3. Legal aid—Great Britain—Automation.   4. Newspaper court reporting—
Netherlands.   5. Justice, Administration of—Netherlands.   I. Title.
KJC3655.G54 2007
343.4109′ 9—dc22

                                                                          2007022683

ISBN-10: 1-84568-101-0 (hbk)
ISBN-13: 978-1-84568-101-2 (hbk)
ISBN-10: 1-904385-33-8 (pbk)
ISBN-13: 978-1-904385-33-2 (pbk)
eISBN 10: 0-203-93727-9
eISBN-13: 978-0-203-93727-3

Contents

Acknowledgements

I owe a debt of gratitude to a great number of people: to Chrisje Brants, Didi Herman, Ronnie Lippens, Brian Simpson and Gary Wilson for their intellectually stimulating and encouraging comments on various draft chapters; to Davina Cooper, Marijke Malsch and Guy Osborn for sharing their thoughts with me at different stages of this project; to Anke Pouw and her colleagues at the Raad voor de Rechtspraak in the Netherlands for their help with organising the fieldwork for Chapter 7. I have also been much inspired by the enthusiasm of undergraduate students at Keele University taking the 'Law, Media and Popular Culture' module.

I am indebted to Peter Farr and Mike Wicksteed from the Judicial Communications Office for England and Wales and to members of the judiciary and communication advisers in the Netherlands for setting aside time in their hectic schedules to talk to me about their work. I want to thank Pertti Alasuutari and Sinikka Hakala for making my stay at the Research Institute for Social Sciences at Tampere University, Finland, such an agreeable experience.

My research has benefited from the financial support given to me by the Socio-Legal Studies Association under the small grants scheme and the AHRC Centre for the Study of Law, Gender and Sexuality at Keele, Kent and Westminster Universities. The AHRC Centre has also provided an intellectually stimulating environment in which I have been able to nurture many of my ideas, as has the School of Law and more recently the Research Institute for Law, Politics and Justice at Keele University. My work has benefited greatly from the sabbatical leave granted to me by Keele University in 2005.

I am very grateful to Chris Marshall for designing the artwork for the cover and to Amreek Dhillon for putting me in touch with such a talented graphic designer.

I want like to thank my friends, João and Patricia de Carvalho, Gary and Sarah Wilson, Els Van Geyte, John McCarthy, Helen Sotiropoulus and Brian Simpson for being so generous with their time, advice and encouragement; and Anna Boogers-Van Lommel for always being there.

Finally, my immense gratitude goes to Didier Meert for helping me prepare the manuscript and master the at times obscure art of word processing but more importantly for his love, support and unwavering belief in me. My father, Felix Albert Gies, passed away last year. As a former freelance journalist, the topic of this book would have appealed to him immensely but sadly time ran out on us and we were never able to have a proper chat about the project. I am dedicating this book to his memory and that of my mother, Jeanne Geeraerts.

Journal acknowledgements

Chapters 2 and 4 are extended and revised versions of 'Explaining the absence of the media in stories of law and legal consciousness', *Entertainment Law* (2003), 2 (1): 19–54 and 'The media and public understanding of the law', in S. Greenfield and G. Osborn (eds.) *Readings in Law and Popular Culture*, London: Routledge (2006). Chapter 5 is a drastically revised version of 'Helping Generation Ex: Divorce, legal advice in women's magazines and DIY law in Cyberspace', *International Journal of the Sociology of Law* (2004), 32 (1): 65–84. Chapter 7 is a revised version of 'The empire strikes back: Press judges and communication advisers in Dutch courts', *Journal of Law and Society* (2005), 32 (3): 450–472.

Chapter 1

Anatomy of a troubled relationship

Pillars of (received) media wisdom

There is undeniably a sense of annoyance – despair even – among legal academics and senior judges at what they see as the mass media's iron grip on the popular legal imagination. Simply put, their fear is that a persistent stream of distorted and sensationalised media portrayals is crowding out sober legal fact and may ultimately prove corrosive of law's authority and autonomy. The urgency of the language used in books, articles and judicial speeches is a measure of such concerns. An imagery of crisis, collapse and blurred boundaries (e.g. Garapon 1996; Stachenfeld and Nicholson 1996; Nobles and Schiff 2000; Sherwin 2000; Haltom and McCann 2004) – which incidentally would itself not look out of place in a breaking news headline – serves to underline the acutely tense relationship between law and the media. This holds particularly true for the way in which the media portray the administration of justice. In Britain, Lord Woolf (2003), the former Lord Chief Justice of England and Wales, asked not so long ago: 'Should the media and the judiciary be on speaking terms?', while Lord Justice Wall (2006: 19), a senior Court of Appeal judge, has called for a 'modus vivendi' between the judiciary and the press to encourage more responsible reporting. Quite wisely perhaps, he immediately cautioned: 'But we should not expect too much. . . . We may try to raise the level of the debate but we must recognise that we may not succeed.' The current Lord Chief Justice, Lord Phillips, recently hit out at some British media for their personal attacks on judges:

> Recently some sectors of the media have chosen to select some judges for personal attacks that have been intemperate, offensive and unfair. A judge who is the subject of such an attack cannot answer back. All here will, I know, share my sympathy for the victims of this abuse, and not just for them. Some of us can grow thick skins, but it is deeply distressing for family members to see those that they love and respect pilloried in the press.
>
> (Lord Phillips 2006b)

He has criticised journalists for their inaccurate and sensationalist reporting of sentencing issues on numerous occasions (Phillips 2006a; 2007b) and his message has also been echoed by the former Lord Chancellor, Lord Falconer (2006).

Judicial and academic concerns are the product of some widely-held ideas about media culture, namely, that the media distort, influence and act as a poor proxy for a proper understanding of what law is about. The issue of distortion and accuracy is a constant preoccupation of academic lawyers studying popular culture (Robson 2004) and it serves as an indication of their unease at the persistent failure of various media, mainly film but also newspapers and television, to paint a truthful picture of the intricacies of legal procedure. Such failures are not just seen as a matter of inadvertent error but in some cases as the result of wilful political manipulation by the media which results in judges being portrayed as soft liberals who are hopelessly out of touch, lawyers as money-grabbing cynics, the police as inadequate and legal doctrine as mind-boggling and absurd. To the trained legal eye, information in the media tends to be simplistic, misleading and superficial. More emotion than fact, legal actors fear that people who mistake media distortions for the truth about law will have their confidence in the legal system severely compromised. The influence of the media is often seen as inescapable and irresistible, targeting unsuspecting audiences who treat media stories as gospel. Public confidence is at the heart of such concerns. It is thought that once distorted ideas have entered people's minds, the latter's perceptions will be skewed in such a way as to erode popular support for key actors in the legal system (e.g. Berlins 2004; Phillips 2006b). Lord Justice Judge (2004), currently President of the Queen's Bench Division of the High Court and the Head of Criminal Justice, explains: 'If the public is misinformed about the administration of criminal justice then that too undermines their belief in and the justification for an independent judiciary.'

An important factor in explaining the media's powerful effects is people's presumed lack of any direct involvement with the law, particularly as regards the actual administration of justice. For example, Garapon (1996: 231) claims that 'for millions of people, the television has become, in the space of 30 years, the main, not to say the sole, source of information, culture and entertainment . . . and therefore, for many, the only contact they have with the law'. This suggests that law is virtually absent from ordinary lay experience, creating ample opportunity for the media to act as a proxy for personal contact with the legal system. According to some commentators (e.g. Garapon 1996; Machura and Ulbrich 2001; Machura 2004), this is quite evident from the fact that people in Continental Europe frequently mistake American legal procedure for that of their own country: in the absence of any direct contact with their own legal system, audiences, thanks to the global impact of Hollywood films, have a greater familiarity with American legal traditions than with their own laws. The reasoning behind this quite clearly is that most people rarely find themselves in court or a police station to experience law first hand and therefore must rely instead almost exclusively on misleading and at best patchy media snapshots of the legal system.

Understandably, concerns about media distortion are much more acute in professions which undergo incessant media scrutiny. Lawyers and judges are not the only victims of the media blame game, as Seale (2002: 33) observes: 'Scapegoating by the media, of course, is the frequent complaint of captains of sunken ferries, drivers of crashed trains, surgeons in botched operations, forensic experts in miscarriages of justice and so on.' Contemporary journalism prides itself on being a watchdog of power, which means that cynicism and distrust are a badge of honour to journalists hoping to expose the next big scandal in public life, trapping media reporting in a vicious cycle of bad news stories. There is, in other words, a 'cynicism bias' (Street 2001: 38) in news making as journalists constantly seek to question the integrity and motivations of anyone holding public office. Not surprisingly, public relations and communication have become an integral part of how the police, prosecutors, courts and the judiciary operate in the glare of a 24-hour news culture. As I will outline in Chapter 7, public education campaigns to limit the fallout of negative media publicity are nowadays a permanent fixture in the administration of justice.

In this book, I intend to unpick the various arguments and assumptions which seem to be holding sway over thinking about law and the media. My aim is not to prove or disprove such assertions – this is not an extensive empirical study – but to confront and contrast them with alternative perspectives on the subject. This, I hope, will enable me to develop an understanding of the tensions characterising the relationship between law and the media and it will also allow me to contribute something by way of assessment of whether there is a need to relieve the most severe pressure points. If the state of play is indeed extremely concerning and the authority of law is at risk of being eroded as a result of media distortions, it would seem that something needs to be done to avert that most alarming prospect of all, namely that of the crumbling of the rule of law under relentless media pressure. I do not mean to suggest that such concerns are entirely unfounded – on the contrary, my decision to write a book about the topic is a measure of how seriously I take them – but I do believe that more gloomy predictions about the total disappearance of the boundaries between law and the media ought to be put into perspective. The media may be exceptionally influential and powerful but so is law: claimants and defendants appearing before a court in Paris or Rotterdam expecting to be the protagonists in a US-style jury trial will no doubt instantly be disabused of their misconceptions and have no choice but to submit to the inquisitorial process.[1] Perhaps the weakest link is not a judge yielding to the expectations of a confused party but the elected politician hastily responding to screaming headlines by initiating a process of ill-considered law reform. I am not claiming that such a knee-jerk response never makes it onto the statute books, but for this to become a pattern would seem to require more than just media pressure alone.[2] Blaming all of law's ills on the media, in other words, is not necessarily the most productive approach because it readily overlooks alternative explanations and may even impair the prospect of excavating the problem to the fullest possible extent.

Everyday life and the popular, or, understanding the mystery of the Italian traffic lights

Everyday life is pivotal to the study in this book as it proceeds on the basis – to paraphrase Williams (1958; cited in Couldry 2000: 24) – that law, just as culture, is 'ordinary'. Indeed, it would be difficult to talk about modern everyday life in a meaningful way without reference to both law and media culture. As Friedman observes:

> Law and legal institutions are absolutely ubiquitous in modern society, and thus, quite naturally in the media. People are involved with law, like it or not. They grumble about legalism, they complain endlessly about lawyers, about the plague of lawsuits, and so on; but in fact these complaints arise out of dependence.
>
> (Friedman 1989: 1587)

Beppe Severgnini (2005) in an introspective travelogue through Italy in which he aims to discover the true Italian mindset, offers a tongue-in-cheek account of the semiotics of the traffic light. He reasons that to expect Italian motorists to stop automatically at a red light would be an insult to their intelligence and national pride. A legal rule is not obeyed in Italy; it is a starting point for debate and analysis. Hence, a red light can be 'relative' or 'quasi-red', that is, it may be legitimately disobeyed if there is no apparent need or reason for motorists to stop, for example, because there are no other road users around.

The unwillingness to take a red light at face value is a typically Italian trait according to Severgnini, but his account arguably also demonstrates something more universal about laws: their meaning is something which we negotiate through our everyday routines, perhaps not always consciously or deliberately, but with sufficient awareness to make us realise their significance in social life. Law is a formidable construct to which we respond through quiet resignation, vociferous contestation and active negotiation. To say that almost everything we know about law comes from the media is to ignore the potential of everyday legal experience to act as a resource which we bring to bear on our interpretation of media contents, so much so that our own experiences may become indistinguishably mixed up with media stories. Everyday legal experience is not necessarily the product of extensive contact with law enforcement agencies but it is more likely to consist of the routine encounter of rules which, if broken, may trigger legal sanctions in the form of fines, injunctions, points on our driving licence, compensation and so forth. In this build-up of an everyday awareness of law, referred to as 'legal consciousness' in some parts of the socio-legal literature (Ewick and Silbey 1998), 'the law' as stated in precedent, statute, codices and doctrine gels with aspects of the popular legal imagination (or 'legality') which includes more diffuse notions of rule-abidingness, power, bureaucracy, justice and order.

It may seem trivial to labour the point that people are not empty-minded when they watch a movie or television. However, the notion that media consumption is something that is only one step removed from sleepwalking has traditionally dominated thinking about media culture. Popular culture more generally is treated with suspicion – not least by the media themselves (McQuail 2000: 38) – not just because it is considered easy and undemanding but also because it is capable of exciting the masses. The unsavoury truth is, as Petley (2001) argues, that such suspicions are invariably riddled with class prejudice. Analysing the panic caused in 1950s Britain by the Marlon Brando movie *The Wild One*, Petley (2001: 173) comments that the gist of officials' reactions was that 'the film is fine for us middle-class intellectuals who will judge it on "aesthetic grounds", but it can't be shown to the plebs in case it gets them worked up'. Scholarly writing on the subject reveals that a significant degree of guilty pleasure informs academics' own consumption of popular culture. Consider, for example, Surette's (1998: xv) prologue to an edited collection on crime and popular culture in which he first 'confesses' to enjoying popular entertainment and then goes on to argue that, 'like candy to cavities, a diet heavy on popular culture will rot one's perceptions of reality' (see also Macaulay 1987).

Old-fashioned reading is seen as much less of a passive process than watching a movie or television: while images appeal to the affective and the emotional, words are thought to activate the mind and stimulate us to think for ourselves. Thus, Postman, who gained worldwide fame for his writings on this subject, comments:

> A written sentence calls upon its reader to say something, upon its reader to know the import of what is said. And when an author and reader are struggling with semantic meaning, they are engaged in the most serious challenge to the intellect.
>
> (Postman 1986: 51)

By contrast, of television he says: 'Television does not expand or amplify literate culture. It attacks it' (Postman 1986: 86) and also: 'Television offers viewers a variety of subject matter, requires minimal skills to comprehend it, and is largely aimed at emotional gratification' (Postman 1986: 88). Similarly, reading a tabloid with its many graphics and pictures is often regarded as less cerebral than reading a broadsheet in which the visual is less prominent. The debate as to whether children should be steered towards reading books and kept away from the television set or PC is a classic example: media culture is often mentioned in the same breath as other ills of our times such as junk food and excessive consumerism (e.g. Postman 1982; Palmer 2006). Such deeply entrenched attitudes towards popular culture explain why the study of law and film remains the poor relative of law and literature, a kind of 'academic fluff', as Robson (2004: 44) calls it, which still has a long way to go before it will be treated as a respectable part of legal studies. One might add that there are many other aspects of contemporary media culture, most notably cyberculture, which have barely begun to register and lag even further behind law and film in their bid to gain reputability in the legal academe.

However, it must also be stressed that taking popular culture seriously is not the same as uncritically celebrating all things popular. Popular culture is not invariably liberating but can also be stifling and unimaginative. The association of some strands of cultural studies[3] with a misplaced romanticising of the 'authenticity' of popular culture and the 'creativity' of media audiences has attracted accusations of populism and collusion with corporate might (McGuigan 1992). It is important not to lose sight of what matters most about popular culture, namely that it is interesting to the extent that is capable of challenging legal orthodoxies and that it is worth studying for what it tells us about continuing struggles over law's ownership, autonomy and legitimacy. Popular culture cannot be omitted from the picture which I am trying to piece together here: the troubled relationship between law and the media stems in part from popular culture's irreverence and its knack for asking uncomfortable questions which doctrine suppresses or marginalises (Thornton 2002). On the whole, it is popular media, and not 'highbrow' or 'cerebral' media, which cause the greatest concern in legal circles. The notion that mass media have created a 'culture' which merits scholarly attention remains a provocative proposition. Fears concerning popular culture are fears about dangerously excitable crowds gathering at the gates of law's empire. The question is not whether popular culture is good or bad; the question is: what makes it such a thorn in law's side?

Case studies

One such potential irritant is reality television. Being ubiquitous in today's television schedules, it represents a form of mass entertainment whose popularity is as great as the opprobrium of cultural critics can be intense. The argument which I will pursue in Chapter 3 is that reality TV embodies much of media culture's fascination with law and order. Indeed, real crime programmes, such as the iconic British programme *Crimewatch*, have played a pioneering role in the development of reality TV. 'Reality television' remains a rather imprecise term denoting 'real life' programmes which aim to depict law enforcement and other public services but also programmes which are less interested in offering a true-to-life portrayal of law and mainly want to experiment with ideas of justice and legality, in the sense of twisting and staging events to provoke something akin to legal consequence. Among the latter is *Wife Swap*, a British reality format in which two women swap families (or perhaps more ambiguously, it is they who are swapped by their men). In the first part of their stay, they have to live by each other's rules but in the second part, they have the power to impose their own rules on their host family. The humiliation which is often meted out to the women in this programme is far from uplifting and emancipatory, but, on the other hand, *Wife Swap* also explores the negotiability of rules in everyday life and gives women the opportunity to acquire the kind of law-making powers from which they are still to a large extent excluded in the official legislative realm. In this sense at least, *Wife Swap* demonstrates the potential of popular culture to 'illuminate otherwise ineffable accounts' (Thornton 2002: 17).

Much of popular culture is concerned with affording a lay audience a glimpse of law's inner sanctum. Law may be something which is largely unavoidable in everyday life, but it is also arcane and deeply mysterious. Legal knowledge connotes power and prestige. Thus, a recent comparative study has revealed that first year law students across several jurisdictions tend to think that law is a very prestigious profession, despite the fact that they do not regard lawyers as particularly trustworthy and ethical (Asimow *et al.* 2005). The notion that law empowers rings particularly true for problem pages in the press and phone-in programmes on radio and television which deal with legal queries submitted by members of the audience, even if this remains a little-studied aspect of media culture, presumably because it lacks the dramatic resonance of news genres and movies. In Chapter 5, I will discuss legal advice media against a backdrop of a growing trend of legal self-help which goes beyond the provision of information by actually encouraging people to tackle their own legal problems without having recourse to traditional tailor-made legal services. In a way, the idea of a law without lawyers is another example of popular culture's heresy, challenging the monopoly of the legal expert: information imparted through media culture competes and may even clash with doctrinal legal knowledge. However, it is also something which is being met with increasing enthusiasm by policy makers and the legal profession embracing the internet in particular as an alternative way of delivering pared-down legal services.

There is a growing awareness among legal actors of the need to address deficiencies in the public's knowledge of the law. It is felt that for too long it has been left to the media to be a gateway to information about the legal system, resulting in the kind of distortions and public confidence issues which I have highlighted above. The internet is not only an indispensable tool of legal self-help; it is also a way in which institutional communicators can bypass the mass media by ensuring that the public has access to official websites acting as a reliable compass for navigating the legal system. Thus, for example, the recently launched website of the judiciary in England and Wales[4] contains various 'myth busting' resources, such as quizzes, statistical information and interviews with senior judges. This proactive approach also extends to the mass media: press releases and 'plain English' translations of judgments are intended to help journalists improve their reporting. For judges in particular, this increased openness towards the media marks a departure from the reserve and dignified silence that they have traditionally displayed in the face of media scrutiny. In Chapter 7, I will study the liaison techniques deployed by Dutch courts which have pioneered the model whereby individual judges are designated to speak on behalf of courts. The challenge that judges face in these situations is how to safeguard their message from the ravages of media sound-bites. Such interventions, which are becoming increasingly common in both civil and common law systems, signal that legal actors are fast reaching the point of being able to manoeuvre tactically and respond swiftly to, and in some cases even pre-empt, any onslaught of media criticism. Some might see the growing emphasis on media and public relations as a capitulation to media pressure, but it is arguably foremost a sign of the legal system's extraordinary institutional resilience and its ability to take on its media detractors.

Reality television, legal self-help media and court-media relations constitute the three case studies at the heart of this book. With this selection, it is my intention to draw attention to areas which have the potential of showing the topography of law and the media in a different light. Any rigid distinction between factual genres and fiction has rightly been discredited since both are liable to extensive dramatisation and freely borrow from each other (see Brown 2003), but the materials of the case studies are undoubtedly situated at the factual end of the spectrum where there is inevitably a degree of contestation over what constitutes legal reality and how facts about law are presented and represented. Whether something is made-up or 'real' matters far less than the conventions of a genre signalling its intention to be read one way or the other. Thus, the 'real' is unmistakably present in reality television, while legal advice pages equally claim to deal with 'real life' problems and the public relations efforts of legal institutions are driven by the aim of showing the public what 'really' goes on, but in each of these instances reality is a highly unstable category.

With these case studies, I also aim to move beyond a strict concern with media contents depicting crime. Granted, issues to do with offending, punishment and fear of crime are at the forefront of the debate about media influences on people's understanding of the law and confidence in the legal system. However, that is all the more reason why we should attempt to situate such concerns in a wider perspective so as to form a more inclusive picture of the law/media nexus.

Making method and theory matter

The study of law and media (film in particular) is rooted in the law and literature tradition (Greenfield, Osborn and Robson 2001), which is in turn influenced by textual critique practised more widely in legal studies. While making sense of how popular entertainment genres operate at a textual level is undoubtedly part and parcel of media analysis, it is also clear that the insights which this yields are inevitably circumscribed: decoding a text's central message is not the same as interrogating its context of production and reception. At a very basic level, this turns on the notion that any text is open to different uses and interpretations. An academic lawyer's reading of a film's legal themes is not necessarily identical to that of other audiences. Attributing wider effects on the basis of the academic lawyer's reading alone is therefore potentially deeply problematic. One might say that there is no need for legal academics to look beyond the confines of the individual text considering that there must be countless surveys and opinion polls which have already clearly established that the media are extremely influential. However, research into media effects is one of the most difficult and contentious areas in the social sciences. Petley comments that:

> People believe that working-class people are more likely than middle-class ones to be adversely affected by media messages because it's true, they are! The answer to that, however, is: prove it. Anyone who tries to read through the literature on this subject will encounter a great deal of confident assertion and bluff 'common sense', but precious little in the way of social scientific research.
>
> (Petley 2001: 183)

Surveying the literature on that most elusive and contentious issue of all, namely whether there is a causal link between media depictions of violence and crime rates, Brown (2003: 108) sighs: 'The twists and turns of policy and academic attempts to research and "prove" effects of media exposure are dizzying in their volume and frequently circular or self-defeating enough to induce migraine.' McQuail's (2000: 48) general assessment is that: 'It has been clear for fifty years that mass media simply do not have the direct effects suggested. It has always been difficult to prove *any* effects' (my emphasis).

Thinking about the media in terms of their effects is as inevitable as it is problematic: indeed, any writing on the media proceeds on the assumption that they are somehow important and influential. This book, I humbly admit, is no different in this respect but it also acknowledges that while the mass media may be ubiquitous in contemporary society, it remains notoriously difficult to pinpoint how particular media portrayals are affecting people's thoughts and behaviour. Studying long-term effects is even more problematic: media axiom dictates that what is the must-see film of the week almost inevitably ends up forlorn in the bargain DVD bin. Ditto of course for newspapers and magazines. Media culture is driven by a quest for novelty. Everything, even the most spectacular, sensational and scandalous, loses its shine eventually. There is no better example of this fickleness than that of the countless celebrities who struggle to maintain themselves in the media limelight. Of course, when it comes to enduring media influences, there is also considerable merit in Silverstone's (1999: 143) argument that 'it is about the drip, drip, drip of ideology as well as the shock of the luminous event'.

Questions of methodology are high on this book's agenda. As I explain in Chapter 4, the groundwork for much of the debate on audience influence has already been laid in media and cultural studies where it has led to the development of different research models. It would be unrealistic to hope to find a solution to problems with which academics in this area have been trying to grapple for decades. However, an awareness of these issues is indispensable if we are to make sense of some important pressure points in the relationship between law and the media. Discarding a concept of mass communication as a linear process of cause and effect (also known as the 'hypodermic syringe' or 'magic bullet' model) has proved an enormous challenge in media studies (McQuail 2000: 47). Indeed, the very existence of media law suggests that mass communication is considered influential enough to be subjected to a regime of legal intervention. However, rather than focusing on the effects of isolated texts, media scholars are becoming increasingly aware of the way in which media culture meshes and interacts with other forms of social experience. This has resulted in a greater emphasis being placed on the ritualistic aspects of media culture that have little to do with any quantifiable impact (McQuail 2000: 54). According to Couldry:

> Surely, to put it crudely, we have to allow for the possibility that a particular text (whether a novel, film or a TV programme) may not matter much at all, or at least not matter in the ways that its 'expert readers' expect or think appropriate. The important question is not what is a text 'in itself', or for a community of expert readers, but how does a text get taken up in particular social and cultural formations? . . . This raises the interesting possibility that our uses of media texts may not always be 'meaningful' at all in which case *textual* analysis can only ever be part of the point.
>
> (Couldry 2000: 68)

Obviously, this hints at the somewhat uncomfortable possibility that specific texts may not be that significant after all, somewhat defeating the purpose of individual textual analysis, but when the matter is as serious as whether particular media portrayals are capable of affecting public confidence in the legal system, it cannot be dismissed without further consideration.

Just as pondering the choice of method involves exploring some new horizons, another issue to arise is where to place the study of law and popular culture in a wider theoretical framework. Is there a conceptual explanation for the fraught relationship between law and the media? A free press is one of the cornerstones of liberal doctrine: the media are thought to have a vital monitoring role to play in a healthy democracy. Freedom of expression attracts special constitutional safeguards. Criticism, even when it is abrasive and unfounded, is acceptable provided, of course, it does not amount to a criminal offence or civil wrong. For the media to be critical means not only to be independent from the institutional exercise of power but also to be aloof towards any form of officialdom. To approach the legal system with a dose of cynicism and distrust is an article of faith for journalists, editors and scriptwriters, meaning that tensions are not just inevitable but also seen as beneficial. However, there is also unmistakably a sense of disenchantment with the liberal ideal: the media, it seems, have abandoned their quest for truth in pursuit of profit, privilege populism over informed debate and would rather please the crowds than challenge them with hard facts.

In Chapter 6, I ask whether the watchdog model may not just be de facto unattainable in a 24-hour news and entertainment culture, but also whether accuracy is ultimately an appropriate yardstick for judging media performance. The routine failure of the media to convey doctrinal legal truth in an undistorted manner hints at a pattern of reality construction which is systemically at variance with the way in which truth is validated in the legal sphere. Whereas the liberal watchdog model views media inaccuracies as anomalous and corrosive of public confidence in democratic institutions, the alternative model which I outline offers a different explanation: using autopoiesis as its principal theoretical framework, it aims to qualify pessimistic projections of the harm which distorted media representations cause to law's authority. A basic tenet in autopoietic theory is that law and the media are autonomous and self-reproducing systems which do not enter into direct contact with each other but which rather communicate about their external environment (see Ziegert 2002). While this lack of a direct interface creates ample scope for miscommunication, it also has a protective effect in that it helps to safeguard the independent working of the systems involved. This raises the possibility that law is to a significant extent capable of immunising itself against the fallout of media distortion and a critical public opinion, offering a perspective which further challenges some of the dominant thinking about the media outlined above.

Law and the media spectacle

'Media spectacle' is an unmistakably pejorative term that encapsulates some of the worst excesses and ills of media culture. It stands for the triumph of emotion over rationality, image over truth, style over substance, ersatz over reality. Drawing on Debord's notion of the 'society of the spectacle', Kellner defines media spectacles as:

> Those phenomena of media culture that embody contemporary society's basic values, serve to initiate individuals into its way of life, and dramatise its controversies and struggles, as well as its modes of conflict resolution.

They include media extravaganzas, sporting events, political happenings, and those attention-grabbing occurrences that we call news.

(Kellner 2003: 2)

He observes that celebrity, public relations and appearance have come to dominate politics, business, culture and everyday life, which are all becoming increasingly staged and contrived. Law is arguably another domain that is being placed under the influence of the spectacular society. Sherwin's (2000) thesis that the boundaries between law and popular culture are vanishing draws heavily on the idea that visual culture has become an indispensable tool of the legal trade. Lawyers, he argues, cannot afford to ignore visual culture's role as purveyor of the definitive images, metaphors and archetypical characters shaping jurors' understanding of reality. To persuade in court means to master the conventions of visual media and to enchant one's audience in much the same way as popular culture does, that is through myths and imagery rather than through logic and rational argument.

Each of the case studies in this book appears to lend some support to the thesis of the media spectacle. The media's facilitation of legal self-help taps into a need to feel emotionally supported by people who speak from personal experience, which could explain the appeal of internet message boards acting as virtual meeting points where people can commiserate as well as advise each other on legal matters. In cyberspace, empathy and personal affinity compete with down-to-earth professional advice. In that sense at least, one could argue that self-help media thrive on drama and emotion, often eclipsing dry legal fact. Reality television is an even clearer exponent of the media spectacle expounding a reality that is elaborately staged and contrived. For example, much of *Wife Swap* is confrontation for spectacular gain and as the unflattering epithet of 'car crash television' suggests, it is the show's unedifying spectacle which explains its broad appeal. My analysis of public relations techniques adopted by courts offers a further perspective on the media spectacle: it seems that even law is not immune against the 'never-ending image wars' (Kellner 2003) of the spectacular society. It too has to repackage itself in order to achieve the desired public image and branding of its 'products'. A cynic might argue that this will only exacerbate the media's spectacular propensities and simply aims to neutralise distorted media portrayals with even more imagery and spectacle.[5]

Amidst such concerns, it would be easy to forget that law is inherently theatrical (see e.g. Aristodemou 2000; Sherwin 2000). Justice, as Garapon (1996) reminds us, requires a great amount of staging and theatricality.[6] His main concern is the potential elimination of law's most important spectacle, namely that of the court process, under the influence of a media culture which is intent on promoting direct justice and which is impatient with the elaborate proceedings required for a proper administration of justice. The thesis which Garapon outlines is similar to the critique of the media spectacle, especially as regards the emotionality which accompanies high-profile trials and which he claims potentially compromises the cathartic effects of court proceedings which appear by media standards to be too slow, too cold and too inadequate to deliver appropriate recompense for victims. Thinking of law as spectacle or theatre, however, does bring something important to the debate about media culture, namely the insight that media pressures do not cause law to become spectacular but that they are merely capitalising on the spectacular qualities already present in legal procedure. Goodrich's analysis of court architecture and the carefully scripted court proceedings is one such reminder of the pivotal role of the legal spectacle:

> The places are mapped according to criteria of ascension and both phys-ically and verbally all points look up to and are directed towards the bench, upon which, after the ushers have demanded silence and respect, it is the Law that sits down in the place of merely human demands. Consider too the forms of dress, the apparel of justice, the order of its coming and going and the restrictions upon the forms in which it can be addressed, the various metonymies as well as the sacral appellations: the court, the bench, your honour, your worship, your lordship.
>
> (Goodrich 1990: 223)

The theatricality of courts goes a considerable way towards explaining the attention which the media lavish on trials in particular. At it most elementary level, news reporting is no different from fiction in its desire to tell a good story (see e.g. Street 2001; Brown 2003) and the real life courtroom drama fits this purpose very well. Thus, what matters in court reporting is not the finer legal details[7] but the basic storylines which law enables news media to relate and the way in which these resonate with established conventions of news making. The conflict between media culture and law is not a clash between media spectacle and sober legal facts; it is about competing spectacles and the concern of legal actors to safeguard the law's own spectacle which they consider instrumental in communicating the legal truth in all its integrity. For example, as I explain in Chapter 7, Dutch courts will prepare detailed scenarios for high-profile trials enabling them to orchestrate the proceedings carefully. One can understand why the exploitation of the legal spectacle in media culture is often seen as sacrilegious. Evidently, the concern of legal actors is to ensure principles of due process, independence and impartiality, but it is also about the belief that safeguarding these principles requires a meticulously executed procedural script which the media almost invariably adulterate and misappropriate.

The quicksand of terminology: public and media

When we speak of 'the public', 'public opinion' and 'public confidence' in relation to the way in which the media depict legal issues, we often do so for lack of a better terminology rather than because we can confidently identify these categories. 'The public' is a very slippery concept. The more we research it, the more mysterious and unknowable it seems to be.[8] Law serves many different constituencies which have interests that are not always compatible and consistent. A more pointed terminology to designate these different interest groups (including victims, claimants, defendants, jurors, citizens, consumers and media audiences) would more adequately represent different forms of public investment in justice and presumably also capture different levels of attentiveness which different publics display towards media communications about law. Perhaps, as I have hinted above, the media's most captive audience are lawyers and others with a professional interest in law: they arguably represent the segment of the public which has every reason to be conscious of media discourses, especially when these concern their professional reputation.

Yet, ironically, these are the very publics which are most likely to deny that the media have any impact on their practices. For a judge to admit to being influenced by the media would threaten the foundations upon which the judicial office rests. Nevertheless, the legal journalist and broadcaster Marcel Berlins observes:

> My feeling, distilled from many conversations, is that judges and magistrates today *are* very conscious of the media, especially the tabloid press, and a little bit apprehensive of what might be the media's reaction to a sentence which appeared – rightly or wrongly – to be over-lenient, or, less often, over-severe. In asking the question: why, when crime is not increasing nor the number of offenders, are sentences more severe? Part of the answer is that judges and magistrates, too, are succumbing to what passes for popular opinion.
>
> (Berlins 2004: 8)

Public opinion is not a construction of the media alone. Street (2001: 53) comments that: 'contained in every news story is an implied audience or readership. Stories are written for a particular group, and the way they are written assumes a particular set of responses or values.' Similarly, legal discourse tailors its message in function of its own imagined public, thereby potentially reinforcing relevant media constructions. To cite Karpin (2002: 56): 'The judge is both audience and *de facto* cultural studies scholar', but in marked contrast with the cultural studies scholar, she also notes that judges have the power to 'transform . . . contestable knowledge into legal "fact" ' (Karpin 2002: 65). One could argue that the insight that public opinion is a mere construction of media and legal discourse – and not necessarily empirical fact – matters very little, if, as Berlins claims, the imagined public has purchase on something that is as important as sentencing. However, by challenging the idea that the public amounts to an independently verifiable variable and by treating it instead as a product of discourse, media reporting on law and justice can be appreciated for what it is, namely a media construct which is not an entirely stable indicator of what people actually think (see Nobles and Schiff 2000; Street 2001). Any attempt at understanding the uneasy relationship between law and media culture must have sufficient regard for the repeated slippage between public opinion, which appears readily identifiable from media coverage, and the actual views espoused by law's different publics.

Law's publics appear inextricably bound up with media audiences. However, traditional concepts of the media audience are rapidly being pulverised by a growing fragmentation of the media landscape and technological innovations which mark a transition from 'passive' audience to much more 'active' users of media products. While old-fashioned 'mass' media may once have involved a predominantly top-down communication by cultural elites and opinion leaders indiscriminately addressing a 'mass' audience, it is becoming much easier for users with no professional skills or ties with the media industries to act as communicators. The convergence of different technologies, such as the internet, mobile communication technology, broadcasting and print media, is erasing the boundaries between producers and consumers of media content. Thus, McQuail suggests:

> We can already conclude that the communications revolution has shifted the 'balance of power' from the media to the audience, insofar as there are more options to choose from and more active uses of media available. Traditional mass communication was essentially one-directional, while the new forms of communication are essentially *interactive*. Mass communication has in several aspects become less massive and less centralised.
> (McQuail 2000: 28)

The decline of mass media in favour of more interactive ways of communicating points to new forms of media consumption: interactivity means that people nowadays browse, select and download the information which most suits their requirements rather than sit back and let themselves be hit by the tidal wave of information transmitted by the mass media. The net result is not necessarily that people are always better informed and more knowledgeable: it may leave them profoundly confused and if anything it may entrench their distrust of mass media sources.[9] Moreover, as I have indicated above, the technological revolution is creating ample opportunity for legal actors to dispense with conventional mass media and reach out directly to their different publics via their own websites. The various institutions involved in the administration of justice are not simply seeking to bypass the media to get their message across but they have become media in their own right by taking advantage of new information and communication technologies.[10] These interventions raise the spectre of legal institutions usurping the role of the media, which would add an interesting twist to the usual concern that it is the media that are usurping law's functions. In short, it appears increasingly problematic to see legal actors as entirely passive and cast the media in the role of exclusive providers of information about law to wider society.

Overview of book content

Acknowledging that media culture's investment in law is often perceived as deeply problematic by legal actors and academics, this chapter has sought to demonstrate that the precise anatomy of the law/media nexus is by no means clear. Concerns that the mass media are responsible for promoting a flawed understanding of law among lay publics relies on the assumption that people have very little direct contact with the legal system. This raises the issue of how important law is in everyday life and how much of its presence can be attributed to media reporting. The interactions between law, media and everyday life will be analysed in more detail in Chapter 2 where it will be argued that both law and media culture are constitutive of everyday experience. As a result, legal experience which people directly acquire in everyday life is traded off against the knowledge which they derive from second-hand media accounts. This means that popular understandings of law may not be entirely shaped by the media alone. Elaborating on the theme of everyday life, Chapter 3 examines how reality television draws its inspiration from the everyday and treats it as something that is of considerable interest to its viewers. I will argue that reality television in its reading of the everyday is often drawn to the storied qualities of law not because the genre is concerned with any actual doctrinal legal content but because law – and law-breaking in particular – is proving a transposable narrative which can be brought to bear upon a diversity of everyday situations.

The presumed influence which the media exert on audiences is at the heart of the problematic relationship between law and the media. The issue of media effects will be subjected to closer examination in Chapter 4, which also engages with the status of law and popular culture as a discipline within the wider field of legal studies and how this has shaped its methodologies. While media effects constitute one of the most controversial and challenging areas of media analysis, technological changes resulting in greater interactivity and increased user involvement mentioned above increasingly belie the model of the passive audience. Chapter 5 offers a concrete example of active user involvement by focusing on the way in which various media outlets are contributing to a growing culture of legal self-help. Spurred on by an already strong therapeutic culture promoted in lifestyle magazines, legal self-help is being stimulated both technologically and by policy initiatives which seek to encourage people to take control of their own legal problems. Legal self-help provides a textbook example of the extent to which the concept of the passive audience has already been rendered obsolete by the availability of interactive technologies.

To say that the relationship between law and the media is rife with tension also raises the question of whether there are any benefits to be derived from this particular state of play. The issue which I pursue in Chapter 6 concerns the media's role as a watchdog of power and the extent to which this means maintaining a distance vis-à-vis the different institutions which the media aim to subject to constant scrutiny. One conclusion to be drawn from this analysis is that it is not necessarily an anomalous situation for the media to give an account of the legal process that is at variance with doctrinal legal truth. The notion that both media independence and judicial independence are important democratic values will also be further examined in Chapter 7, which focuses on attempts by courts and judges to educate both media and public in order to foster greater understanding of the administration of justice and improve public confidence. Such interventions inevitably raise the question of how to strike a balance between maintaining the media's independence and correcting or steering their reporting. Finally, Chapter 8 offers a summary of the main points and a reflection on the way in which the relationship between law and the media is likely to evolve in light of the developments studied in this book.

Chapter 2

Media, everyday life and legal consciousness

Introduction

Everyday life has been the object of considerable theoretical interest in cultural studies (see e.g. Gardiner 2000; Chaney 2002; Highmore 2002). Similarly, in the socio-legal field it is at the heart of research which aims to document how our everyday experiences of law shape what is called our 'legal consciousness'. Everyday life therefore offers an interdisciplinary vantage point from which to analyse the question that concerns me most in this chapter: how important are the media in explaining people's familiarity with the law? The claim that media culture accounts for people's main source of legal experience will be subjected to some closer scrutiny: I will argue that such a perspective is problematic in that it appears to suggest that law, predominantly being the object of vicarious experience, rarely manifests itself in daily life in a direct way. The task in hand is therefore to identify law's presence in everyday life and examine the extent to which this presence is attributable to audiences' consumption of media culture. In the first instance, this calls for a clarification of where we want to locate law. If law is seen as only encompassing formal legal institutions, this obviously restricts the incidence of law in everyday life, unless we mean to include only the everyday lives of judges, lawyers, prosecutors, academics and other relevant professions. However, this would overlook law's ability to be at the frontline of everyone's daily life where it acts as an interpretive prism through which we view the world. We experience law vicariously through the media but law also affects us in more direct and personal ways. A parking ticket or a speed camera may be sufficient to unsettle our routines and bring home law's inescapable grip on our lives.

Secondly, to say that law is an inherent feature of everyday life does not of itself reveal how people relate to this formidable presence in their day-to-day existence. This is where 'legal consciousness' will be introduced as a concept which seeks to capture different ways in which law is instrumental in shaping people's notion of self and their being in the world. Thirdly, the media's ability to act as a gateway to law in everyday life will be examined. Media culture constitutes an integral facet of popular experience, furnishing everyday life with the kind of semiotic wallpaper that many have come to take for granted. The media offer reassurance, structure day-to-day existence and endow it with what Silverstone (1994) – following Giddens (1990) – calls 'ontological security'. By the same token, the media also have the ability to punctuate our lives with the extraordinary and the unusual, opening up a world of ideas that would otherwise be slow to penetrate our day-to-day existence. Law's inherent ability to be spectacular and captivating makes it a particularly suitable ingredient for the almost indistinguishable diet of news and entertainment with which the media seek to spice up everyday life. However – and this insight is equally important – the media are not uniformly influential. Media consumption is a process of enormous complexity whereby we have, on the one hand, many different communicators vying with each other to influence the media message and, on the other, a dispersed audience whose reactions to the worldviews and ideas presented to them through various media channels have traditionally been difficult to gauge. I will explore two factors that are relevant to the way in which media representations of law are received in everyday life: the extent to which law is experienced as a disruptive factor in day-to-day existence and the extent to which media texts are able to resonate with personal legal experience.

The conceptual framework of law and everyday life

Theories of the quotidian: a brief sketch

Everyday life, as several authors have noted (e.g. Featherstone 1992; Fiske, 1992; Langbauer 1992; Felski 1999; Seigworth and Gardiner 2004) is notoriously difficult to conceptualise. For Featherstone (1992: 160), everyday life 'appears to be a residual category into which can be jettisoned all the irritating bits and pieces which do not fit into orderly thought'. Everyday life is hard to define because it defies language (Lefebvre 1984), referring to an inarticulate part of human experience that is almost too obvious for words. According to Felski (1999: 15), 'everyday life simply *is*, indisputably: the essential, taken-for-granted continuum of mundane activities that frames our forays into more esoteric or exotic worlds. It is the ultimate, non-negotiable reality, the unavoidable basis for all other forms of human endeavour'. The inescapable and all-encompassing qualities of everyday life almost inevitably make it a symbol of oppressiveness, boredom and existential drabness. The point is not that only ordinary people have an everyday life while a privileged few are able to escape from it entirely to lead an altogether more exciting or extraordinary life; rather there are the few who, on account of their status or wealth, are able to make much more of the 'forays into more esoteric or exotic worlds' highlighted by Felski. Nowhere is this more obvious than in respect of the gender and class divide which is considered a key characteristic of everyday life (Lefebvre 1984: 35).

To understand this close identification with women and the working classes, it is important to draw attention to the entwinement of everyday life with the conditions of modernity. Gardiner (2000) and Chaney (2002) remind us that the everyday is not a-historical. Much of its problematic is associated with a process of intense commodification and relentless rationalisation, for example through technologies enabling time, production output and consumption patterns to be measured.[1] Such rationalisations allow for people's existence to be broken down into standardised and cyclical units, generating uniformity and repetitiveness which result in the apparent loss of identity for individuals who all live their life to a similar rhythm and pattern. The assembly line, according to Highmore (2002), is a powerful symbol of the fusion of everyday life and modernity, thereby touching upon a familiar argument in the analysis of the exploitation and alienation of the proletariat in Marxist theory. However, while the debilitating monotony induced by the assembly line may be the most extreme in the manual labourer or the unskilled worker, other social groups are not spared the tedium of the everyday. Nevertheless, it appears that the perceived benefits of an orderly regimentation of the ordinary and mundane are distributed unevenly across the social spectrum. Suburbia, as Silverstone (1994: 59) points out, represents one of the most identifiable symbols of everyday monotony but it also provides the kind of secure environment that is craved by the middle classes in particular. Everyday life also has an undeniably gendered dimension, as Featherstone (1992: 161) explains: 'The everyday is regarded as the sphere of reproduction and maintenance, a pre-institutional zone in which basic activities which sustain other worlds are performed, largely by women.' In an ambivalent move that has not gone unnoticed in feminist circles (Langbauer 1992), Lefebvre singles women out as being worst affected by, but also the most unaware of, the repetitiveness and aggressive commodification of the everyday (Lefebvre 1984: 73). Having undergone its own process of rationalisation, the home operates as the equivalent of the assembly line in the private sphere. Everyday life is embedded in the world of domesticity, with its interminable chores and its focus on the most basic human needs creating a burden which continues to befall women in a disproportionate manner (MacKinnon 1995: 109).

The cyclical, the monotonous, the domestic, the habitual and the temporal mean that everyday life is something that we usually take for granted. 'Everyday life simply is the routine act of conducting one's day-to-day existence without making it an object of conscious attention', comments Felski (1999: 27). It is the inconspicuous, the invisible and the unremarkable which make our habits all the more powerful. Thus, as I discuss below, it is law's extraordinary ability to nestle itself into much of what we take for granted which renders its presence in everyday life so formidable. However, the oppressiveness of the quotidian is only part of the story. There are as many paradoxes to the everyday as there are ways of accommodating the conditions of modernity. The coldly rational does not expunge the irrational from daily life.

Everyday life has been identified as a hugely creative force and a site for resisting the oppressive conditions to which it gives rise in the first place. For Gardiner (2000: 17), everyday life is both 'an alienated and potentially liberated state'. The everyday has a redemptive and emancipatory quality that cannot be overlooked: its endless array of mechanisms of regimentation and rationalisation also provides the groundwork for heterodoxy and subversion. The prospect of total rationalisation is kept at bay through moments of inventiveness and gestures of defiance, making the everyday simultaneously a site of emancipation and subordination. Resistance is central to the work of de Certeau who is best known for his theorising of people's 'make-do' approaches to everyday life. His main concern is with:

> ... suggesting some ways of thinking about the everyday practices of consumers, supposing from the start that they are of a tactical nature. Dwelling, moving about, speaking, reading, shopping, and cooking are activities that seem to correspond to the characteristics of tactical ruses and surprises: clever tricks of the 'weak' within the order established by the 'strong,' an art of putting one over on the adversary on his own turf, hunter's tricks, manoeuvrable, polymorph mobilities, jubilant, poetic, and warlike discoveries.
>
> (de Certeau 1988: 39)

Lacking a calling for revolutionary or heroic deeds, the individual in everyday life simply works with what is available, investing mass-produced cultural artefacts with personal meaning often by inventing usages which defy the rationalisations imposed by capitalism. Apparently, we were never meant to make cheap text messaging central to our usage of mobile phone technology because it is the least profitable for network operators, but many users prefer it to more expensive voice communication. Today, the humble SMS has given rise to an entirely new set of social and cultural practices.[2]

Similarly, for Fiske (1992: 157), a cultural theorist whose work seeks to flesh out the liberating potential of the everyday, popular culture is not about passively suffering everyday life; for him, grassroots cultural production seeks actively to endow the everyday with meaning and 'texture'. This celebration of the resistive dimension of popular culture is a central theme in cultural studies and it is one that has also been embraced in socio-legal analysis (see further below). However, this focus on resistance has also given rise to staunch and growing criticism that goes to the very heart of the cultural studies movement. I will attend to such criticism in Chapter 4. Suffice it to say here that a perceived weakness of the celebration of resistance or *bricolage* is its lack of a critical engagement with social and cultural inequalities. For Highmore (2002: 27), cultural studies simply ends up telling the same story all over again, one that seeks out the resistive in the oppressive but which may paradoxically also end up legitimising oppression which is invariably perceived as being receptive to creative means of subversion. Gardiner (2000: 8) sums up the sense of frustration with the paucity of cultural critique in the following way: 'Increasingly, the "everyday" is invoked in a gestural sense as a bulwark of creativity and resistance, regardless of the question of asymmetries of powers, class relations, or increasingly globalised market forces.'

Law and the rationalisation of everyday life

A central argument of this book is that we cannot understand the relationship between law and the media without considering the extent to which law is part of the fabric of everyday life. The underlying idea is that the media represent only one way in which law manifests itself in our lives on a day-to-day basis. But how valid is this claim? To what extent is law a feature of our personal experience? How often do we come up against it and how much more often do we simply ignore it? And what does it mean to live our lives in law's shadow? These questions require a clarification of what is meant by 'law', or, more precisely, an exploration of the various sites which law occupies. As a set of rules, derived from a body of doctrine, case law, legislation and other sources, law can be found in a wide range of locales, its reign being most visible in highly institutionalised settings such as courts, law firms, police stations and probation offices. It is probably true to say that relatively few people come directly into contact with such places on a regular basis, but we should not be too hasty to assume that this indiscriminately holds true because of the disproportionate extent to which some minorities are exposed to law enforcement mechanisms.[3] Moreover, it is clear that law is performed in a variety of social settings and not just in the context of the institutions that are most visibly associated with it. Sarat and Kearns (1995b: 8) argue that 'without the everyday, law is a voice never heard, a memory never known. Without the everyday, law is a living impossibility'. We may be largely oblivious to law's presence but that is precisely a sure sign that it is essential in everyday life to the point of being unnoticeable. Being subtly woven into our habits and practices, law succeeds in remaining largely invisible until such moment when there is a breakdown in the social relations governed by it: divorce, a breach of contract, a neighbour dispute. Law has a tendency to express itself in a discursive register, an arcane and much-dreaded jargon, which is quite alien to everyday life, but its presence is nevertheless important to the way in which we structure our routines and go about our day-to-day activities.

One way of making law stand out from the routines of everyday life is through a process of 'making strange' (Highmore 2002), which aims to dislodge law from the taken-for-granted patterns of the everyday, for example, by keeping a diary to record one's day-to-day legal experiences. Students participating in such an 'estrangement' exercise as part of the undergraduate and postgraduate law curriculum at Keele University (UK) usually express genuine surprise at how much of a common occurrence law is in their own daily lives. Group discussions of the diary exercise offer an opportunity for unravelling everyday tactical moves such as those explicated by de Certeau. A standard example is the habit of slowing down when approaching a speed camera. Being an almost unconscious response to what has become a familiar feature of the built environment, slowing down to avoid being caught speeding by a machine captures so many of the things which scholars of everyday life find fascinating: the technocracy of law's panoptical presence (even down to the ruler-like marking on the road), the regulation of speed, the engrained habit of slowing down only to pick up speed again afterwards and the small gesture of defiance which the slowing down and the subsequent accelerating constitutes. Also noteworthy is the impact of the speed camera on people's use of time and space, which is evident from another potential irritant in everyday life: the parking meter. 'Witnessed an altercation between a motorist and a traffic warden. Apparently the driver had parked in a premium rate bay but was only displaying a standard rate ticket' reads one entry in a student's diary. We may often be oblivious to such incidents, but the ability of law to regulate our use of time and space in everyday life in such minute detail remains an amazing achievement.

Traffic offences, TV licence renewal notices and library fines are just a few of the little pinpricks which law administers as part of the cycle of everyday life. Law, just as the everyday, is a dense and multi-layered experience. Its visual impact on the material landscape is undeniable, contributing to what de Certeau (1988) calls the 'scriptural economy' in which the medium of the written word has come to overshadow oral communication. The everyday under the scriptural regime transforms itself into text: the lawn in suburbia is not just a private stretch of greenery; it is a signifying practice which socially positions people and has the effect of zoning their identity. Law overlays the everyday with its own signifiers, contributing to the intense scripting of everyday life. 'Keep out: authorised personnel only!', 'The owner cannot accept responsibility for any damage to the vehicles or their contents left in this car park', 'Danger: weak roof' and other visual disclaimers constitute fleeting reminders of extensive networks of legal relations and responsibilities physically mapped out in everyday life (see Blomley and Clark 1990). Acts which are routinely and unconsciously executed, such as leaving our car in a car park or entering a building, do not occur in a legal vacuum, but they assimilate us into a pre-defined legal framework that seeks to spell out and pre-empt the consequences of our actions, however banal or mundane. Indeed, the disclaimer prevents the legally uneventful from turning into something legally eventful, thus ensuring the kind of social stability and continuity that is vital to the realisation of the project of modernity.

The issue that needs to be emphasised here is that law's pervasiveness is not incidental but constitutive of the conditions of everyday life. Max Weber (1954) pointed to law's crucial position in the rise of modernity and capitalism in particular. His thesis was that only a formal rational legal system was capable of creating the right conditions for capitalism to become a viable economic regime. This included the institution of a bureaucratic apparatus applying rules in an impersonal and predictable way. Weber painted a pessimistic picture of the disenchanted subject trapped in the iron cage of modernity and its unstoppable bureaucracy. Predictability and stability of legal norms exact a hefty price: the individual risks becoming a mere 'cog' in law's machinery which affords little space for his or her individual desires (Milovanovic 1989: 123). MacKinnon describes law's oppressiveness in the following way:

> To most women, law is a foreign country with an unintelligible tongue, alien mores, secret traps, uncontrollable and unresponsive dynamics, obscure but rigid dogmas, barbaric and draconian rituals, and consequences as scary as they are incomprehensible. Actually, this is true for most men as well.
>
> (MacKinnon 1995: 109)

Law is a familiar building block of the everyday but at the same time it also constitutes a bewildering labyrinthine force with which individuals struggle to relate in a meaningful way (Cowan 2004).

Parts of everyday life which were once largely untouched by law are rapidly undergoing a process of what Habermas (1986) calls 'juridification'. The everyday can be roughly equated with the Habermasian 'lifeworld' (Habermas 1984). The self-reproducing lifeworld forms the inevitable backdrop for communicative action which is grounded in intersubjectivity and which is ultimately aimed at mutual understanding between social actors through the achievement of a consensus in which participants find each other not in the substance of a decision but in the procedure by which it was arrived at. By contrast, the system, which for Habermas constitutes a separate social sphere, is dedicated to the pursuit of economic and political goals through instrumental and strategic rationality. Put crudely, the excesses of modernity can be witnessed from the gradual colonisation of the lifeworld by the system, resulting in increased bureaucratic control that disrupts the spontaneity of communicative structures. Law contributes to this process of colonisation through juridification which is often associated with a 'quantitative growth of law or legal interventions' (Cooper 1995: 507).

Juridification manifests itself most acutely in the interventions of the welfare state (Habermas 1986), for example, resulting in the institution of care for the elderly, thus distorting the communicative resources of the lifeworld (for example, mutual aid) and stifling the intersubjective basis of social interactions. Excessive regulation of everyday life accounts for the perception that law is unnecessarily interventionist, imposing itself in situations which ideally should be governed by the lifeworld's own resources. The thesis of juridification underscores the expansionist tendencies of law in everyday life. In popular discourses, the term 'nanny state' is commonly used to designate an excess of state interference in people's health and lifestyle choices. Paradoxically, however, the development of ever more legal rules seems to be the only conceivable solution in modern society which struggles to adjust to new challenges and therefore simply expands the use of familiar regulatory mechanisms (Beck, Bonns and Lau 2003). Thus there seems to be a clear link between the intensification or deepening of modernity and law's colonisation of everyday life.

Legal consciousness

The everyday stands for what is familiar and repetitive but it is also considered ungraspable and unknowable. Modernity has transformed daily life into a site of alienation and subordination to rationality but, simultaneously, commentators attribute an extraordinary creative and resistive potential to the everyday. Having assumed a near inescapable presence in day-to-day interactions, it follows that law must similarly be a target for contestation and resistance. Despite Weber's pessimism, the individual resists being reduced to a mere cog in the system by circumnavigating law's iron grip. This section examines the dynamics of resistance and compliance from the perspective of legal consciousness research, which will subsequently provide a framework for explicating the media's ability to act as a gateway to law in everyday life.

The notion that law is constitutive of, instead of being external to, everyday life is slowly coming to fruition. The discussion very much turns on whether we should adopt a law *and* society approach or, by contrast, a law *in* society approach which places law firmly at the very heart of social life. Law *and* society coincides with what Sarat and Kearns (1995a) call an 'instrumental' perspective which typically regards law as a set of distinct norms which are situated outside society and which can be deployed as an external instrument for forcing through important societal changes. Much of the research in this tradition is concerned with studying how effective law is in shaping and regulating social life. By contrast, law *in* society represents a constitutive perspective which focuses not on how law influences society from outside, but on ways in which law is active in processes of meaning and self-understanding. Instead of looking at how law 'as an external, normative missile' (Sarat and Kearns 1995a: 29) changes people's behaviour and attitudes, the constitutive approach is interested in how notions of legality manifest themselves in the way in which people see themselves and interpret the world around them. In the words of Ewick and Silbey (1998: 16), law 'has a commonplace materiality pervading the here and now of our social landscape'.

To understand law's presence in everyday life requires an analysis which goes beyond the purely attitudinal and the cognitive. Consciousness, not knowledge or attitude, seems to be the crucial issue. Thus, Sarat (1990) in his study of the legal consciousness of welfare recipients did not aim to find out what the participants in his research knew or how they felt about welfare services and social laws. Instead, he was interested in what law meant to them. Similarly, ethnographic studies of small claims courts and local courts (Merry 1986; Yngvesson 1989) have taken it upon themselves to uncover a struggle of a profoundly ideological nature, focusing on the way in which litigants challenge dominant legal ideology by invoking alternative meanings and beliefs. The theme of struggle and resistance runs as a central thread through these analyses. Bureaucracy is a web-like enclosure in which people, welfare recipients in particular (Sarat 1990), find themselves trapped and from which they seek (temporary) relief, deploying tactics which give them some respite from law's grip on their lives. Hegemony and resistance are two sides of the same coin: on the one hand, people, particularly those at the margins of society, accept dominant ideas of law and justice, while on the other hand, they also constantly seem to be challenging these ideas by engaging in resistive practices.

The dynamics of compliance and resistance shape people's legal consciousness. According to Trubek (1984: 592), 'Legal consciousness is that aspect of consciousness of any society which explains and helps justify its legal institutions', while for Sarat (1990) legal consciousness is synonymous with ideology. In the case of the welfare recipients whom he interviewed, the ideological underpinnings consisted of a mixture of ideas confirming and contesting dominant principles of law. In spite of repeated disappointments when appealing to the welfare system, those seeking assistance somehow manage to remain hopeful that one day they will be successful in obtaining effective redress for their never-ending housing and debt problems. Legal consciousness is therefore much more than the product of individual experience. Law's mythical and ideological qualities keep individuals' faith alive even if experience tells them otherwise. As Engel (1998: 112) points out, 'there is an individual aspect to consciousness ... but an individual's consciousness is shaped by the structures and relationships of which she or he is part', something which is also reflected in Ewick and Silbey's (1998: 36) definition of legal consciousness as neither a set of conscious attitudes nor an entirely 'epiphenomenal' by-product of structural conditions. Instead, they see it as a cultural practice in which individuals activate a set of cultural codes to make sense of the world around them. Legality, in its structural sense, 'consists of cultural schemas and resources that operate to define and pattern social life' (Ewick and Silbey 1998: 43), but at the same time, it is dependent on individual action for its reproduction and application. Moreover, the various codes of legality are not exclusively legal; they comprise a wide and diverse set of rules and principles which are not limited to law alone. Some of the examples that Ewick and Silbey cite include notions of competition and fair play which manifest themselves in a variety of social contexts.

Ewick and Silbey identify three patterns of legal consciousness which enable them to conceptualise potentially significant variations in the way in which legality as a structural feature of the everyday is open to individual agency. A first way of experiencing the presence of law in everyday settings is what Ewick and Silbey define as 'before the law'. This emerges when people see law as authoritative but also as something which is removed from ordinary social interaction: they recognise law for its importance in daily life, but for them it never appears to integrate itself fully in the everyday because it ultimately remains an independent force which exerts its influence from the outside. Law is therefore typically experienced as a parallel universe which overlaps very little with everyday life. The emphasis in the 'before the law' stance is on law as something distant, leaving people feeling powerless to deploy legal remedies and procedures which they believe are largely beyond their reach. The second dimension of legal consciousness in the classification which Ewick and Silbey put forward is 'with the law'. It refers to the belief that law is a kind of game that individuals play in their daily activities. From this perspective, law operates as a strategic resource: it is something that is available to people when safeguarding their interests in their dealings with others. This suggests that individuals will feel to a large extent able to control the presence of law in their lives, even though Ewick and Silbey (1998: 135) emphasise the importance of contingency and unpredictability in the perception of 'law as a game'. Finally, there is what Ewick and Silbey call the 'against the law' dimension of legal consciousness in which the emphasis is on people's resistance, often in the form of 'make-do' tactics and usually involving small gestures of subversion. The main purpose of such resistance is, as Ewick and Silbey (1998: 48) point out, to 'forge moments of respite from the power of law'.

Law from a constitutive 'law-in-society' perspective is considered ubiquitous. The resources to be mobilised in legal consciousness can be found everywhere, although law's influence may also be hardly discernible because it shares many of its interpretive codes with other areas of social activity. The question that is of particular interest here is: where do we situate the role of the media in this 'commonplace' conception of law and legal consciousness? A difficulty with studies of legal consciousness – and this is in marked contrast with research traditions which have taken the issue of media influence as their primary concern – is that the role of the media tends to be somewhat neglected, not because media input is seen as unimportant, but because it is treated as self-evident. It is striking that, for example, in the stories which Ewick and Silbey (1998) collected, the media seldom explicitly come to the fore. In fact, this seems to be the case for the majority of studies of legal consciousness and law in everyday life (see Hirsch 1992: 854).

As Vine (1997: 125) argues, it is a truism to say that the media are influential. The issue is not whether they are important, but the extent to which they are important and the manner in which their influence is felt. The challenge is to generate a critical awareness of the role that the media may play in furnishing and sustaining various codes of legality without slipping into a media-centric account (see Chapter 4) in which legal consciousness would be explained entirely through the media. We seem to know relatively little about the relationship between the interpretive models routinely supplied and reproduced by the media and other resources used by individuals to construct legal meaning. How compatible are mediatised sources of legal consciousness and personal experience? What kinds of readings of law do media representations inspire? Do media images make people feel overawed by law or do they bring out the resistive dimension in their legal consciousness? Do they encourage people to think of law as a self-interested game of risks and benefits perhaps against their better experiential judgment? Obviously, the answer to these questions depends in part on the specific type of media one chooses to focus on, requiring a text-by-text analysis. However, in the next section, I also want to suggest that a more general explanation resides in how the media's place in everyday life is envisaged and conceptualised.

Media, legality and identity

The contribution that the media make to our sense of familiarity with law is in several ways commensurate with their ability to structure our overall experience of daily life. Broadcasting in particular has been noted for its ability to integrate itself seamlessly into the rhythm of the everyday. Scannell (1996) goes even further by arguing that modern life derives its cyclical and ritualistic character from radio and television through carefully designed scheduling which provides for time-specific slots to mark different periods of the day, from early breakfast shows to late evening and night time programmes.[4] The advent of internet radio, for example, means that it is now possible to live on 'home time' even when abroad just by tuning into familiar programmes broadcast over the internet. Periodical media other than radio and television undoubtedly have a similar structuring effect on dailiness: a regular publication rhythm creates a sense of repetitiveness and familiarity. Importantly, this reinforcement of the cyclical through a continuous supply of fresh information is considered instrumental in the media transforming current events into past memories (Silverstone 1994). Traumatic or dramatic events are relatively rapidly forgotten because they are inevitably overtaken by new and often unrelated developments. This for many represents a problematic aspect of media culture, revealing a degree of superficiality which impedes the kind of in-depth discussion and analysis which one would expect in an ideally working public sphere (see Chapter 6).[5] However, the cyclical and transient character of periodical media arguably also fulfils an important role in negotiating risk in everyday life. It is an effective way of domesticating (often literally through consumption in domestic settings) the unknown and grounding it into what is known and familiar.

Silverstone (1994: 198) considers television 'a contributor to our security' and there is little reason why this should not apply to the mass media more generally. The media are often noted for their ability to create anxiety, which is, for example, detectable in an irrational fear of crime (see e.g. Sparks 1992). However, it is more or at least equally important to understand that the media also act as a security blanket, offering reassurance, continuity and a sense of community even in times of great upheaval. Thus the next chapter is devoted entirely to reality TV as a genre in which ordinary, everyday experiences take centre stage. The media lend themselves perfectly to domesticating law's more exotic qualities and reinforcing the taken-for-granted and structured aspects of legality. The media's bread-and-butter is the eventful and the disruption of the familiar as well as its continuity. Law with its many moments of upheaval is a gripping media subject, but more importantly, the cycle of transforming the extraordinary into the taken-for-granted state of affairs also makes the media a great restorer of law's normalcy. Even profound, media-driven moments of crisis tend to leave few dents in the overall fabric of the legal system (see Chapter 6). When media interest has ebbed away (as it invariably tends to do) and public interest has waned law is returned to its original state. The media enable us to satisfy our curiosity about law from the safety of our living room and behold the legal maze in a risk-free way: law in media discourse is invariably something that happens to other people. Even the most majestic and institutionalised spaces of law, which for some people overlap only sparsely with the routines of their day-to-day existence, acquire thanks to media a familiarity which Thompson (1995) has famously termed 'intimacy at a distance'. As Chaney (2002:14) observes: 'The boundaries of the "normal" are thus constantly being expanded or changed by interactions with the exotic spectacles made available by mass culture industries.' In other words, without the media, familiarity with law's more exotic aspects would be almost impossible to achieve.

Yet, I also want to argue that such a 'second-hand' familiarity cannot be treated as the principal or overriding factor in the constitution of legal consciousness. Media culture has not superseded the network of social relations embedded in everyday life but it has become inextricably entwined with it (Jansson 2001). As Moores (2000: 37) argues, living in a media-dominated environment does not mean that face-to-face interaction is no longer relevant to our sense of self and our perceptions of the world. This calls for an analytical perspective that is sensitive to the way in which the media merge with direct experience. The mediation role of the media depends on their ability to fulfil a hinge function between two interconnecting spheres of experience, which Scannell (1996: 172) terms the 'great world' and 'everyone's my-world' and which leads him to conclude that broadcasting represents a 'doubling up of place': in addition to the site of an event itself, it also occurs in the site where it is heard or seen (Scannell 1996: 76). Neither site seems sufficient in itself to create eventfulness: the place of the event and the place where it is received by an audience form an indissociable entity. For Scannell, this represents the true magic of broadcasting as it means that the 'here' and 'there' and the 'then' and 'now' have undergone a fusion, something which Moores (2004) believes to be true of all electronic media. Similar observations can be made about the media's role in integrating law's there and then with daily life's here and now. Law belongs to the 'great world', coming across as something distant (very much in evidence in the 'before the law' dimension of legal consciousness), menacing, reassuring or simply irrelevant but, at the same time, it also has a visceral presence in the here and now of the lifeworld. This means that in dealing with the innumerable media stories about law which people routinely encounter in their daily life, we cannot discount the importance of the context of reception, more specifically the element which Moores (2000: 39) terms 'selective and reflexive appropriation'. Thompson offers the following description of this process:

> Non-local knowledge is always appropriated by individuals in specific locales and the practical significance of this knowledge – what it means to individuals and how it is used by them – is always dependent on the interests of recipients and on the resources they bring to bear on the process of appropriation.
>
> (Thompson 1995: 207)

The ability of law in its mediatised form to gel with local legal experience and the extent to which it is selectively appropriated and made meaningful by people in everyday settings depends on the intervention of what de Certeau (1988: 31) calls the 'consumer-sphinx'. The key to understanding this enigmatic figure resides in the explication of (media) consumption as another moment of production:

> A rationalized, expansionist, centralized, spectacular and clamorous production is confronted by an entirely different kind of production, called 'consumption' and characterized by its ruses, its fragmentation, . . . its poaching, its clandestine nature, its tireless but quiet activity, its quasi-invisibility, since it shows not in its own products . . . but in an art of using those imposed on it.
>
> (de Certeau 1988: 31)

Scholars of both media and law in everyday life have been much inspired by de Certeau's approach, which, as noted above, is informed by the problematic of modernity. We seem capable of resisting mass culture just as we are capable of resisting legal authority. Usage appears to be the critical factor: both our media consumption and legal consciousness involve moments of agency, making us active media users and legal subjects. For all its taken-for-granted aspects, legality needs to be reproduced and put into practice. This invites practices of *bricolage* and ultimately also resistance, making the obvious not that obvious after all. Similarly, for all their efforts to make us see reality in a particular way, the media, *pace* de Certeau, fail to control their audiences' understanding of the world. The epistemological issues arising from the study of media effects and audience resistance will be fleshed out in greater detail in Chapter 4. The question which is of immediate relevance here is this one: once we accept that neither legality nor the media's definition of reality meets with uniform acceptance or appropriation and that both are potentially subject to great variations in take-up and usage, how do we then account for such differences? Which factors underpin the different ways in which people reproduce legality and call upon, or fail to call upon, the resources on offer through the media? Two elements which are potentially relevant in addressing these questions merit some closer attention: firstly, the extent to which law is experienced as a disruptive presence in everyday life and, secondly, the extent to which media are able to resonate with first-hand legal experience.

Social identity is important in accounting for differences in audience reception of media texts (see Chapter 4) but it has proved similarly significant in explaining variations in legal consciousness: research suggests that under-privileged groups are most likely to have a legal consciousness which is characterised by a 'before the law' perception or a feeling of being up 'against the law' (Ewick and Silbey 1998; Nielsen 2000). Law for them can become the overwhelming web-like enclosure which Sarat (1990) describes in his work on the legal consciousness of welfare recipients, while for ethnic minorities in urban areas, simply venturing out onto the street can be sufficient to expose them to law's suffocating presence, for example, in the guise of vexing stop-and-search procedures (see e.g. Clancy, Aust and Kershaw 2001). This suggests that, depending on their social status, people feel more or less comfortable with law's presence in their lives, which would explain why some perceive the law to be on their side while others experience it as a constant hindrance. Race, class, gender and the mere fact of residing in a suburb as opposed to the inner city therefore tend to give rise to different legal experiences and, hence, arguably also a different form of legal consciousness.

Furthermore, negative personal experiences also impact on the way in which different social groups use the media as a resource for making sense of law. Although Dowler's (2002) analysis was not specifically concerned with legal consciousness, his US survey of perceptions of police effectiveness underscores the importance of first-hand experience: his main conclusion is that people's satisfaction regarding their own personal contact with the police is capable of overshadowing media influence, making it the overriding factor in accounting for public confidence in the police. It could be said that when people have predominantly negative personal experiences of law, this will somehow have a much greater impact on their legal consciousness than any media coverage has. The injury of personal confrontation runs deeper than any indignation at particular media portrayals. The extent to which law is seen as a disruptive force in everyday life, actualised in a strong 'against the law' type of legal consciousness, may therefore be an important element in accounting for possible differences in the interpretation of media texts. Moreover, it could be hypothesised that media messages create further opportunities for entrenching the belief system of individuals who are inclined to adopt an 'against the law' stance, provoking disbelief, cynicism and outright rejection of media portrayals which attempt to promote a particular legal ideology. Silbey's comments on the meaning-making process in operation in courtroom dramas are particularly useful here:

> First, trial films, as a group, contain identifiable patterns of narrative structure, cinematic features, and character development that manifest assumptions, embolden expectations, and reproduce ideological notions of legality. These patterns – marks of a genre – induce specific expectations of law in the films' community of viewers, expectations of their own subjective and authoritative role in making meaning and meting out justice within the American legal system. Second, in order for these patterns to be influential (as I argue that trial films are in the production of popular legal consciousness), as embodied by the trial film genre, these patterns constitute and encourage the identification of a specific kind of film viewer, what I call the trial film's viewer-subject. This viewer-subject is one end-effect of the trial film genre: an experience through which the spectator (inscribed by the filmic text) interacts with the social viewer (audience member) and is asked to assume certain positions within and by the film in order to make sense of it. This viewer-subject is one way trial films help sustain the power and legitimacy of legal institutions.
>
> (Silbey 2001: 97)

The key point, however, is that the 'social viewer' may choose not to endorse the position of the 'viewer-subject' inscribed in the text, thereby limiting the text's ability to further a legal ideology because of the discrepancy between its pre-programmed interpretations and those actualised by the social viewer.

A second, related factor in explaining the significance of the media as a resource for legal consciousness is the extent to which media representations manage to resonate with first-hand or local legal experience and meet the expectations of audiences. Making sense of audiences' preferences represents particular difficulties because it inevitably turns on the very difficult question of whether the media direct people's preferences or, vice versa, whether audiences' preferences direct their choice of media. Yet, preference is important in interpreting media influence: for example, having established a correlation between the type of newspapers that respondents prefer to read and their perceptions of crime, O'Connell, Invernizzi and Fuller (1998) were subsequently unable to exclude the possibility of this being a bottom-up (readers' perceptions of crime guide their choice of newspaper) rather than a top-down phenomenon (newspapers determine readers' perceptions of crime).

Furthermore, there is evidence to suggest that social identity is responsible for what Sasson (1995) calls a 'differential attentiveness to media discourse', which was evident from the different accounts that individuals of various social backgrounds produced when questioned about their perceptions of crime.

A sharp contradiction between media images and personal experience may result in the media being discounted as a source of legal consciousness. Someone from a minority background may be relatively indifferent towards mainstream cultural representations of law, as Ewick and Silbey (1995: 220) have suggested. Conversely, individuals may be motivated to specifically seek out media contents which resonate with their own first-hand legal experiences. Dowler (2002: 236) suggests that audiences consciously select media messages that are consistent with preconceived views they hold of a specific issue such as police effectiveness. Schrøder (2000: 245) highlights the vital role of the 'link of relevance' between the personal sphere of a reader/viewer and the sphere represented by media texts, suggesting that the interlocking of text and experience is extremely important. Thus it could be argued that what people see on television or encounter in other media has to relate to their own experiences in order to be relevant as a resource with which they can make sense of law. Moores (2000: 38), drawing on Giddens (1991), suggests that the desire to contribute to an ongoing narrative of the self is a strong factor in accounting for people's selection of media resources. Similarly, Ewick and Silbey (1995) identify storytelling as a prime location for observing the interactions between hegemony and resistance: the symbolic resources called upon by individuals, for example when accounting for their experiences of the social, need to fit in with the narrative which they wish – and often feel compelled – to recount.

I was able to observe such processes at work in my own research (Gies 2003a). Set in an inner-city environment, this particular project sought to address the question of what law meant to residents of the estate. Their local encounters with the law were multifarious and often confrontational, so much so that first-hand and hearsay anecdotes dominated their many stories about law. One of the (few) media resources which they appropriated in their accounts concerned the high-profile case of the racially motivated killing of the black teenager Stephen Lawrence, focusing on the failure of the police to bring his alleged white killers to justice and the subsequent public inquiry. This case undoubtedly represents one of the most significant turning points in race relations in Britain of the last decade.[6] As a media event, it was at its height at the time I conducted my research. It struck a particular chord with Afro-Caribbean residents who were able to integrate it quite easily into their biographies of selfhood and community which centred on their experiences of institutional racism in their own contacts with law enforcement agencies. The way in which mainstream media largely embraced the findings of the Lawrence Inquiry was remarkable because it was exceptional. The dominant media narrative was a symbolic resource which, for once, offered an almost seamless fit with the personal experiences of ethnic minorities.[7]

There are undoubtedly numerous inescapable media events, which Fiske (1984: 7) defines as 'sites of maximum visibility and maximum turbulence' to which we are virtually all exposed. The Stephen Lawrence case had such moments of intensity. Even individuals who try to avoid the most cataclysmic of media events, for example through a conscious decision not to watch television or read any newspapers, may find these somehow inescapable because they have become a talking point in every context of social interaction. Short of isolating themselves completely from social life, people may have very little choice but to take notice of these major events. It is tempting to argue, in analogy with Gerbner's theory of the distorting effect that prolonged and intense exposure to television has on perceptions of crime (Gerbner and Gross 1976; Gerbner 1996), that media events portraying a major upheaval within the legal or political system are bound to impact upon everyone's legal consciousness. While there is evidence to suggest that, regardless of social position, members of the same society tend to share some important cultural resources (some of which are media-related, see Sasson 1995), factors such as class, race and gender may still affect the level of attentiveness that individuals display towards cataclysmic media events. If the link of relevance between media discourse and experience is absent or very weak, the ability of these omnipresent media stories to direct someone's legal consciousness may be severely compromised. As Bird (2003: 2) notes: 'Images and messages wash over us, but most leave little trace, unless they resonate, even for a moment, with something in our personal or cultural experience.' The resonance factor could explain why major media events may be not relevant at all to the legal consciousness of some social groups while being overwhelmingly present in that of others. For example, Sasson (1995: 156) found that, despite significant media coverage of the incident, the story of the beating of Rodney King by LAPD Police was rarely referred to by white participants in his research while it figured prominently in the accounts of black participants. This points towards the role of resonance or fit as a decisive factor in the way in which individuals negotiate the interplay between personal experience and mediatised events.

Conclusion

Everyday life is, to quote Langbauer (1992: 49), 'a position or marker rather than a stable referent'. The everyday is impossible to grasp or conceptualise in an even way because it inevitably falls apart into contradictory fragments of experience. Everyday life is considered both a site of liberation and oppression. Celebrating the everyday for its authenticity runs the risk of ignoring its underlying exclusions and inequalities, while simply dismissing it as a pathology of modernity risks devaluing the lived experience of ordinary people.

Set against this complex theoretical backdrop, this chapter has tried to give some insight into where to situate two of modernity's most important off-shoots – law and media – in everyday life.

Law often comes across as remote, irrelevant and unresponsive to human wants and needs, but this does not stop it from steamrolling through many people's lives with little consideration for their dignity and right to self-determination (see Cowan 2004). The formidable presence of law is an opportunity to some who align themselves 'with the law', while others seek to resist it and try to minimise its disruptive potential. The media, replete with stories about law, have the ability to intensify both law's remoteness and its uncomfortable proximity. Through the media, we are offered the possibility to partake in law's other worldliness and to express surprise, bemusement or indignation at its machinations in a way which may come to reinforce the overall perception that law is simultaneously something which we will never be able to comprehend and which feels very real and important in our own lives.

Yet, at the same time, we also have the ability to simply ignore the media and let them wash over us because some of their messages will have limited relevance to our own existence. I have sought argue that our perception of and alertness to the media is not totally random or unpatterned. Direct experience is traded off against mediatised resources: the extent to which law is felt to disrupt daily life and the ability of the media to resonate with our personal experiences of law are arguably crucial factors. These, in turn, are often determined or influenced by social and cultural differences. The fact remains that, in comparison with an older white middle-class woman, a young black or Asian man tends to be much more visible to the law. Similarly, welfare bureaucracy has the strongest hold over the lives of society's most deprived groups. People struggle with law to varying degrees. Some will find that media stories resonate with their own experiences, while others will reject the same media narratives as completely unrepresentative.

An important conclusion which emerges from my discussion concerns the unpredictable nature of people's media consumption. The relationship between law and the media is uncomfortable for many reasons, one of which undoubtedly involves the volatile interventions of the consumer-sphinx. If only this enigmatic figure were more knowable and transparent, markets could be directed to strike a perfect balance between supply and demand, pollsters would be able to call the results of elections well in advance and policy makers would be relieved of their many anxieties about the way in which the media are influencing audiences. In short, taking the sphinx out of the consumer would represent a complete realisation of modernity's most nightmarish ambitions. Everyday life, however, is – mercifully – much more messy and less easy to tame.

Given the relative opacity of everyday practices, it is perhaps not surprising that law's presence in everyday life is often thought of as the exclusive realm of media representation: law is seen as too solemn, too technical and too arcane to be the object of ordinary experience. Consequently, what the media say about law is routinely conflated with what people think about law (or, to use Silbey's terminology again, the viewer-subject is conflated with the social viewer). This chapter has sought to argue that the better view is one which is sensitive to the way in which the representational and the experiential are mutually constitutive. Reality television, which will be discussed in the next chapter, offers a particularly interesting illustration. The coming together of cultural representation and everyday experience is the hallmark of reality television which, more than any other genre, has made it its mission to elevate ordinary people to a celebrity status and which derives its main inspiration from the everyday, thereby bridging the gap between the representational and the experiential. Not coincidentally, reality television narrates law as something in which ordinary people actively and extensively participate in everyday life. Far from being too banal for portrayal, day-to-day encounters with the law are the object of spectacle and drama in reality programmes focusing on seemingly ordinary and very recognisable situations.

Chapter 3

Reality TV and the jurisprudence of *Wife Swap*

Introduction

Over the last two decades, reality television has spawned some of the most noteworthy contributions to the growing 'juridico-entertainment complex' (Reed 1999 quoted in Haltom and McCann 2004: 11) providing further confirmation, if any was needed, of how strongly entwined law and media culture have become. In Britain, the quintessential real crime programme *Crimewatch*, which invokes the help of the public in solving crime through reconstructions and testimonials, has been joined by an endless array of other shows, such as *Clampers* (featuring traffic wardens), *Bailiffs* and *A Life of Grime* (featuring environmental officers from Salford City Council), all offering variations on the law-and-order theme. The popularity of the genre shows little sign of waning. In the US, *The Law Firm* in which young lawyers compete with each other by arguing 'real' cases before a retired judge and a 'real' jury hit the television screen in the summer of 2006, while the BBC recently broadcast *The Verdict*, a similar reality programme featuring a fictitious rape case tried by a retired judge and a jury consisting of celebrities. Meanwhile, in post-invasion Iraq, one of the most successful shows is *Terrorism in the Hands of Justice* in which suspects are paraded on television to confess to acts of terrorism, a form of publicity which is ostensibly aimed at maximising punishment and deterrence.

What is particularly remarkable about reality TV is the way in which everyday situations, incidents and events in which ordinary people are caught up take centre stage. In the previous chapter, I challenged the notion that the media must be instrumental in shaping people's knowledge and opinion of law because media culture constitutes their main, if not only, contact with law on a day-to-day basis. It has been my contention that law is actually strongly present in ordinary everyday experience where it shapes individuals' legal consciousness. The present chapter seeks to reinforce this point by showing how law is an integral aspect of the spectacle of the everyday in reality television. On the whole, reality TV is not concerned with offering viewers an escape to an exotic world that is far removed from the humdrum of everyday life but it seeks to enable identification with everyday situations in which law is acutely relevant.

The everyday in reality shows does not occur spontaneously: events are routinely engineered or staged for the benefit of making television. If law is to be understood as an 'internal feature of social situations' (Ewick and Silbey 1998: 35), that is, as 'legality', reality television is instructive about the way in which law, just as everyday life itself, can be subjected to a process of reality staging. Law often is the story to be told in reality TV, providing a narrative engine[1] which is at its best when transgressive behaviour occasions the invocation of the show's rule book, for example, when a 'fraudulent' participant is exposed and removed for a breach of established regulations or when a contestant in a talent show is punished for being 'in contempt of court' by showing a lack of deference to the experts acting as 'judges' of their star quality.[2] Although there is little to suggest that these shows want to be representative of the 'official' legal process – they may interface very little with law in a formal sense – I will argue that they nevertheless are part and parcel of reality television's spectre of legality.

The principal case study in this chapter is the British show *Wife Swap* (Channel 4, produced by RDF media) in with participants engage very actively in the reproduction of legality in a domestic setting. Domesticity, as we have seen in the previous chapter, is arguably everyday life's most prominent stage, involving responsibilities which have a habit of disproportionately burdening women. *Wife Swap* portrays the distribution of household work as a performance of gender scripts which are subject to informal rules of family life but which interestingly the show seeks to formalise and subject to a process of negotiation, thereby rendering them more legalistic. The show's premise is that two women who do not know each other swap families and spend the first five days living by each other's rules which they themselves appear to have articulated in a detailed manual. In the last five days of their stay, it is their turn to lay down their own rules and act as legislators to their host family.

Wife Swap is unusual in that it appears to give the participating wives considerable input, yet the title of the programme, with its sexual connotations, is also deeply ambivalent, suggesting that the women are objects to be exchanged. An important source of the women's disempowerment is the fact that they are the principal target of the highly codified set of rules that they impose on each other. Often unable to persuade their host families to comply with the legal regime they seek to institute, the wives struggle to assert their authority. Rather than being empowering, their legislative experiment often ends in failure and despair. One of the most significant moments of the show is the finale when the wives and their partners finally meet, an encounter which is often particularly confrontational for the women and which underscores *Wife Swap*'s unsurprising failure to embody a more progressive 'fantasy of women as law-makers' (Aristodemou 2000: Chapter 7). Yet, the point which the show eloquently conveys is that even when legality is at its most inconspicuous in everyday life and takes on the guise of taken-for-granted domestic routines, it can be disrupted in such a spectacular way as to foreground its importance as a battleground for social and legal equality.

Reality TV and everyday life

Reality[3] television spans a broad spectrum of programmes which range from 'docusoaps' and real crime shows to the confessional entertainment of chat shows and elaborately staged game shows in which the prizes are often equally varied: participants may be competing for a recording contract (*X-Factor*) or cash (*Big Brother*) – invariably coupled with short-lived notoriety and fame – but also the more intangible reward of self-betterment[4] or simply the excitement of playing with another identity.[5] News and current affairs documentaries are among the most important precursors of the reality format: just as reality TV, news nowadays is 'made' rather than reported, or as Brown (2003: 53) puts it, 'presented' rather than simply read out to the audience. According to Hill's genealogy (2004), reality television or 'popular factual television' has roots in tabloid journalism, documentary television and popular entertainment, three very diverse genres which came to the rescue of programme makers at a time when increased competition and deregulation made it necessary to cut production costs and make cheaper television.

What makes reality television instantly recognisable as a genre – notwithstanding its enormous hybridity – is its preoccupation with everyday life. As Hill explains:

> Many of the topics addressed by popular factual television are topics about ordinary people and their everyday lives. Popular factual programmes interconnect with people's everyday lives, addressing issues people are curious about, interested in, or care about. For British audiences the most popular types of reality programmes are about issues that are relevant to them – healthcare, crime, work and leisure, personal relationships.
>
> (Hill 2004: 191)

As a cultural phenomenon, reality television represents a milestone in the recognition of the everyday as something that is worthy of publicity and commentary, further eroding any remaining boundaries between the public and the private sphere (Van Zoonen 2001). Docusoaps which specialise in the activities of 'ordinary' people in 'ordinary' occupations such as traffic wardens, bailiffs and midwives are perhaps not that different from programmes which focus on the lives of (minor) celebrities who are often shown in rather unglamorous situations as they struggle with household chores, wayward offspring and unruly pets. Of course, it is highly debatable to what extent the antics of *Big Brother* contestants and the lead characters in *The Osbournes* (documenting the domestic life of the rocker Ozzy Osbourne) can be considered ordinary and mundane. Reality television may have brought about the Warholian prophecy that everyone can be famous for 15 minutes, but it is questionable whether the genre does indeed offer a voice to a genuine cross-section of 'ordinary' people (Couldry 2002; Tincknell and Raghuram 2004).

Moreover, it would be a misconception to say that reality television is about everyday life pure and simple. More often than not, participants find themselves in situations which are unfamiliar and unsettling (Jermyn 2004), allowing them to experiment with different lifestyle[6] choices and face up to extraordinary challenges. Thus, for example, the wives in *Wife Swap* are removed from their familiar home environment to live with a family whom they have never met before, taking a leap into the unknown. The break with everyday life rather than everyday life itself provides the thrill and drama around which so many reality shows are crafted. The appeal of the format for contestants is the promise that they will be whisked away from their everyday existence to fulfil their talent and ambitions by becoming a pop star, a fashion model or simply a celebrity. It is the juxtaposition of the ordinary and the extraordinary, the promise that no life is too dull or too ordinary to be turned into an object of nationwide fascination, which appears to explain the success of reality television.

The democratisation of technology is a significant factor in the foregrounding of the everyday in reality shows. The hand-held and self-operated camera has reduced production costs and increased the media visibility of everyday activities that would otherwise remain obscure. Thanks to websites such as YouTube amateur footage of events (and non-events) can be instantly uploaded onto the internet. We now live in the 'cam era' (Koskela 2004), which is the result of a technological explosion allowing for around-the-clock surveillance and self-observation, throwing even the least noteworthy aspects of everyday existence into the media limelight. Both our ontological security and discomfort hinge on the presence of CCTV cameras in public spaces and, not coincidentally, it is CCTV footage which provides such rich pickings for real crime shows (Jermyn 2004). Surveillance technology figures prominently in the toolkit of reality genres, making grainy CCTV footage the hallmark of authenticity and realism across the entire spectrum of reality TV. Whereas professional camerawork only suggests to a media-literate audience that an event was staged for the benefit of the broadcast, poor quality amateur images from CCTV cameras and portable surveillance technology have become synonymous with authentic representations of everyday life which only accidentally made it onto television and therefore have a greater cachet of credibility (see Jermyn 2004).

The long-term consequences of this mainstreaming of technology may be difficult to fathom and it is always wise to avoid broad-sweeping predictions about the impact of any new technology. However, it would certainly appear that the domestication of technology has permanently discredited thinking which involves seeing media audiences as a passive and meek crowd of atomised individuals (see Chapter 4). For Brown (2003: 55), 'soon, the term "audience", always imprecise, already anachronistic, will disappear altogether', while according to Koskela (2004: 1999), 'ordinary' people are 'reclaiming the copyright of their own lives'. People may often have very little control over the technological gaze which they undergo in public spaces and reality television is often accused of being exploitative, but some individuals obviously relish the opportunity to turn their own everyday existence into a spectacle. Moreover, reality television routinely solicits and commercially exploits the audience's active participation, for example to vote off contestants, through interactive technology such as text messaging and the internet. This takes the audience's input into media culture to a level which even the most ardent supporters of the resistive audience thesis (see Chapter 4) could have hardly thought possible about a decade ago.[7] The audience no longer just watches from the sideline; it has become the text to be consumed and it is often the most important protagonist in the story. Tincknell and Raghuram explain:

> A viewer sitting at home is not only invited to identify *with* the actors; she or he can *become* one of them by volunteering to tell her story, become a contestant, or by taking part in the show as one of the studio audience. Such programmes thus constantly solicit the audience to 'be the text', through their necessarily extensive and repeated appeals for participants.
>
> (Tincknell and Raghuram 2004: 258)

Law and reality television

It is clear that reality television is greatly indebted to pioneering factual programmes featuring emergency services such as the police, fire fighters and ambulance crews (Hill 2000). Moreover, the reaction of cultural commentators to real crime shows when they were first broadcast in the mid 1980s prefigured current moral concerns that reality TV exploits participants and panders to audiences' unhealthy curiosity (Jermyn 2004). The real crime format is interwoven with the narrative structure of reality television. Brown (2003: 39) observes that reality television genres are 'in essence extensions of a logic which has always been present in popular cultural representations of crime and law' (see also Sparks 1992). Indeed, even lifestyle shows, which at first glance occupy an entirely different niche in the television schedules, mobilise what Brown (2003: 43) terms 'crime metaphors'. The 'naming and shaming' on television of 'offenders' of good taste or hygiene by the 'fashion police' (for example, *What Not To Wear* on BBC 1 which mimics a police line-up of potential makeover candidates), interior decorators (for example, *How Not To Decorate* on Channel 5) and professional cleaners (for example, *How Clean is Your House?* on ITV) are an undisguised emulation of the exposure of criminals in crime appeal programmes. The use of cameras to catch 'offenders' (who are sometimes unaware that they are being filmed) in the act as they go about their daily routines or to film other people's reactions to an alleged aesthetic 'offence' (for example, bad interior decorating) constitute a favourite shock tactic of lifestyle programmes aiming to demonstrate how much participants are in need of a makeover, the lifestyle format's equivalent of offender rehabilitation.

Programmes enlisting lab technicians and other people in white coats to establish how unhygienic someone's house is (*How Clean is Your House?*) or how unhealthy someone's diet is (for example, ITV's *You Are What You Eat* in which significant attention is given to the lab analysis of participants' bodily fluids) strongly echo the minutiae of forensic analysis featured in real crime programmes. Truth established through scientific means and sanctioned through the process of law commands a level of respect and credibility which sets it apart from the uncorroborated personal opinions of lifestyle experts. Trinny and Susanna, the style gurus of the BBC fashion makeover show *What Not To Wear* do not just opine that their makeover candidates have terrible taste in fashion; they have forensic-style evidence (including footage from a near strip search in front of a 360 degree mirror) to back up their claims. Kim and Aggie, another television duo featuring in the home makeover show *How Clean is Your House?*, use detailed lab results as a trump card to prove to participants just how germ-ridden their houses have become. By emulating a legal-panoptical approach to evidencing truth, even seemingly subjective and taste-specific topics such as what is stylish or clean acquire a gloss of universalism and objectivity, authorising experts to lay down the rules which the successful makeover candidate must obey.[8]

Crime and law metaphors are important not just in lifestyle programmes but also feature prominently in reality talent contest shows. One example is the use of expert panels which evaluate the talent of contestants in phenomenally successful talent shows such as *Pop Idol* and *The X-Factor* (both broadcast by ITV in the UK). The experts are systematically referred to as 'judges', evoking a type of authority which transcends that of a mere assessor or auditor of a talent competition. The experts in *The X-Factor* have to deal with the acute dilemma of being put in a position of being a judge in their own cause. Acting as mentors to an assigned category of contestants, the experts also act as judges of their own and each other's acts, providing a master class in judicial bias. The judges act tactically while claiming neutrality and their decisions fuel much speculation in the press and on fan websites as to what motivated them to vote off or keep in a particular contestant. As a commentary on the performance of judges, the picture could hardly be more critical: the expert-judges are revealed to be flawed individuals who are driven by ulterior motives and display a spurious sense of justice. Yet, there is a distinct lack of indignation at this unflattering portrayal on the part of (other? real?) judges. While there are precedents of fictitious miscarriages of justice in soaps moving fans to campaign for the release of the wrongly convicted character (Brown 2003: 53), to date this has not been paralleled by audience mobilisations around reality talent contests. This may well be because shows of this kind tend to engage with legality in a different way: unlike fiction or factual reporting, reality talent contests do not purport to portray an external referent. Instead, they belong to a consciously self-referential universe.

As Couldry (2002: 84) observes, there is an obvious ambiguity in reality shows which is often deliberately left unresolved: reality television is only a game but it is one which appeals to veracity. The truth to be revealed, however, is mostly an immanent reality which reality television seeks to provoke rather than depict in a transparent manner. Taken-for-granted patterns and routines (such as a bad fashion sense, unhealthy diets and the distribution of household chores) are revealed to contestants and makeover candidates by virtue of their participation in the experiment or game that is the reality programme. Without the programme, such routines and habits would have remained unquestioned and therefore they would have continued to be an unknown un-reality. There are obvious echoes here of Boorstin's 'pseudo-events' (1961) and Baudrillard's (1983) 'hyperreality' which attributes to media culture an ability to create a heightened sense of reality which appears to be more vivid, more thrilling and more actual than is actual empirical reality (Hill 2000; Brown 2003; Jermyn 2004). Reality television has come of age by making such great strides in its invention of the real that it no longer needs any symbolic gesturing to a stable external referent. As Brown (2003: 17) points out, 'the news media is more and more constituted by news *about* the media' while soaps adopt major current affairs topics such as domestic violence and racism as storylines that are consequently recycled again by news media. That media culture is in many ways circular and self-referential is a point which will be considered in more detail in Chapter 6.

Social experiment programmes (which differ from talent contest shows in that it is not always clear what type of talent or skill is being tested) are another noteworthy case of such self-referencing. To study social experiment television as something that is representative – or more commonly fails to be genuinely representative – of reality is somewhat misguided. There is no 'slice of life' to be represented in such shows; they are a creative force in their own right merely offering what Hill (2004: 177) terms a 'staged reality'. The celebrities which emerge from these programmes, bar a few, tend to disappear from sight as soon as they are deprived of the oxygen of publicity generated by the programme which made them famous. The contemporary celebrity is the figment of reality television's imagination, a type of brainchild who can never live an independent life because reality formats take a minimal interest in cultivating their relationship with anything other than their own reality.[9] For example, there is no suggestion in *Big Brother* that in the real world a group of strangers voluntarily would spend months together locked away in a house to win a cash prize, just as *Wife Swap* does not claim that wives habitually swap places to go and live in each other's homes in a bizarre pact to lower their own and each other's self-esteem. Such realities are staged because it allows programme makers and participants to tease out a truth which could not be articulated without an intense process of surveillance. *Big Brother* and *Wife Swap* do not *represent* but merely *complement* a social reality (such as that of reconstituted families or friends forced to cohabit because of rising rent and house prices) in which people increasingly grapple with intimate relations that are not exclusively constructed around kinship or heterosexual desire.

What are we to make of this realm which fits neither the category of fact nor that of fiction? This question requires new light to be shed on the problematic that figures prominently in this book: the failure of media culture to do justice to legal truth by means of factually accurate representations. Concerns about media distortion and misrepresentation proceed on the assumption that the media fraudulently suggest that they are representative of reality. However, reality genres have reneged on television's promise that it can offer a window on the world: most reality TV is merely introspective or indeed 'implosive' (Brown 2003: 64). This points to an alternative economy of legal signification. Reality television stages and arguably upstages law's reality by creating its own parallel universe. In doing so, reality genres move into a utopian and dystopian terrain which is usually reserved for visionary political fiction.[10] Reality TV taps into law's 'deep structure' (Milovanonic 1992), articulating what is often an inarticulate residue in law.[11] The *X-Factor* shows what happens when judges give in to the temptations of passion and personal preference, *Big Brother* addresses the implications of 24-hour surveillance in the name of authority and *Wife Swap*, as I discuss below, asks how women fare when they attempt to lay down the law. Reality television magnifies the micro drama of such everyday struggles and gives these an intensity that they are often denied in the official legal realm.

Wife Swap

Wife Swap *as watercooler TV*

Wife Swap can be described as 'part social experiment, part makeover, and part gameshow' (Hill 2004: 36). The show aims to transform participants' lives by letting them experience for the duration of a 10-day period different lifestyle choices pertaining to child rearing, the allocation of household chores and work–life balance issues. The show was an instant success when it was first broadcast by Channel 4 in 2003 and the programme has received numerous awards, including the prestigious BAFTA award for Best Features Programme in 2004. As with so many other reality shows, *Wife Swap* has also proved a hit with the tabloid press making some of the participants minor celebrities whose fame is extended thanks to regular appearances in the gossip columns, reinforcing the programme's quality as 'watercooler TV' (Holmes and Jermyn 2004: 14). While supporters and critics[12] cannot agree on whether *Wife Swap* offers a fascinating insight into the pressures of modern life, women's lives in particular, or whether it is voyeuristic and exploitative of women's insecurities regarding their position in the home, the show's underlying legal narrative has received far less attention. Bearing a suggestive title with unmistakable sexual connotations, *Wife Swap* is foremost an exploration of the 'sexual contract' (Pateman 1988) in which agreements serve to simultaneously entrench and question the taken-for-granted distribution of domestic chores.

As we have seen in the previous chapter, everyday social interactions, including those in the domestic sphere, are of particular interest to legal consciousness research which seeks to move beyond a narrow preoccupation with formal law. Ewick and Silbey comment:

> It is increasingly clear that to know the law we should expand the range of material and social practices and actors that constitute it. We need to discover not only how and by whom the law is used, but also when and by whom it is not used. We need, for that matter, to reassess what we define as using the law. Moving away from a focus on use as exclusively the mobilisation of formal or official legal actors, we must consider legal use in other contexts, within family and neighbourhoods, workplaces, and for purposes unintended by formal lawmakers.
>
> (Ewick and Silbey 1998: 34)

Wife Swap is brilliant at exploiting the pettiness of everyday domesticity and the seemingly trivial injustices which accompany it: the grating unfairness of having to pick up someone else's dirty socks, clean up after others or do the dishes just because you are told this is your place as a spouse, parent or child. Unremarkable as such matters may be, they are the stuff of everyday experiences of inequality, yet they are often obscured in the official legal canon.[13] How such ordinary experiences are mapped out in media discourse is therefore a worthwhile enquiry if we are looking to broaden legal analysis in the manner envisaged by Ewick and Silbey.

The use of agreements to iron out imbalances in domestic relations or, by contrast, cement inequality manifests itself in different ways in *Wife Swap*. At one level there is the contract between the participating families and the programme makers in which the former are rewarded with celebrity and greater self-knowledge – familiar rewards of reality television – (Couldry 2002), in exchange for agreeing to have their experiences broadcast to the nation. It is not clear if participants receive any money. The chance to appear on television, the excitement of being able to live someone else's life for a 10-day period and the possibility of re-evaluating one's own domestic life appear to be the main incentive for participants. The execution of this script is very formulaic:[14] programme makers seek to maximise differences between participants, and thereby the potential for antagonism and confrontation, by staging an exchange between families of very different social backgrounds, most importantly in terms of their class and lifestyle but occasionally also their race and nationality. A contrast which is routinely sought after by programme makers is that of an industrious wife used to toiling in the home with little support from her partner trading places with a woman who expects her partner do a substantial share of the housework. A variation on this theme is that of the submissive wife trading places with a domineering wife generating contest and strife around differing notions of femininity. The couples who trade places for the purpose of the experiment are either married or cohabiting and they are overwhelmingly heterosexual.[15] Very exceptionally, husbands will exchange places but the majority of episodes involve a swap between wives.[16]

Renegotiating the sexual contract

The programme is surprisingly silent on whether there is a sexual aspect to the exchange. The newly constituted couples occasionally are shown to be engaging in romantic activities such as candlelit suppers but the extent to which *Wife Swap* is a sexual exchange is left unexplored.[17] Nonetheless, to fully understand how the programme operates, it is important to highlight its performance of what Pateman (1988) has famously termed 'the sexual contract' which is embedded in the very notion of marriage and the private sphere, inextricably linking it with the status of wives. By calling the show 'Wife Swap' – and not, for example, 'Family Swap'[18] – its central narrative appears to negate the women's autonomy and agency in the decision to spend time with an unknown family. *Wife Swap* undoubtedly deserves a nuanced reading: the women are the object of the contractual exchange staged by programme makers, but at the same time they also appear to be very much in control as it is they who write the household manuals to be followed in the show. However, by uprooting the women from their own domestic, social and cultural milieu and placing them in the unfamiliar territory that is the other (wo)man's home, programme makers also systematically put them at a disadvantage vis-à-vis their host family, which undermines the women's position and often saps their morale.[19]

The roots of the sexual contract, the necessary precondition for marriage, are not an agreement between a man and a woman but foremost an agreement between men giving each other sexual access to women and the logical possibility of this resulting in fatherhood and a range of assorted rights (Pateman 1988; Aristodemou 2000). With the word 'wife' connoting sexual status and 'swap' hinting at an exchange of sexual partners, the very presence of the wives in the men's respective households in *Wife Swap* is suggestive of the women's sexual availability. The sexual politics of the programme clearly lends itself to quite contrasting interpretations. That for some on the Right the show represents an unacceptably permissive stance on traditional family values was very much evident from the reaction of the American Family Association, which was swift to condemn plans for an American version of *Wife Swap*, arguing that it was unacceptable for Christians that a married woman should go and live with someone else's husband.[20] On the other hand, a feminist reading of *Wife Swap* cannot ignore the fact that the programme has the dystopian ring of Margaret Atwood's *The Handmaid's Tale* (1986) in which by way of punishment for the sexual freedom they enjoyed in a pre-revolutionary era, 'fallen' women are sent from one home to the other in order to be impregnated by the man of the house, invariably a high-ranking official wielding power in a post-revolutionary society which is based on strict biblical teachings.

Menial household tasks are the most pronounced focus for the bargaining in *Wife Swap*, allowing for the sexual contract to be fleshed out in very minute detail. The programme tends to focus on the many chores with which the 'liberated' wife struggles as she adjusts to the life of her toiling counterpart and the void which the latter experiences when she is suddenly relieved from the yoke of her usual domestic work pattern. This is not an unequivocally liberating narrative but a source of much divisiveness: the toiling wife is often shown in the programme to be spending much of her time berating the woman whom she replaces, criticising the standards of cleanliness in her new home and commenting disapprovingly on the take-away and microwave dinners served up to the family under the regime of the 'lazy wife'.[21] The programme immerses itself with much gusto in major private sphere issues, focusing attention on labour inside as opposed to outside the home. While such attention is indicative of a growing cultural recognition of everyday life, it also means that viewers are given limited insight into the non-domestic aspects of the women's lives such as their careers, hobbies and social circle (Fairclough 2004). By contrast, the men in *Wife Swap* are at times mainly there as extras because their identity is not bound up that strongly with home life.

Pateman's observations are very relevant in unravelling this gender divide as she argues that what distinguishes marriage from an employment contract is the deployment of the wife as an unpaid labourer in the home:

> A (house)wife does not contract out her labour power to her husband. She is not paid a wage – there is no token of free exchange – because her husband has control over the use of her labour by virtue of the fact that he is a man. The marriage contract is a labour contract in a very different sense from the employment contract. The marriage contract is about women's labour; the employment contract is about *men's* work.
>
> (Pateman 1988: 135)

One wonders if *Wife Swap* would work as a television show if it routinely involved a husbands' swap. Because the women in their capacity as wives or partners are unwaged labourers, the contingencies of supply and demand in the marketplace can be completely ignored in *Wife Swap*: no matter how much work or how little work each woman is used to doing, there is no bargaining taking place to compensate for any differences in their workload. The ease with which women can be 'slotted in' makes it possible for the swap to occur without disrupting the normal rhythm of the household.

Wives at war

The most troubling aspect of *Wife Swap* is that it is unashamedly geared to fostering distrust and intense rivalry between the wives, routinely singling out the women's insecurities. The most common source of the women's vulnerability is the programme's panoptical scrutiny of their performance as domestic workers: having cameras constantly following participants around is undoubtedly instrumental to the formula. The personalities of the wives are usually portrayed in a very unfavourable light and they often come across as highly dysfunctional, neurotic, pathological and over-emotional.[22] The toiling wife is typecast as a sad and uptight woman who is obsessed with cleanliness and who deserves to be pitied. It is not uncommon for her to be told by the other wife that she should learn to lighten up if she wants to be more fun as a partner and a mother. By contrast, the 'liberated' wife tends to be exposed as a sloppy, uncaring and lazy housewife who should make a greater contribution to the household by doing more cleaning, cooking fresh meals and prioritising her role as homemaker over her career. The domineering wife is told to be less assertive while the submissive wife receives patronising advice about how to be a more 'modern' wife. In short, there is usually a staggering lack of solidarity between the participating women. They routinely compete with each other to be the better wife (and woman) and often fail to show any understanding of each other's lifestyles. This divide is also often exacerbated by the class differences between families who have a very different approach to issues such as child rearing and the allocation of household chores.

The finale of each episode, a variation on the theme of the 'reveal' which is characteristic of reality programming (Hill 2004), when the couples meet to discuss their experiences, does not provide the kind of deliberative space in which the women are able to validate and transcend their differences. Instead, the programme is edited in such a way that the encounter frequently ends in an unedifying shouting match (and even physical aggression) between the women while the men take a back seat. Consider, for example, the following exchange at the end of an episode from series 5 between Wilma and Sharon when they meet to discuss their experiences:[23]

Wilma:	My house is beautiful. If I had your house, I wouldn't want to clean it.
Sharon:	What are you saying about our house? [Turns to her husband] You know what: six hours of cleaning every Thursday. Right, and what's not finished on the Thursday, finishes Friday.
Wilma:	At least I clean.
Sharon:	And then every single night . . .
Wilma:	At least I clean.
Sharon:	Our house is so dirty. Our house is so dirty!
Wilma:	You have no idea about life. At last I can put a face . . .
Trevor, Sharon's husband:	[Loud laughter] We have no idea about life?!
Sharon:	What planet are you off from? I think you're from fucking planet Z . . . because you're really not normal . . .
Wilma:	To sleep as long as you do. To do nothing. A wife? A mother?
Sharon:	Aw . . .
Wilma:	Yeah, you are nothing.
Sharon:	Aw, right.
Wilma:	You are in the gutter . . .
Sharon:	You're a piece of shit I wouldn't even stand on, you know that?
Wilma:	You're in the gutter.
Sharon:	You're a fucking shit.
Wilma:	You have a beautiful, beautiful girl. All she sees is alcohol.
Sharon:	Why don't you go and sit up there on your fucking pedestal cause you're trying to sound like you're a fucking martyr.
Wilma:	[Pointing to the floor] Cause you're down here, that's where you are.
Trevor:	[To Wilma] You're really talking crap.
Sharon:	I'm actually gonna go fucking mental in a minute. I am. Because she's like . . .
Trevor:	She's talking crap . . .
Sharon:	I tell you what [throws her glass of water in Wilma's direction]. I fucking can't stand it.
Mark, Wilma's husband:	[Jumps up] OK, that's it.
Sharon:	[Walking away from the table] I'm not having her. Fucking contrary fucking . . .
Wilma:	It's hard to hear the truth . . . It's hard to hear the truth. That's what's wrong.
Mark:	[Walks up to Trevor, seeks eye contact and shakes hands with him] Listen, listen, please, all right?
Sharon:	[Retreating from the room] Get off your fucking pedestal.

In the exchange above, the camaraderie and solidarity between the husbands, symbolised by the gesture of the handshake, contrast sharply with the verbal abuse the wives direct at each other. Indeed, there could not be a greater difference between the composure of the men and their wives' outbursts:

while the men, almost as if by tacit agreement, treat each other in a civilised way, they are content to look on as the reveal escalates into a catfight between their wives. Brown's (2003: 116) consideration that many reality formats offer a portrayal of understated violence makes great sense here: 'These examples demonstrate much more clearly than perhaps "slasher" movies do, the extent to which bodily violence is subtly and not-so-subtly implicated in everyday life, but always already media-created.' Although her comments mainly refer to reality programmes involving dieting and cosmetic surgery, they are equally applicable to the outbursts of verbal and occasionally physical aggression witnessed in *Wife Swap*.

Rule changes

The failure of *Wife Swap* to foster solidarity between the participating women stands in sharp contrast with the experiment's promise of enlightenment and broadening participants' horizons by means of a role reversal. One important moment of reversal occurs when the women, having lived by each other's rules for the first half of their stay in their host family, are given the opportunity to create their own regime for the remainder of the time which is aimed at enlightening family members as to how home life could be organised differently. The changeover is a very formal process whereby the legislating wife assembles her host family and proclaims the rules that are about to come into force. This allocation of rule-making powers to the women serves as a reminder that the home is traditionally women's sphere of decision making but more subtly it points to the idea that the sexual contract is negotiable.

The question is: why do the women's legislative efforts so spectacularly and so consistently founder? A very prosaic answer is undoubtedly that this is how programme makers want the show to function on a narrative level: they choose to focus on moments of conflict and despair because they believe that this makes compelling viewing, although this does not fully answer the question of why they should think that showing the women in a non-confrontational light would make bad television.[24] Even devoted viewers, it seems, are at a loss to explain the appeal of the show, as the following entry on Channel 4's online discussion forums acknowledges:[25]

> I suppose maybe the show is good watching in sort of an 'automobile wreck' kind of way. You know that it's horrible, yet you still can't help but look. It damages and hurts people (the participants) while onlookers drive by to rubberneck.

A viewer on another website concurs:[26]

> Wife Swap is appalling for many reasons, not least the participants. Both series have been sprinkled with swearing, sexism, prejudice and snobbery.

You definitely feel slightly nauseous, even dirty, after watching Wife Swap. But there is something endlessly fascinating at looking at the different ways that people live their lives.

The show's car crash aspect (another metaphor of violence) in large part derives from the unfavourable circumstances in which the wives invent and reinvent the household rulebook. The women impose their regime without consulting each other or their host families, which means that their laws are severely lacking in legitimacy. Rebellion against the new regime that the wives attempt to establish in the second week is commonplace: the women, who living in a strangers' home are literally on unfamiliar territory, are isolated from the start and their attempt to impose their own rule without consultation or debate isolates them further, crumbling the little power they hold and exposing them as very ineffectual law makers. Under the show's formula the result of the rule changes is often that the new rulebook is ignored, making the women even more vulnerable than before as the limited authority they have is completely undermined by the host family's lack of compliance. What is perhaps most troubling about this portrayal is its apparent suggestion that women have neither the authority nor the nous to be able to become successful legislators.

Promoting traditional womanhood?

The clash between different lifestyles which the show subjects to a codification exercise is undoubtedly aimed at giving viewers some food for thought and inviting them to reflect on their own lifestyle choices. Amidst all the upheaval and confrontation, the show is a makeover narrative in which there is considerable emphasis on how the swap changes participants' family life.[27] However, it is striking that the lifestyle changes which some participants appear prepared to make at the end of each episode often produce shifts which are sufficient to rein in the equality claims of the 'liberated' wife but which are insufficient to bring equality for her unliberated counterpart. Men who are accustomed to doing very few household chores count their blessings when their wives return home at the end of the exchange and they vow not to 'take them for granted' as much as they used to do, but changes in their conduct are usually slight and their wives still end up doing the lion's share of the housework. By contrast, it is not uncommon for the 'liberated' wife to return home in a much weaker position, feeling pressure to be more involved in the housework.

For example, in episode 2 of the first series of *Wife Swap USA*, Kym, an 'unorthodox working woman who believes her husband should rule the kitchen',[28] swaps with Dawn who gets up at 5:30 am to make her husband's coffee before she embarks on her own day of doing household chores and her full-time job as a medical transcriber working from home. At the end of the episode, Dawn who believes that a 'real' man should have gainful employment outside the home, causes a radical rethink in Kym's household resulting in her partner giving up his position as house husband to find a job as a painter-decorator. While Dawn's husband, a self-confessed 'redneck', also undergoes a transformation by showing a greater commitment to household chores, his position remains fundamentally unchallenged. The greatest change took place in Kym's household, which now resembles a more conventional heterosexual family unit. In *Wife Swap*, the 'radical' principles embedded in the laws of the 'liberated' or the domineering wife are often treated as problematic and in need of invalidating while the submissive wife's codex of household politics usually only requires amending.

Holmes and Jermyn argue that many lifestyle programmes which set out to document women's experiences are distinctly normalising:

> Rather than empowering these ordinary people by giving them a platform from which to share and celebrate their personal experience, these programmes co-opt their stories into a discourse in which the overwhelming drive is to contain and deny difference in order to embrace the apparently universal female desire for conventional marriage and motherhood.
>
> (Holmes and Jermyn 2004: 24)

Similarly, from a narrative perspective, the lifestyle experiment in *Wife Swap* more often than not aims to blunt differences between the swappers, mainly in such a way that their outlook on family life gravitates towards a normative middle ground of womanhood.[29] *Wife Swap* could easily be interpreted as the expression of a worrying desire to turn back the clock in an age of greater formal gender equality, as indeed Fairclough suggests:

> Unfortunately, after the quantifiable progress that has been made in terms of the representation of women within visual media, a programme such as *Wife Swap* is intrinsically negative and even threatens to undo this progress due to its harking back to an outdated and conservative representation of wives and mothers.
>
> (Fairclough 2004: 345)

However, it is perhaps too easy to dismiss *Wife Swap* as some kind of anachronism that is an affront to gender equality, just as it would be wrong to judge the show in terms of how representative it is of domestic politics in the early twenty-first century. The issues with which the families struggle are undoubtedly recognisable. Applying the thesis that reality television tends to stage legality rather than represent it, the often unedifying spectacle that is *Wife Swap* could be seen as nothing more than a piece of improvised theatre. The reactionary domesticity of *Wife Swap* (and similar programmes) is not that different from the 'playful misogyny' of men's magazines which became a phenomenal success in the 1990s (Stevenson, Jackson and Brooks 2000: 377) and which offer readers a non-politically correct way of negotiating the uneasy questions which present themselves in an age of profound social change. *Wife Swap* bears testimony to the adjustments which are required from individual men and women in the private sphere in an age of greater legal equality. The show's paucity of imagination – portraying women as either dominatrix figures or as 'exploited doormats' (Fairclough 2004: 345) whose different lifestyle choices are a cause for great conflict – is a measure of the problems involved in the cultural re-scripting of the sexual contract and the difficulty of envisaging strategies for dislodging both the habitual and normative dimensions of everyday life.

Conclusion

While it is difficult to predict whether reality programmes will continue to dominate the television schedules – even media experts were caught out by the rising success of reality genres in the 1990s – it is a phenomenon which undoubtedly has profoundly changed media culture. There is a close connection between the introduction of CCTV footage when real crime shows first hit our television screens and the widespread use of surveillance technology in reality television today, enabling programme makers to take the minutiae of everyday life as the focus of their reality creations. It is not just crime and deviance which undergo the panoptical treatment; domesticity (no less violent perhaps) also attracts around-the-clock observation, generating hugely popular programmes among which *Wife Swap* undoubtedly takes a place of honour. However, the use of surveillance technology is not the only legacy of real crime shows. Even more important is the adoption of law-centred narratives across a very diverse range of programmes, including the ubiquitous lifestyle format which is interwoven with everyday legal experience.

The argument which I have made in this chapter is that to understand reality television, it is important to avoid seeing it as a distortion of an external reality because that suggests that it is simply a failed attempt at portraying what goes on in the outside world. Many reality programmes are not interested in representing reality; they are in the business of manufacturing their own reality. Reality television does not seek to compete with or measure itself against a set of independently verifiable facts or situations. The social experimentation in which many reality shows take part is indicative of a self-created and hyperbolic realism. Understandably, *Wife Swap* invites speculation as to how representative the programme is of women's position in contemporary family life: both the submissive doormat and the bossy wife are easily constructed as an affront to middle-class sensibilities. However, such an assessment proceeds on the basis that reality television has a slice of life quality which makes it a faithful depiction of what goes on in wider society. *Wife Swap* certainly does its best to cultivate sharp contrasts, but it could not in any way pretend to be a statistical measurement of family life. The programme manages to showcase reality television's potential to stage reality rather than to slavishly represent it. In the long run, this could prefigure new ways in which media culture defines the very category of legal reality.

This issue will be explored more fully in Chapter 6. However, one approach which is already worth flagging here involves Brown's suggestion that rather than assessing media representations in terms of their realism, it is preferable to think of them as maps in the cartographic sense:

> Thus it is with the contemporary mediascape; it is analogically comprehensible as a mosaic of maps. The maps of the actual, 'natural' physical world bear no more or less relationship to it than do media representations to social reality. The mediascape is at once more and less than the real; it could never correspond to it, and vice versa, because the media creates reality in the way maps create landscapes: partly in relation to the practical objectives and normative practices of institutions, partly in relation to the expressive signifiers of inexpressible lusts and longings, fears and hopes, hedonisms and nihilisms of cultures.
>
> (Brown 2003: 181)

As a map to social reality, *Wife Swap* tells us that domestic arrangements are no less stubborn and immutable than is formal law, even when women are given carte blanche to change the rules overnight. However, as a map, it is also imprisoned in its own reality whose capability to re-image and re-arrange the socio-legal fabric of everyday life is inherently constrained.

Chapter 4

Method, audience and social practice

Introduction

Any attempt at understanding the uncomfortable relationship between law and the media cannot be complete without considering legal actors' concerns about the impact that distorted media representations have on lay publics. We saw in Chapter 1 that media influence on public confidence in the administration of justice lies at the heart of this debate. Judges, lawyers and legal academics are not alone in assuming that the media generate powerful and usually adverse effects which are responsible for a wide range of social problems. Jewkes comments that:

> Whether assessing the effects of advertising, measuring the usefulness of political campaigns in predicting voting behaviour, deciding film and video classifications or introducing software to aid parents in controlling their children's exposure to certain forms of Internet content, much policy in these areas is underpinned by media-centric, message-specific, micro-orientated, positivist, authoritarian, short-term assumptions of human behaviour.
>
> (Jewkes 2004: 11)

In other words, social anxieties about the media very narrowly centre on audiences' responses and behaviour but they tend to ignore the complex social and cultural backdrop against which media culture operates. This lack of context is most vividly illustrated by the hypodermic syringe model which holds that the media act as a set of powerful stimuli which are 'injected' into people, generating inescapable and predominantly negative effects (Gauntlett 1995; Jewkes 2004).

Indeed, almost as soon as a new medium enters the mainstream and becomes commercially available, concerns about its effects crop up and force their way to the top of the policy agenda, but interestingly new media technology also tends to create high expectations regarding its ability to make more critical, more knowledgeable and more vigilant citizens of us all

(Schoenbach 2001). That has been the story of contemporary popular media such as the internet, video games, television, film and, going further back in media history, printing and writing (Sutter 2000). Indeed, Schoenbach (2001: 363) reminds us that 'Socrates was the first to complain about the decline of memory because of the new medium "written texts" and about the treacherous nature of black marks on white' while Thornton (2002: 15) argues that 'fear of the effect of popular culture on law today would seem to be analogous to Plato's fear of the corrupting effect of profane poetry on philosophy in Classical Athens'. What pessimists and optimists have in common is a shared belief that, for better or for worse, the media touch and transform people's lives (Couldry 2004: 117).

Researching audiences is one of the most challenging tasks in media studies and related disciplines. The stakes are undoubtedly very high. As Schoenbach (2001) argues, the hypodermic syringe model may be no more than a myth of convenience which lends itself very well to promoting and safeguarding policies that are designed to contain media effects, suggesting that some of the foundations of regulation would have to be rethought if there were to be any retreat from the idea that the media trigger powerful effects. This is not to deny that the media are an important social force; the point is merely that their impact is not proving simple or straightforward to explain. This chapter aims to demonstrate that the way in which the role of audiences should be examined, interpreted and conceptualised is a deeply contentious issue.

The task in hand is to examine to what extent legal actors' specific concerns about media effects have an epistemological grounding in relevant literatures. This will be approached by outlining the various methodologies that have been deployed to make sense of processes of media consumption. One of the most momentous interventions in this field has been that of cultural studies in the 1970s and 1980s, which turned traditional effects research on its head by approaching the audience not as passive dopes hypnotised by manipulative media but as active and creative participants in the communication process whose input in the production of meaning was to be treated on a par with that of creators of media texts themselves. Audiences, in other words, were seen as capable of resisting the power of the media. However, cultural studies' celebration of audiences as active and creative has in turn sparked the criticism that this is too optimistic an understanding of media culture. This has been instrumental in triggering a profound crisis in cultural studies. For a field that was once heralded as the only possible future orientation for the humanities (Baetens 2005) and which significantly has also been embraced by socio-legal scholars (Sarat and Simon 2003), the decline of cultural studies raises issues that are clearly of wider importance.

If the writing is on the wall for the cultural studies paradigm, where does this leave the effort to develop a way of grappling with the interleaving of law and media culture in everyday life which is not driven by a media effects model? I will suggest the answer to this question resides in the adoption of a methodological pluralism which incorporates the legacy of cultural studies, but it also requires a decentring of the relatively narrow concern with the interaction between particular media texts and audiences in favour of the study of media culture as something which is interwoven with a wide range of social practices. First, however, I will explore some of the factors that have been instrumental in shaping the methods and approaches adopted in the wider field of law and popular culture. A central issue to be considered here is how legal scholars see themselves as consumers of popular culture.

Studying law and popular culture: method and reflexivity

Methodology, or the 'overall epistemological approach adopted' (Gray 2003: 4), is a topic that remains somewhat under-explored in the field of law and popular culture. While the study of media and popular culture does not require specifically designed methods and can instead easily adapt tried-and-tested approaches from the social sciences and the humanities, the broader epistemological issues to have arisen in these cognate disciplines have clear relevance. A not insignificant part of the research process is concerned with identifying methods that are suitable for the research questions one is pursuing, but it is important to note that the choice of method is also partly governed by extraneous considerations. What counts as the 'right' method in studying media audiences has varied greatly over time: while treating audiences as lab specimens or survey samples was once seen as the only 'scientific' way of studying media effects, recent influences from ethnography and anthropology have resulted in favouring more 'authentic' field studies which have seen researchers despatched to people's homes to observe media consumption *in situ*. While such paradigmatic shifts constitute evidence of researchers' willingness to subject their methods to continuing scrutiny and evaluation, the changing climate in research funding politics is a more prosaic but nevertheless important factor in all this. For example, Gray (1999: 32) points out that ethnographic approaches involving small-scale projects were originally nurtured by researchers who by reason of their marginal position in academia (for example, in the early days of women's studies) were unable to secure large research grants.

Considering the relative marginality of the study of law and popular culture in the wider domain of legal studies, one might wonder how this is shaping its methodology. For example, Greenfield *et al.* (2001: 196) suggest that one of the reasons why film analysis has proved hugely popular with legal scholars may well have something to do with issues of scale and available resources: it is easier to analyse a film than it is to study an entire series of television programmes which may be more difficult to access and usually amount to a much larger sample of analysis. This in turn suggests that this type of research is typically conducted without much funding, pointing to a resource problem which potentially influences scholars' choice of method and materials. Such factors are therefore relevant in elucidating the various approaches which structure the study of law and popular culture as a field of enquiry within the wider socio-legal domain, making it necessary to grapple with the question of where to place such research in the pecking order of funding priorities and the prestige it generates.

The concern is therefore not just how to ensure that we align the 'right' methods with the 'right' questions but to render visible the many elements which guide researchers in making these choices and ultimately also help justify a particular methodological framework. Increased reflexivity concerning one's research position and value judgments is undoubtedly an integral part of such a process, as Alasuutari (1999) has argued in relation to audience research. For example, Sparks (1992: 2) in his analysis of crime and television declares from the outset that he does not want to speak 'from a lofty and dispassionate height but rather in the belief that we are all swayed by emotions and capable of mistaken impressions'. In other words, when it comes to something that is as ubiquitous and taken-for-granted as media culture, it is important to acknowledge that scholars may be as impressionable as other audiences. Moreover, a concern about the effects of media culture, usually on other people, is a preoccupation which the social scientist shares with the lay person. Alasuutari (1999: 11) speaks of an awareness of a 'moral hierarchy' which underpins the audience's own normative stance on media culture. People tend to be apologetic and defensive about their enjoyment of popular entertainment genres (for example, soap operas) while they have markedly fewer problems with their consumption of more 'serious' programmes (for example, current affairs). As I explained in Chapter 1, fears about media effects also have a clear class dimension in that it is often assumed that lower and less educated classes are more vulnerable to being taken in by distorted media representations (Petley 2001; Jewkes 2004).

Such hierarchies of taste are also in evidence in the socio-legal field. Macaulay (1987: 214) in his pioneering assessment of why legal scholars should concern themselves with the study of popular culture jokingly remarks: 'Perhaps, best of all, I no longer need feel guilty as I watch the Badgers, Bucks, Brewers, and Packers struggle with so little success. It's not wasting time. It's research.' What seems like a throwaway comment may well be indicative of the way in which popular culture is judged as an object of research and the methodological choices to which it is subjected. The idea that dipping one's toe in popular culture is just a bit of fun reflects the standing of such endeavours in the research community. Studying law and popular culture is like 'dancing on the edge' (Redhead 1995: Chapter 1): it appears lightweight in comparison with more 'serious' research such as doctrinal analysis or socio-legal research with an articulated policy dimension. Banakar (2000) suggests that law may not be as receptive to other disciplines as it could be, hampering the latter's ability to contribute to legal knowledge, whereas Hillyard (2002: 648) mischievously observes in respect of differences in standing between law and social policy studies: 'Lawyers . . . view much social policy on a par with basket weaving or line dancing and maintain that non-lawyers cannot "do" law.' If social policy and its robust methodology are struggling to be taken seriously, this does not bode very well for the ability of disciplines most closely associated with the study of the media to make much of a difference. This not helped by the fact that media culture has been caught up in a discourse of social harm ever since it came to scholars' attention: while the study of law and literature is usually seen by lawyers as a noble pursuit because literature is considered enlightening, the same cannot always be said of popular mass media which are overwhelmingly associated with negative effects. The place of media effects in audience research will be discussed next.

From passive dopes to the active audience

Audience research has come a long way. From a historical perspective, the 'tap on the knee' or hypodermic syringe approach to media effects is the oldest tradition which has shaped the idea – prevalent at times not only in media studies but also in other disciplines, for example in criminology and sociology – that the media are able to exert an influence on their audiences which these find somehow both irresistible and inescapable. The possibility that audiences have some way of controlling the role that the media play in structuring their worldviews and thoughts does not enter the equation in classic media effects research. As Stuart Hall puts it:

> Though we know the television programme is not a behavioural input, like a tap on the kneecap, it seems to have been almost impossible for traditional researchers to conceptualize the communicative process without lapsing into one or other variant of low-flying behaviourism.
> (Hall 1980: 131)

This preference for the hypodermic syringe model in explaining the relationship between media and audiences can be traced back to media research in the first half of the twentieth century when it was predominantly rooted in sociology and behavioural psychology (Jewkes 2004), disciplines which research determinants of individual behaviour through the prism of methodologies derived from the natural sciences (Gauntlett 1995: 9). Moreover, the political climate of that age also provided support for a strong media effects hypothesis. The two World Wars were the age of propaganda in which governments discovered the media's potential as a weapon of persuasion that could be used to manipulate public opinion. The Frankfurt School, for example, which was subsequently very influential in European and North American media research, explained the descent of German society into fascism through the influence of the media functioning as a potent agent of mass propaganda. In unravelling the media's extraordinary powers, much emphasis was placed on the atomisation of industrial societies, which meant that their fabric had disintegrated to such an extent that the individual's only meaningful social relationship was with the mass media, thus eliminating intermediary levels of interaction which would otherwise be provided by interpersonal relations (Morley 1992: 45). Although the hypodermic syringe model was challenged and refined after the Second World War, it was not until the late 1970s that audience research witnessed the kind of methodological and epistemological shift that was necessary to dethrone behaviourism and to break the spell which the question of media effects had had on generations of researchers (McQuail 2000). Even today, the tap on the knee metaphor is unmistakably present in contemporary efforts to locate and explain the importance of the media (Heins and Bertin 2003).

Research into law and media is by no means an exception. The language used is often reminiscent of the hypodermic syringe metaphor. For example, Friedman (1994: 129) asserts: 'The ceaseless flow [of media images] puts ideas into people's heads. These are the basic stuff of legal culture, and legal culture is the architect and the mechanic of law.' When Sherwin (2000: 21), aiming to establish the (negative) impact which popular culture has on lawyers' conduct in the courtroom, asks the question 'what stories, what recurring images and metaphors, what stock scripts and popular stereotypes help us through the day? And where do they come from?', he does not hesitate: 'For most people, the source is not difficult to ascertain. It is the visual mass media: film, video, television, and to an increasing degree computerised images. . . . In a sense, we "see" reality the way we have been trained to watch film and TV.' Schoenbach (2001: 365) talks of 'a pessimism so strong and self-evident that until the 1940s scholars hardly bothered to do systematic research on the effects of new media'. Similarly, the media often stand accused of inculcating people with a flawed and distorted understanding of the law. The problem is not that this claim is entirely untrue or implausible but that it involves a level of generalisation which treats media effects as largely unmediated by factors such as age, class, race and gender (see also Chapter 2). Moreover, the emphasis on negative media effects makes it difficult to envisage that popular media may actually make a positive contribution to people's understanding of the law, for example by acting as a valuable source of public information. In short, the media's 'pro-social effects' (Ang 1996; Livingstone 1996; Mason 2000) are routinely ignored.

In the light of this enduring preoccupation with negative media effects, one might be forgiven for thinking that the hypodermic syringe model is still the undisputed and only possible way of conceptualising the relationship between the media and their audiences. This, however, flies in the face of evidence suggesting that other areas of audience research have evolved enormously since the early days of studies of media effects. The work of the

Centre for Contemporary Cultural Studies at Birmingham University (UK) in the late 1970s and early 1980s provided the breakthrough which proved instrumental in transforming audience analysis. The question to be asked was no longer 'what do the media do to people?', but 'what do people do with the media?'. As Curran (1996: 124) points out, this change in emphasis was in itself not new: as early as the 1930s more 'liberal' voices in media research emphasised the idea that 'audiences [were] not empty vessels waiting to be filled'. Moreover, the notion of the active audience can be traced back to a much earlier tradition, which is known as 'uses and gratifications', owing to its focus on the uses that audiences make of the media for the purpose of 'gratifying' or fulfilling specific needs, for example, the need for information, companionship and entertainment (Schrøder 1999).

However, whereas the uses and gratification tradition from the late 1950s onwards was unable to sever its link with an experimental research design, the Birmingham School can be credited for promoting a radically different methodology which disposed of the idea that media audiences could be treated as lab specimens to be isolated from their everyday social context (Vine 1997). It became clear that an experimental setting was inadequate in exploring the relationship between the media and their audiences because it overlooked the vital link with everyday life. The living room, not the psychologist's lab, became the focus of attention. Audiences' relationship with television, a medium heavily embedded in domesticity, could not be studied in isolation: domestic rituals, family relations and even the interior design of people's living rooms, in short people's everyday environment, were treated as relevant in explaining audiences' interpretation and use of television (Livingstone 1996). The preferred methodology for uncovering the importance of the domestic in media use was ethnography. 'Clinical empiricism' (Morley 1992: 174) was out and field research became the preferred method.

From a conceptual point of view, the change in focus from effects to meaning, or from behaviourism to semiotics, was as important as the change in setting from laboratory to the living room. This paradigmatic shift is largely attributed to Stuart Hall's (1980) model of encoding and decoding, signalling a new dawn in qualitative audience research which has become known as 'reception analysis' and which is closely associated with a cultural studies approach. What was at issue was more than just the question of whether media audiences either passively or actively engaged with media texts. The emphasis in Hall's paper was on the possibility of audience resistance in the process of making sense of the media. The audience was not only active; it was also potentially involved in a subversive pattern of unseating the hegemonic subtext of media texts.

Hall's model is very simple, but as Alasuutari (1999) observes, it is this very simplicity which makes it one of the key references in contemporary audience analysis. The basis of this model is that encoding (the way in which media professionals shape a text) and decoding (the way in which encoded messages are subsequently interpreted and understood by audiences) are seen as two very different moments in the production of meaning that do not necessarily coincide. A media text on its own is a half-finished semiotic product which reveals little about the way in which audiences actually interpret it. In Hall's model, audiences might partly ignore the meanings embedded in encoded texts by producing an 'oppositional' reading, which means that the ideological underpinnings of a text are read 'against the grain'. Although the model also includes the possibility of a dominant-hegemonic reading in which the decoder faithfully reproduces the encoded message, its significance lies in the fact that it envisages a scenario in which media influence is not inescapable, but actively resisted by the audience. This has inspired an entire generation of researchers in media and cultural studies to examine the significance of class (Morley 1980), but also gender (Radway 1984) and ethnicity (Liebes and Katz 1993) – tell-tale signs of the cultural turn in media research – in subverting dominant meanings embedded in media texts.

Historically, the cultural studies paradigm constituted a resolute departure from the type of literary criticism traditionally practised in language departments. The elevation of mass culture to an object of serious academic inquiry, a status traditionally reserved for the canons of high culture, sent shockwaves through the academic community at the University of Birmingham where the experiment began in the 1960s (Webster 2004). An anti-elitist stance was part and parcel of the cultural studies ethos, challenging received wisdom that media audiences must be either hopelessly gullible or hopelessly lazy. The emphasis on the active audience in reception analysis rendered it hugely problematic to judge the reactions of an audience by the media texts it consumed: meaning ultimately remains an unstable construct which is in constant flux. To cite an example used by Hall (1980: 131), the media generate images of violence but these images are not violent in themselves. They are merely a set of visual signs to be decoded by audiences whose interventions are crucial in making these images meaningful. This tempered the pessimism underpinning traditional research into media effects: a particular media text, when looked at in isolation, may not be the most refined cultural artefact, but thanks to the creativity of its readers, it may acquire a level of sophistication which one could not envisage on the basis of the text alone.

The liberating potential of reception analysis was most strongly felt in relation to media texts that are typically consumed by women, for example, soaps (e.g. Geraghty 1991; Brown 1994), women's magazines (Winship 1987; Hermes 1995) and romance novels (Radway 1984). The traditional feminist stance was strongly reminiscent of classic research into media effects: early feminist analyses portrayed women as victims of patriarchal media whose strong influence served to reinforce gender stereotypes and reconcile women with their subordination (Ang and Hermes 1996). However, in the 1980s, there was a remarkable turning point: the stigma attached to women's media, it seemed, had been lifted thanks to the new insights into audience research offered by reception analysis. Even feminist academics confessed to liking soaps and women's magazines (Van Zoonen 1994). Pleasure was an amorphous but widely used term in describing women's experiences of media texts, emphasising the non-judgemental philosophy underpinning reception analysis. Women's media were not something to be despised or dismissed. Reading *Cosmopolitan* or watching *Eastenders* was taken seriously by a new wave of feminist researchers who sought to identify ways in which female audiences subverted the patriarchal subtext of various media portrayals.

Cultural studies: crisis and critique

The entire cultural studies paradigm is in deep crisis today (Baetens 2005). In Britain, the unceremonious closure of the Department of Cultural Studies and Sociology at Birmingham University in July 2002 represented a striking symbol of cultural studies' changing fortunes (Webster 2004). Cultural studies has come under attack on several fronts: it has been decried for its 'unscientific' character and its lack of methodological rigour (Gray 2003; Webster 2004), while its commitment to interdisciplinarity has been dismissed as an anti-disciplinary tactic (Baetens 2005) which effectively undermines and delegitimises established disciplines. The fluidity of cultural studies and its refusal to pin down its object of inquiry, once praised as the only effective strategy for overcoming stubborn disciplinary boundaries, now appear a major weakness. For Baetens (2005: 5), 'as things are now, cultural studies can be just about anything, which means that in fact it is just about nothing', while for Bourdieu and Wacquant (1999: 47) cultural studies is simply a 'mongrel domain'. The most trenchant criticism is reserved for what is seen as a watering down of the political radicalness of cultural studies: the price of its success seems to have been a rapid institutionalisation and a mainstreaming of what was once regarded as a potentially radical form of critique.

Some of the shortcomings associated with cultural studies have important implications for the methodological analysis at the centre of this chapter. Moreover, the problems which have beset cultural studies do not only raise issues for the study of media and popular culture, but they also strongly resonate with some of the concerns involving the methodological orientation of socio-legal studies more generally which has undergone its own cultural turn. Hillyard (2002), for example, criticises the postmodern appetite for deconstructive theory, which he believes risks leaving the socio-legal endeavour in a state of relativism and also hampers a much-needed and principled stance on material inequalities. He also expresses concern for the methodological 'slightness' of the preoccupation with overly theoretical analyses.[1] An awareness of the perceived weaknesses in the cultural studies approach therefore forms an indispensable part of the effort to advance the methodological debate on how to study the complex relationship between law and media culture. The main weakness I want to address here concerns the perception that by emphasising and celebrating resistance, cultural studies greatly exaggerates the power of media audiences.

Underpinning our daily diet of media images, advertisements, political marketing, song lyrics and product branding are some of the most powerful institutions and industries in contemporary society. While the political economy of media industries is the focus of a well established research tradition in media studies (see Golding and Murdock 1996), there are concerns that cultural studies' preoccupation with the interpretation of media messages by a supposedly critical audience may inadvertently obscure the enormous power deficit in the relationship between the individual viewer or consumer and the institutions and corporations behind the encoded message. As Bird (2003: 168) points out, 'we cannot pretend that the power of corporate media can somehow be vaporised by the magic wand of audience creativity'. To give an example, it is infinitely more likely that a John Grisham novel be selected for a Hollywood adaptation than would a novel by the Belgian crime writer Georges Simenon, which inevitably means that global audiences partial to a Hollywood diet will get to mull over the adversarial system a great deal more than they do over continental penal traditions. This, of course, does not diminish the fact that Simenon has a worldwide fan base which is very well represented on the internet and that his *Maigret* novels have been the subject of several film adaptations and television series. However, the issue remains that media consumers are mostly dependent on the huge machinery which commissions, finances and distributes programmes and films for them to be given access to specific materials and ideas.[2]

The question therefore is whether audience creativity can ever be a match for corporate might. Critics have argued that audience resistance amounts to little more than a pyrrhic victory as it fails to contribute in any meaningful way to redressing the balance of power in processes of media consumption (see e.g. Curran 1996; Philo and Miller 1997).[3] The emphasis on resistance in cultural studies, as I have discussed above, was a reaction to the cultural pessimism that pervaded the traditional media effects paradigm which was dominant until well into the 1970s. For Gray (1999), Hall's encoding/decoding model has to be evaluated against that particular backdrop. The paper in which he outlined his thinking was a 'position' piece which was not intended to serve as a polished model for empirical research. Furthermore, Gray points out that very few actual studies support the extreme glorification of the active audience which has been so heavily berated by detractors. In other words, her argument is that the majority of studies are much more nuanced and cautious than has been made out by critics.

Nevertheless, the underlying worry for critics is that too optimistic a judgement of audience activity could undermine carefully constructed policy arguments as to why some form of regulation and state intervention in the cultural industries is necessary to safeguard the public interest. Some believe that the active audience paradigm is a capitulation to market forces promoting an anti-public service media agenda: the traditional justification for public service broadcasting is its mission to deliver high quality programmes, but placing too much emphasis on audience resistance and the indeterminacy of meaning makes quality judgements virtually impossible. Hence, it has been argued that reception analysis plays in the hands of those who want greater media deregulation because, after all, audiences distil their own meanings and interpretations irrespective of the intrinsic qualities of the cultural goods they consume (Corner 1996; Morley 1996). What argument, for example, would be left to challenge the corporate dominance of a few media moguls and press magnates if it is the prevailing belief that the decision on the value and meaning of cultural goods ultimately lies with the audience (see Philo and Miller 1997: 49)?

To be criticised for supporting a populist version of neo-liberalism is undoubtedly an ironic fate for a research tradition firmly rooted in the kind of neo-Marxist analysis which clearly inspired Hall's seminal encoding/ decoding model. However, it remains something of a *non sequitur* to argue that research documenting audiences' enjoyment of what the media have on offer necessarily promotes an agenda of deregulation and laissez-faireism in the media industries. We could also make the argument that people are found to be enjoying specific programmes thanks to the care that has been given to certain quality criteria in broadcasting schedules which are reinforced by regulation, meaning that there is scope for further enhancing people's choice and satisfaction with what is on offer through regulatory techniques. In countering the optimism of cultural studies involving the wholesale celebration of the audience's pleasure and creativity, critics must be careful to avoid the equally one-sided argument that the pleasure which audiences derive from media contents necessarily spells disaster for the public interest.

The charge of cultural relativism can be cited as another factor in cultural studies' reversal of fortune. For Philo and Miller (1997: 18), the 'discursive bubble' of cultural studies which leads to an almost religious conviction that there is no reality beyond the text invites 'political acquiescence'. By adopting the position that all ideas and viewpoints have equal value (or no intrinsic value at all), scholars deprive themselves of the opportunity to take a critical and normative stance on issues which are most in need of their evaluation. The influence exerted by postmodernists is seen as the main culprit in this wholesale abdication from important ethical responsibilities (see also Chapter 8). Philo and Miller also highlight the failure of cultural studies research to account for the potential of resistance by audiences with more troubling views. 'We hear very little of the pleasure of fantasies of power and domination' (Philo and Miller 1997: 37). There are indeed few analyses of the resistive decoding by the white supremacist, the rapist and the homophobe, but that presumably also means that for all its supposed relativism, cultural studies does stand for specific values and beliefs. It should be recalled that the work of de Certeau (1988), who pioneered many of the ideas which have become the mainstay of cultural studies, is explicitly concerned with the cultural practices of the disempowered who are driven to a make-do politics because they lack more radical means of resistance. This explains why the focus in cultural studies has been predominantly on the activities of the subordinate and not so much on the forces of domination. However, this obviously does not mean that cultural studies should not seek to fill this gap by giving attention to the more troublesome practices of some audiences.

Capturing the wider picture: the 'holism' of media practices

It is interesting to note that media studies is steadily evolving towards a holistic methodology, which is undoubtedly in part a response to some of the shortcomings of the cultural studies approach. The underlying idea is, as Deacon (2003) has argued, to resist the artificial partitioning of aspects of the mass communication process which are in effect inseparable from each other. The criticism that audience research in cultural studies tends to ignore the political economy of mass communication processes may be justified to some extent, but this does not necessarily mean that what is known as 'production analysis' (the analysis of the media industries) can simply dismiss the questions that have come to the fore in reception studies. Audience research in the cultural studies tradition has brought into view traditionally neglected cultural practices. This is a not unimportant achievement which has foregrounded the views of people on whose behalf and for whose benefit scholars claim to be speaking. This 'multiplication of voices' (Couldry 2000: 37) is a key legacy of cultural studies. The deployment of a diverse set of methods in a complementary fashion accompanies an increasing realisation that no single approach on its own is capable of grappling with media culture in all its complexity and richness (see e.g. Bird 2003). There appears to be a growing acceptance that media research is a sufficiently broad church with space for humanities-oriented textual analysis, social sciences survey methods and qualitative approaches.

The case for methodological diversity is at least as strong – if not even stronger – in the socio-legal field. There is considerable scope for enhancing the 'social' side of socio-legal research through the development of a methodology which takes researchers out of the law library to study on the ground what Hillyard (2002: 650) calls 'the material realities of life'. This equally applies to the study of law in media culture: while the analysis of various media texts is well developed, the equivalent of media studies' production and reception analysis – with some notable exceptions, see for example Asimow et al. (2005) – has yet to emerge. The case for more research into the interaction between media reception and ordinary legal experience was explored in Chapter 2 where I argued that law's presence in everyday life should frame the endeavour to unpick the relationship between law and media culture. Talking from a media studies perspective, Gray (1999: 33) points to a 'need to take account of and pay attention to the messiness of the everyday, the dull thud of the commonplace, the routine and routinised nature of daily life in all its complexity, and into which media forms are enmeshed'. This mission statement applies with the same vigour to the study of law and the media; indeed it is thought to be of benefit to the entire socio-legal field (Cotterrell 2002).

In a similar vein, there is also scope for exploring aspects relating to media production processes, which, again, cannot be simply read off from specific texts or representations. We know that stories about law form part of the media staple diet, we can make an informed guess as to why this is and we can lament the many inaccuracies that we can detect in the media's treatment of a highly specialist area such as law, but how much do we really know about the process of media production in this particular context? Who decides what constitutes a worthwhile story and in view of what aims? What kind of obstacles and challenges do journalists, film-makers and programme makers face when transforming the raw legal data in front of them into a palatable media story? What makes law so newsworthy and gripping in the first place? How is law scripted for non-specialist audiences? We may suspect rampant commercialism and sensationalism: a crime of passion helps to sell news-papers while the dry administrative decision taken on typically 'technical grounds' has significantly less commercial appeal. We may also point the finger at political and ideological forces which stand to benefit from the hard-hitting law-and-order story (see e.g. Glasgow University Media Group, 1976; Chibnall 1977; Hall et al. 1978) and over-the-top accounts which 'expose' law's unduly liberal side (see e.g. Haltom and McCann 2004). However, on the ground the workings of contemporary media culture have been noted for revealing a subtle and complex set of dynamics, which suggests that there are different elements at play that require a rich explanatory framework (see e.g. Schlesinger and Tumber 1994; Mawby 1999).

My final suggestion may seem somehow contradictory: I want to argue that to understand the relationship between law and media culture, it is important to stand back and take a non-media-centric position. Media centrism can be defined as 'giving undue prominence to media rather than other causal factors in explaining social phenomena' (Couldry 2007: 8). Put differ-ently, it means that the power of the media in orienting society tends to be inflated in such a way that other relevant factors are neglected or marginal-ised. It cannot be ignored that modern societies are media saturated, but that does not necessarily make the media the cause of all that is good or bad. Nor does it mean that our media consumption is the only determinant of our social or cultural identity, as it appears increasingly doubtful whether there is an 'audience' waiting to be studied[4] (Bird 2003). Striking the right balance is notoriously difficult: on the one hand, researchers do not want the media to disappear entirely from their radar (and for the study of media to cease to be relevant), but they also want to avoid explaining the social exclusively through the media.

For example, it is tempting to attribute the lack of public confidence in legal institutions to the distorting effects of media which tend to paint the legal process in a particularly sensationalist or stereotypical light, but this risks glossing over what may be genuine problems hampering public understanding, such as the use of jargon and obscure rituals in the administration of justice, which have little to do with the nature of media reporting. Media discourse may be merely echoing public concerns about justice. Such epistemological problems are not new or unique to the law/media nexus: do the media initiate or merely reflect broader social trends (including relations of power and domination)? Are they a prime mover in social processes or do they mainly react to events? For Silverstone (1999: 145) it is a bit of both: 'Media technologies, like other technologies, have the social behind them, the social in front of them and the social embedded in them', while Stevenson (1995: 184) suggests that 'media cultures are both autonomous from and yet interwoven into other activities and practices, which in turn have a structuring impact upon them'. Focusing on the social in its broadest possible sense remedies the limitations of media centrism, meaning that the socio-legal tradition is particularly well-placed to provide an intellectual home for the study of law and media culture. How prominently the media should feature in unravelling and clarifying the relationship between law and other social structures then becomes the first, but not necessarily the only, research question that is worth pursuing.

In media studies, recent analyses have suggested that the main emphasis should not be on the production or consumption of texts (or indeed on texts themselves), but on social practices that are media-oriented in nature and acquire a ritualistic character in everyday life. Couldry (2004: 125) gives the example of watching a football match: although such an activity is clearly oriented to a media broadcast, we cannot assume that everyone who watches it is passionately 'consuming' a text or is busy 'being' an audience. As many of us will have experienced ourselves, watching television can be a sign of celebrity devotion and fandom, but it can equally constitute a way of killing time, be an expression of respect for another person's interest in a programme or it could be ignored in such a way that it simply fulfils a wallpaper function while we carry on with other activities (preparing the family meal, making telephone calls, having a drink in the pub and so on). However, it is important to note that a greater emphasis on social practice does not mean that the media disappear from view altogether; instead one of the main questions becomes: 'Do media practices have a *privileged* role in anchoring other types of practice because of the privileged circulation of media representations and images of the social world?' (Couldry 2004: 127). This conjures up the possibility of examining whether there is a hierarchy between media practices and other social practices that has specific potential in clarifying the relationship between law and media culture: is law's authority at risk because of subtle shifts in the social hierarchy which mean that media practices have now become the dominant way of 'anchoring' or 'ordering' legal experience? The question does not necessarily demand to be answered in the positive: as I demonstrate in Chapter 6, the input of socio-legal theory could be important in determining the direction of this enquiry.

Conclusion

This chapter has examined how knowledge about media audiences is produced. An important issue to have been highlighted involves concerns about media effects, more specifically, the concern that the media are capable of affecting people in a profoundly negative way. Jewkes (2004: 11) comments that 'it is surprising to witness how much contemporary popular discourse about the power of the media rests on assumptions that are very close to those underpinning the hypodermic syringe model'. Similar observations can be made about the debate as to whether the media are capable of undermining public confidence in the administration of justice. Where research has been undertaken, it tends to reveal a rather complex and even contradictory set of public attitudes (Allen 2006: 69). Surprisingly, for example, 'the public' has been noted for having less punitive attitudes than is often thought. The issue of cause and effect regarding the media has eluded and confounded media analysis since its inception. Allen's (2006: 77) assertion that 'people who watch TV most tend to be most fearful, and watching crime programmes increases the desire to see offenders punished' is a textbook example. Could it be that people who are fearful (for example, the elderly and the frail) are more likely to stay in and watch more television or are the programmes which they watch the root-cause of their fears? This question once again points to the complex relationship between media and the everyday, which was explored in Chapter 2.

When looking at the development of relevant methodologies, it is clear that the analysis has shifted away from the hypodermic syringe model to consider what people do with, and more recently, do *in relation to* various media. Audience research is constantly evolving: experimental research in contrived lab settings was discredited in favour of a reception analysis that was truer to life; cultural pessimism had to make way for optimism, which itself was repudiated for being politically and methodologically problematic; a celebration of audience resistance for a while replaced uncomfortable questions about the media's political economy; quantitative analysis was traded in for qualitative methods. The recent emergence of a holistic approach to the wider media picture represents a realisation that in matters as complex as media culture, a very diverse range of approaches is necessary. The interdisciplinary credo is as strong as ever in media studies 'desperately seeking the audience' (Ang 1991).

I highlighted the potential of a non-media-centric perspective that promotes a reading in which the social significance of the media is not explained entirely by reference to media effects. This led me to explore the argument that more needs to be done to understand social practices which are oriented to, but which are not exclusively constituted by, the media. The next chapter is devoted to the study of one particular example, namely the journey which people embark on when they are confronted with a significant legal problem, a trajectory which may in some cases involve turning to media sources dispensing legal advice. This quest for legal knowledge and information could be regarded as a very literal example of audience activity. It also resonates with a wider culture of self-help that receives its impetus not just from the media but also from the sphere of policy making where people are increasingly encouraged to tackle their own (legal) problems with the aid of self-help resources. Internet technology in particular has made legal self-help a more realistic prospect but its interactive properties also signal the rise to prominence of the media user, a triumphant figure capable of overshadowing the passive crowd traditionally associated with the hypodermic syringe model. As a result, the domestication of the internet is providing yet another twist in the long-running saga of the study of media audiences.

Chapter 5

Cultures of legal self-help

Introduction

The mass media are routinely noted for their problematic relationship with the legal truth and the extent to which they are in the business of embellishing the law as well as consistently distorting it. The most widely studied examples are undoubtedly news reporting of high-profile trials, the ever-popular courtroom drama and crime fiction. However, the media's engagement with law cannot be reduced to sensational headlines, blockbuster movies and bestsellers alone. It clearly has a much wider remit. Thus in this Chapter I seek to highlight how various media outlets, such as problem pages and advice columns in magazines, radio phone-ins and increasingly also internet websites, act as a prolific source of popular legal advice. The example of legal advice media is instructive in much the same way as reality television is (see Chapter 3): firstly, it has the ability to evince the mutually constitutive dynamics of media and everyday legal experience because legal advice media explicitly seek to address the everyday legal problems of audiences and, secondly, it also provides strong evidence of how the audience is constructed in media discourse as actively seeking legal information, corroborating the active audience model explored in the previous chapter.

The variety and extent of popular legal advice in the media is such that its role in the rapidly developing culture of legal self-help cannot be ignored. The rise of legal self-help, whereby clients rather than seeking tailor-made professional advice resort to helping themselves by using information resources specifically designed for this purpose, is simultaneously a cause of great optimism and concern. While the prospect of legal self-help has been embraced by policy makers and academics alike as a way of facilitating the delivery of legal services (Widdison 2003), there are also doubts as to whether people are indeed capable of successfully helping themselves in tackling their legal problems (Giddings and Robertson 2003). It is unavoidable that legal self-help should at least in part rely on the input of mainstream media in making people aware of the options that are available to them when they are faced with a legal problem, notwithstanding the fact that the accuracy of media portrayals is often called into question. This calls for a much greater understanding of the role of various media in assisting the legal self-helper.

Two features immediately stand out when surveying the breadth of popular legal advice. First, it is important to point out that the legal profession plays a highly visible role in legal advice media. It is not uncommon for an advice column in a newspaper or magazine to be authored by a legal practitioner showcasing his or her skills, while cyber-advice is often dispensed by members of the legal profession who use it as a way of advertising their professional services. This raises the spectre of the legal profession using its contribution to popular legal advice media as a promotional tool with which it can shape and influence its own public image.[1] One of the questions to be pursued in this chapter concerns the type of image that lawyers seek to project in such channels, focusing specifically on advice targeted at people who are confronted with the legal implications of divorce.

Secondly, new information and communication technology (ICT) and the World Wide Web in particular have given an unparalleled impetus to the growth in legal self-help.[2] Not only has the internet created an almost unlimited information capacity, it has also transformed legal self-help into a much more attractive and realistic proposition by making information more accessible and user-friendly. The challenges of new ICT for legal practice are well documented (see Susskind 1996). New ICTs may have brought the fragmentation of the profession (Francis 2004) a step closer, especially considering the ease with which new players are deploying technology to enter the legal services market. For example, in Britain, the supermarket giant Tesco has become a much feared competitor[3] who even gave its name to the terms 'Tesco lawyer' and 'Tesco law', which have become shorthand for far-reaching changes in the delivery of legal services (Clementi 2004). From the perspective of the mass media, the increasing volume of user-generated contents on the internet is eroding their monopoly to act as conduits for public opinion and carriers of information. As a 'disruptive technology' (Mountain 2001: section 3), the internet therefore evidently has the potential to impact strongly on both conventional mass media and the traditional model of legal practice.

Self-help is about taking responsibility for one's own problems. It also means risk-taking, in the sense of 'confronting a diversity of open possibilities' (Giddens 1991: 75). The internet has transferred much of the responsibility for seeking out reliable information onto users. While traditionally the mass media perform the role of gatekeepers of information on behalf of their audiences, internet users exert much more autonomy by virtue of their access to a range of unlimited information resources. Information has been dislodged from familiar accredited sources of expertise: anyone with access to the internet is able to circulate information. Consequently, legal self-helpers have to be sufficiently enterprising and discerning when searching for a solution to their problems. While self-help packages will structure this process to some extent, self-helpers undertake a range of tasks which lawyers would traditionally perform on behalf of their clients. An indispensable characteristic of legal self-help is therefore the expectation that people will take charge of their own problems. This trend towards the 'managerialisation' of everyday life (Hancock and Tyler 2004: 621) and individual responsibilisation, exhorting people to help themselves and realise their own potential, has been closely identified with the burgeoning market of lifestyle magazines which will form the focus of the first part of this chapter. In the second part, I will discuss the impact of the internet on the fledgling culture of legal self-help.

Legal self-help in mass media

Self-help as a lifestyle choice

Legal advice in the media concerns itself with seemingly ordinary problems which people are likely to experience in their own everyday life. Audiences are guided through a maze of legal issues, which includes home-ownership, employment, parenting, finance, marriage and consumer rights. This is hardly a new phenomenon. For example, Lanctot (1999) examines the popularity of *Good Will Court*, a radio show in 1930s America which involved lawyers and judges hearing and settling 'real life' legal disputes. As an early reality programme providing some basic legal education, the huge popularity of *Good Will Court* bore testimony to the unmet legal need of that particular era. However, pressure from the Bar Council meant that the experiment was short-lived: the legal profession cited a range of concerns, including the unreliability of the advice and the negative impact on the image of lawyers and judges, in its hard-fought campaign to have *Good Will Court* and similar radio shows banned from the airwaves. Lanctot points out that opposition against lawyers dispensing professional advice in written legal advice columns was equally strong, although imparting generic legal information has traditionally been deemed acceptable.

As this historic example illustrates, legal advice media undoubtedly have some role to play in meeting people's legal needs and they map onto a much wider phenomenon which Susskind (1996) has termed the 'latent legal market'. This represents a segment of the legal services market in which there is a demand for inexpensive and readily accessible legal advice which was until relatively recently ignored by legal practice. In the 1970s and 1980s, legal self-help books and packs first started to appear in book shops, signalling that some in the legal profession (as well as those on the margins) were tentatively starting to explore the latent legal market:

Regarded by many practitioners as laughably inappropriate, these texts sought expressly to demystify the law and to encourage non-lawyers to undertake a variety of tasks, all of which were previously thought to be the exclusive province of duly qualified legal advisers.

(Susskind 1996: 209)

Similarly, it is not uncommon for legal advice pages in magazines to act as a gateway to further sources of help such as premium telephone lines and self-help manuals.[4] It is interesting to note, for example, that Esther Rantzen, a well-known British agony aunt who used to counsel people on lifestyle problems in her own television show, was chosen by the personal injuries firm 'Accident Advice Helpline' to front their advertising campaign, which features a mock advice column in which Rantzen advises a victim of negligence to contact the company.[5]

The culture of self-help underpinning the latent legal market has been nurtured most prominently by the ubiquitous lifestyle magazine which vigorously promotes the idea that readers should take active control of their everyday life and constantly seek to better themselves. Hancock and Tyler explain:

'Lifestyle magazines' . . . tend not to focus on what might traditionally be regarded as hobbies or 'pastimes' involving 'doing' things (gardening, interior design and so on) but specifically on broad issues of 'being'-style, self-presentation, interpersonal relationships, consumer culture and so on; all issues relating to the pursuit of the 'project of the self'.

(Hancock and Tyler 2004: 622)

Lifestyle magazines help readers to tackle what Giddens (1991: 14) calls the 'how shall I live' question, which 'has to be answered in day-to-day decisions about how to behave, what to wear and what to eat – and many other things'. As for the concept of 'lifestyle' itself, Giddens (1991: 81) defines it as 'a more or less integrated set of practices which an individual embraces, not only because such practices fulfil utilitarian needs, but because they give material form to a particular narrative of self-identity'.

The traditional women's magazine has always considered it to be its role to act as a manual of domesticity, providing readers with a wealth of lifestyle advice (Ballaster et al. 1991; McRobbie 1991; Winship 1987). In the late 1980s the magazine market was revolutionised by the arrival of the phenomenally successful men's lifestyle magazine, addressing issues such as health, fashion and relationships which had until then been the preserve of women's magazines (Stevenson et al. 2000). The philosophy of self-help now cuts across the gender divide, representing the bread and butter of the lifestyle magazine which portrays everyday existence as a sphere of social experience that is worthy of managerial intervention and rationalisation. Hancock and Tyler observe:

It [the popular lifestyle magazine] seemingly draws upon the language and efficiency imperatives traditionally associated with organizational management as a cultural resource, one that we can utilize in order to invest rationally in ourselves (by being 'in control of . . . ideas, feelings and actions') and hence, maximize the likelihood of capitalizing on the investments we make.

(Hancock and Tyler 2004: 623)

Managing the self only becomes possible when readers are sufficiently aware of problematic areas in their everyday life and are prepared to take responsibility for improving their own situation. Legal issues fit this pattern of reflexivity, as Gross and Pattison (2001) established in their study of pregnancy magazines, which they found devote considerable attention to giving readers advice on employment issues surrounding pregnancy and birth. A striking feature of the legal advice dispensed by such magazines is that claiming rights in pregnancy is represented as a relatively easy process which largely depends on women's willingness to take responsibility, suggesting for example that all women have to do to assert their rights is write a letter to their employer (Gross and Pattison 2001: 519). The message to readers is that it is very much down to their own initiative to ensure that they obtain the protection and benefits to which they are legally entitled.

Reader activism is also most strongly encouraged in the area of consumer rights. Some women's magazines offer readers a powerful ally in the guise of their in-house expert who contacts companies to help readers obtain redress for their problems. For example, the British women's weekly *Bella*[6] features a consumer consultancy page in which the expert, in addition to giving advice, also takes up the issue with the store or the company involved in a reader's complaint. *That's Life!*, another weekly, features the combatively entitled consumer column 'Is it a rip-off? Ban the scam – we fight for your rights!'. The column editor encourages readers to assert their rights, awarding £25 to the 'moaner of the week', this being a reader who has successfully complained to a company about a consumer issue. The message which this is trying to send is clear: readers should not expect that big corporations will respect their rights of their own volition but they should themselves be prepared to take responsibility for safeguarding their interests as consumers. Such assertiveness is of the essence in a self-help culture encouraging people to be rights conscious and take charge of their own legal affairs.

Obviously, the advice pages featured in most lifestyle magazines take an extremely reductionist approach: the questions which (sometimes fictitious) readers ask are usually short and the answers are equally terse. They are part of what Winship (1992) calls the 'dip-in and dip-out' character of hands-on magazines such as *Bella*, which cover such a diversity of issues that their approach is inevitably superficial.[7] As Carter (cited in Winship 1992: 101) has argued: 'The conventions of problem-page writing demand an encapsulation of complex thoughts and emotions in minuscule autobiographies, hopelessly compacted.' So too do legal problem pages offer minuscule biographies of letter-writers whose problems are devoid of any complexity. On balance, the value of such columns does not so much reside in their ability to offer adequate and comprehensive legal advice as in their promotion of the self-help philosophy which coalesces with policy efforts to alleviate the burden on the legal system, and legal aid in particular (Hanlon 1999), by exhorting people to help themselves.

'There is life after a break-up': a case study

Of all the lifestyle magazines to have been brought onto the British market in recent years, the magazine *Vive* deserves a special mention. Launched in 2000, its unique selling point was that it focused its advice almost exclusively on issues surrounding divorce. Its slogan that 'there is life after a break-up' illustrated the magazine's philosophy that marital break-up represents something of a rebirth: a new self, a new relationship, a new family, a new look, in short, the chance of a new lifestyle were seen as part of the unintended side-effects of divorce that readers should embrace. That divorce should be selected as an overarching theme for a lifestyle magazine is no coincidence: divorce concludes one phase in life but it also heralds the start of a new one, generating both anxiety and further opportunity for self-actualisation which presents itself as a potentially bewildering range of lifestyle choices (Giddens 1991).

Unfortunately, it is impossible to offer an extensive analysis of *Vive* for the simple reason that the magazine ceased publication after only four issues, thereby failing to emulate the success of its North American counterpart *Divorce Magazine* (see further below). Nevertheless, *Vive* was noteworthy because of its determination to help readers to cope with the psychological, the financial and, significantly, the legal aspects of divorce with the aid of a multidisciplinary team of specialists. The family law expert was particularly prominent in *Vive* and law firms specialising in divorce appeared its most important advertisers. Marcel Berlins approvingly observed in his legal column in the *Guardian*: '*Vive* . . . offers a strong line in legal advice for splitters, and I was delighted to see it fulminating against the wrong and dangerous use of the term common-law wife' (Berlins 2000).

Vive's 'divorce doctors' (as they were called) tackled a range of issues. For example, in the July 2001 issue, we find a two-page article entitled 'Dad's the word' with as the subtitle: 'When it comes to children in divorce, are fathers less likely to be given a fairer deal than mothers?' Another two-page feature article on cross-cultural divorce asks: 'Consideration for the children is always a priority in divorce settlements. But how much more difficult is it when separate lives also means living in separate countries?' The question-and-answer theme is also prominently present in a three-page article on 'standing up to domestic abuse', which takes readers through the legal remedies available in a question-and-answer format. For example: 'My partner is being violent and abusive to me. Is there anything I can do to stop it?', 'So what is an injunction?', and 'Should I consider leaving the home?'.

As Currie (2001: 274) argues, the question-and-answer style in magazines serves a particular purpose in that it seeks to engage the reader directly and suggest that the issue under consideration is a matter of dialogue between expert and reader. It also encourages readers to take active control of finding a solution to their problems, making it a suitable mode of address for self-help magazines (see also Leman 1980). Using questions to draw in readers, *Vive* gave the appearance of being a tool of self-diagnosis. The remarriage quiz featured in the July 2001 issue is a case in point: it offered readers a self-assessment of their prospect of remarrying in church, asking questions 'that you will be asked to consider when interviewed by your parish priest'. The score explanation at the end of the test allowed readers to establish whether they were likely to be granted a church wedding. Another article entitled 'Learn how to master your life' featured a 'life coach' prescribing practical exercises for readers.

The self-help philosophy permeating the articles also clearly extended to legal issues. Hancock and Tyler (2004: 633) note that quantification is the 'common currency of rationalisation' on which the lifestyle magazine thrives: an important stepping-stone towards taking control is to break a problem down into a number of easily manageable components. The 12-step guide to 'DIY divorce' featured in *Vive* is a good example of how the magazine, by dividing divorce up into an exact number of stages, attempted to make legal self-help a less daunting prospect. The 12-step guide starts again with a question: 'Are you eligible to divorce?' and ends in step 12 with the granting of the decree absolute. The guide reads like a flowchart of divorce closing with the phrase 'YOU ARE NOW DIVORCED'.[8] In the 12-step guide, readers are encouraged to obtain a divorce without the help of a lawyer provided their case is 'straightforward', which is exactly the kind of scenario that is covered by Susskind's definition of the latent legal market. *Vive*'s upbeat message to readers was that they could take control of their own legal problems, sending out a clear message of self-empowerment.

Whereas, generally speaking, legal advice pages in lifestyle magazines do not pretend to be a substitute for professional help, *Vive* appeared to be breaking new ground, taking the self-help philosophy much further by trying to reduce the need to rely on professional advice if the circumstances allowed this. Some of the legal advice it featured was remarkably detailed and it even included case commentaries. The family lawyer was visibly involved, which suggests that self-help law does not turn the qualified lawyer into an endangered species. On the contrary, the latent legal market represents a fertile domain for the expansion of professionalism, for example, as I discuss below, by reinventing the professional as a 'lifestyle expert' or 'doctor'.

However, the real growth capacity for the latent legal market resides less in traditional print media such as self-help books and magazines (and this may have been the reason for *Vive*'s commercial failure) than in internet technology which appears much better suited to satisfying the demand for inexpensive and easily accessible legal services. It is to legal advice on the internet that I turn my attention next.

Legal self-help and cyber-advice

The internet and the delivery of legal services

Self-help is a broad cultural phenomenon which in the lifestyle magazine expresses itself through the promotion of a 'with the law' type of legal consciousness (see Chapter 2): law is portrayed as being very much on readers' side but they need to apply themselves actively to asserting their rights, just as they have to make the required effort to improve their health, career and relationships. That self-help in some cases conceivably means that people take charge of their own legal problems was illustrated by *Vive*'s attempt to encourage readers to take a pro-active role in the many lifestyle issues thrown up by divorce. Obviously, the fact that lifestyle magazines do their best to promote a discourse of self-help does not necessarily mean that people are indeed tackling legal problems unaided. However, there is strong evidence to suggest that legal self-help is not just a fashion fad or lifestyle choice driven by media culture. Thus, for example, a 1999 survey in England and Wales showed that 35 per cent of people who are faced with a 'justiciable problem', that is a 'problem for which there is a potential legal remedy' (Pleasence *et al.* 2003: 14), resort to some form of self-help (Genn 1999). A 2003 follow-up survey confirmed that people seek help from a wide range of sources which include the media (Pleasence *et al.* 2003). In marketing terms, this represents a sizeable target for the development and promotion of self-help products, especially because it appears unlikely that self-helpers in the near future will be able to fall back on universalistic legal aid provisions to access custom-made professional help (Moorhead and Pleasence 2003). Instead, we see that public resources are being diverted into the development and improvement of more cost-effective self-help resources.

Whereas in the past such self-help resources consisted mainly of books and leaflets containing basic legal information, the internet allows for a much more sophisticated and user-friendly dissemination of legal knowledge. As Widdison (2003) notes, simply generating an electronic version of print self-help media would vastly under-utilise the potential of internet technology: online self-help resources have to be designed in such a way as to maximise the structured and interactive properties of new ICTs. Thus, for example, the Court Service's website[9] in England and Wales presently already allows claimants to bring a money claim online and defendants to respond to any money claims brought against them without either party physically having to go to court.[10] For proponents of technologically assisted self-help, such initiatives represent a new dawn in the delivery of legal services that holds the promise of lowering the threshold for accessing justice. Others, on the other hand, have yet to be convinced of the merits of an increasing reliance on self-help technology. For Giddings and Robertson (2003: 115): 'Rather than being empowered by the availability of such services, they [consumers] may end up being abandoned to navigate a complex legal map without the necessary knowledge, skills and confidence.'[11] The authors believe that while self-help resources are useful for pointing people in the right direction by providing some basic legal information, they are less suitable as 'A to Z maps' leading users to a tailored solution for their legal problems.

What undoubtedly increases the uncertainty for self-helpers is the sheer volume of information available on the internet and the difficulty of assessing the trustworthiness of online sources. An online transaction is an anonymous, distant and virtual process which deprives users of the 'vocabularies of bodily idiom' (Goffman 1963) that accompany face-to-face interaction. This raises the broader social and regulatory problem of identity deception in cyberspace, which maps onto the issue of the pace and extent of change in what Giddens (1991: 16) terms the 'runaway world'. The overwhelming fear is that the internet constitutes a playground for fraudsters exploiting the possibility of presenting oneself online in a manner which is not constrained by the offline corporeal self. Adults posing as children to groom potential victims for sexual abuse represent the danger *par excellence* of disembodied social interaction in online settings (Simpson 2005). However, in the literature on online identity construction, there is also growing scepticism about the extent to which users adopt and change an identity at will. Empirical research suggests that the presentation of the self online is much more stable and much more subject to social control (mainly from other users) than is often assumed (Bakardjieva 2003; Lee 2006). Moreover, it has been argued that internet users who are free from the constraints associated with face-to-face communication may in fact be encouraged to reveal more about themselves and consequently be more honest and open in online settings (Hardey 2002; Pauwels 2005). The effect of a possible 'identity play' – however much over-hyped it may be in academic writing (Pauwels 2005) – is not unequivocally negative or positive. On the one hand, the ease with which outsiders to the profession are able to set themselves up on the internet as providers of legal information undoubtedly raises legitimate concerns about deception and fraud.[12] On the other hand, as I argue below, the internet also creates scope for different strategies of self-presentation by professionals, including lawyers, for example, to reposition themselves as lifestyle experts.

For Harshman *et al.* (2005: 231), the explosion of information on the internet nevertheless poses a fundamental challenge to traditional conceptions of professional expertise:

> The democratization of information via technology . . . de-anchors information from its source. Because sources of data and information can be disguised in cyberspace, people can claim to be anything or anyone. A lack of face-to-face encounters in communities of virtual information removes a considerable number of the cues ordinarily used to assess validity claims.
>
> (Harshman *et al.* 2005: 231)

To put it differently, in addition to challenging professional monopolies and exposing users to the risk of fraudulent claims of expertise, the internet also deprives practitioners of their traditional insignia of credibility and trustworthiness. The case of an American teenager who began dispensing online legal advice at the tender age of 12 without ever having done so much as open a law textbook yet who scored high satisfaction ratings from users embodies the nightmare scenario of self-helpers falling victim to pranksters and fraudsters to the fullest possible extent (Harshman *et al.* 2005).[13] Such dangers make conventional mass media seem beacons of reliability because at least their information has been processed by journalists who are regulated by professional standards and who operate in an institutional framework. On the internet, by contrast, much of the information has been cut loose from such accountability safeguards, resulting in the overwhelming impression that users are left to fend for themselves when it comes to determining what information to trust.[14]

Despite such concerns, the potential of the internet to act as an alternative gateway to the general public is considerable. Creating a website is an attractive strategy for bypassing mass media filters which are often linked to distortions in reporting. In this respect, the internet is not so much a medium of deception as a welcome corrective for misinformation promoted in mainstream media and a way of promoting a desired public image. Institutions, companies and pressure groups understand the potential of the internet as a way of 'narrowcasting' their messages to citizens and consumers only too well. A well designed website is today a vital tool of institutional transparency (or spin?), corporate branding and political mobilisation. Evidently, however, there is more to the internet than institutional, corporate and political actors seeking to address their constituencies. Private bloggers publishing logs or diaries on the internet, self-helpers and anyone who takes the trouble of designing a personal website occupy the same communicative space as the big players. The growth of user-generated contents means that the internet has a radical influence on what Livingstone (1999: pdf) calls the 'reframing of knowledge hierarchies' in which lay people actively participate in the production of knowledge and even compete with the experts. As my example of self-help in print magazines suggests, it would be too simple to claim that self-help culture is a product of the internet alone but it is clear that the internet has deepened this phenomenon as users increasingly turn to websites to seek help and support with everyday problems ranging from ill health to bad debts (Orgad 2004). Despite the information overload, the internet brings together sources of information and support which would be much more difficult to obtain in an offline environment. Focusing once again on the topic of divorce and self-help in the next section, I want to elaborate on two features of online self-help: the importance of professional empathy and the validation of users' own experiences.

Online legal self-help forums: lawyers as lifestyle experts?

The expert/reader relationship in lifestyle magazines is closely modelled on the notion of a partnership of equals: experts are not directly solving readers' problems but they try to incentivise them to help themselves. According to Hancock and Tyler:

> Western industrial societies appear to be almost defined by an obsession with the need to seek out experts and sources of life planning in order to make it through the complexity and uncertainty of contemporary exist-ence. What is perhaps most notable about today's examples of such expert advice, however, is the emphasis they place not so much on instructive imperatives, but rather on the facilitation of self-improvement. That is, they appear to allow us to 'manage' our own lives more efficiently and effectively, than to provide expert solutions per se.
>
> (Hancock and Tyler 2004: 631)

The importance of the expert being able to demonstrate empathy and solidar-ity with readers' problems cannot be underestimated if their partnership is to be successful.

The North American Divorcemagazine.com, which is the website of the eponymous print magazine and which also caters for the UK market through hyperlinked partner websites, provides an excellent example. The contributing experts, varying from relationship therapists to lawyers and accountants, do not shy away from drawing inspiration from their own experiences of marital break-up and baring their own soul in the process. Thus, the relationship therapist, Dr Love, writes in her January 2007 column:

> Since the last time my column appeared in Divorce Magazine I have been through the most difficult year of my life. If you had told me this time last year that I would be going through a divorce, I would have said 'I'm sorry . . . you have me confused with someone else.' And yet, here I stand. My heart has suffered; my health has suffered; my family and friends have suffered. I thought seriously about not continuing to write this column. So why did I?

> I continue for the same reasons I've been writing here in this place for the past ten years. I continue because I want a happy marriage to be available to anyone who wants it, regardless of social or economic status. And I continue because I hope that my experience, as well as my research, can be of benefit to you and those you touch.[15]

Another contributor, in a feature in which she counsels users on how to find a suitable lawyer, advises:

> You don't have to become best friends, but you must be comfortable enough with your attorney to be able to tell him or her some of your deepest, darkest secrets. If you can't bring yourself to disclose information relevant to the case, you'll be putting your attorney at an extreme disadvantage. Your lawyer isn't your therapist or confessor, but he or she does need to be aware of all pertinent facts in order to do a good job for you.[16]

Despite the warning not to confuse a lawyer with a therapist, the expertise that users should be looking for clearly involves more than legal qualifications alone. The 'added value' is professionals' ability to reassure and empathise. Lawyers should not invariably occupy the position of a detached and emotionally neutral professional but they must be able to demonstrate an understanding of how it feels to be embroiled in a custody battle or to have to go through painful negotiations to reach a financial settlement. This suggests that the competent lawyer is someone who successfully combines professionalism and personal insight. She or he is well versed in both the grammar of law and the language of emotions, a fluency that is required to appreciate the complex ramifications of divorce. Thus, for example, one lawyer advertising on Divorcemagazine.com describes her strengths in the following words:

> Experienced New York divorce attorney Susan Kunstler has a reputation for determination to reach the best result possible, coupled with great compassion, for her clients. She is tough enough to fight for you yet sensitive to what you are going through.[17]

The talents we see being showcased here differ somewhat from the traditional analytical skill of disentangling legal issues from the web of emotions and irrelevant diversions presented by the client: lawyers have been described as translators who find a suitable legal expression with which to reconfigure social experience (Cain 1979; Bourdieu 1987). However, such an approach risks discarding much of what lay people consider important about their experience of divorce. In her survey of how people cope with legal problems, Genn (1999: 249) notes that divorce is often experienced as part of a larger cluster of problems. Moreover, her findings suggest that divorce ranks very highly among problems that have a strong and predominantly negative impact on people's lives (Genn 1999: 193). For example, in her survey, 52 per cent of respondents with experience of divorce and separation reported that it led them to suffer from sleeping difficulties. This serves as a confirmation that divorce has a pervasive effect on many people's lives, giving rise to problems which cannot be confined to the strictly legal implications of marital break-up alone. Divorce and separation are dramatic and life-changing events presenting people with problems which require more than just legal advice by way of solution. Indeed, this may be true of other areas of law as well. Widdison (2003: section 2) observes that: 'It is becoming widely accepted that legal guidance needs to be orientated towards "life episodes" rather than traditional legal categories.'

The internet, with its interactive and hyperlink properties, lends itself particularly well to the reframing of legal problems as 'life episodes'. That this can be exploited to the commercial advantage of law firms can be seen from the success of the UK based online divorce firm Divorce-online.co.uk, which blends legal self-help with lifestyle solutions. Divorce-online.co.uk claims to be 'the largest online divorce service in the UK, having dealt with over 35,000 successful divorce cases since we began the service in 1999' and proudly states: 'We invented online divorce in the UK.'[18] The website actively promotes a self-help philosophy, selling do-it-yourself divorce packages as well as offering low-cost 'managed divorce services'. There is also free 'community' content available, including a bulletin board and a downloadable 'divorce diary', offering users an online therapeutic space. Divorce-online.co.uk also features a wine store and (like Divorcemagazine.com) a dating service. The virtual family lawyer, it seems, provides a one-stop destination for those wishing to terminate their relationship and embark on a new one.

This suggests that lawyers (and paralegals) are keen to utilise their presence on cyberspace as an image-building tool,[19] profiling themselves as relationship experts who intervene not just when a relationship has come to an end but also in the prevention of marital breakdown. One of the most high-profile family lawyers in the UK is Vanessa Lloyd Platt. She is a regular contributor to newspapers and television shows dispensing relationship advice, making her a minor celebrity. She has also written a book on relationships (Lloyd Platt 2001), enabling her to profile herself as a lawyer with a very broad range of skills and expertise. Her holistic philosophy is also prominently present on the website of her firm Lloyd Platt & Co,[20] which features not just divorce related information but also a recipe section which states that 'food, relationships and happiness are very much interlinked'. As noted above, the broad range of skills on display here confirms that some family lawyers have found an additional vocation as 'divorce doctors', acting simultaneously as legal experts and 'pop' psychologists (Ehrenreich and English 1979) who are perfectly placed to help clients grapple with the different facets of divorce.

Strikingly, for example, in the aforementioned Divorcemagazine.com feature on how to find a suitable divorce lawyer, one of the lawyers quoted under the heading 'Legal tips to help you through your divorce' has surprisingly little legal information to impart but much more by way of lifestyle advice: 'Hire the best professionals you can afford. Keep busy and physically active. Talk and socialise with friends, get adequate rest, eat and drink wisely, spend quality time with your children, and commit to getting on with your life.'[21] What is significant is that this attempt at re-orienting the image of lawyers is not limited to the area of divorce law alone. In the UK, the shift from law to lifestyle in the promotional materials of law firms has also been observed in the recruitment documentation of corporate law firms aimed at law graduates: here, as Collier (2006: 38) suggests, the stuffy or 'bookish' image of lawyers is often downplayed in favour of extensive references to consumerism, a hedonistic youth culture and urbanism.

Users-turned-experts

According to Bakardjieva (2003), internet users typically range from 'info-sumers' to 'communitarians'. The infosumer expects to find reliable information on the internet and shies away from online exchanges which seek to cultivate intimacy, solidarity and community. The communitarian, by contrast, is a self-helper who uses the internet as a way of giving and receiving emotional support and who values the solidarity of others. Divorce-online.co.uk and Divorcemagazine.com satisfy both the infosumer and communitarian with a user content ranging from the purely informational to the communitarian. Self-help is practised most notably by offering users message boards to discuss their experiences and for giving and obtaining advice. For some, message boards may be a way of easing the isolation that is part of their post-divorce status. Bakardjieva (2003: 291) uses the term 'immobile socialisation', an inversion of Williams's (1974) notion of 'mobile privatisation': online discussions are a means of cementing a bond of solidarity among users drawing on their personal shared experiences (see also Parr 2002).

The distinction between experts and users is easily blurred in an environment in which experts try to relate to users as much as possible and users have their own valuable expertise to impart. However, the exhortation to help oneself, both in online and off-line cultures, should not be treated as unequivocally empowering as it represents a potentially extensive commodification of users' experiences. Attractively packaged websites which promise guidance on every imaginable facet of a legal problem are often a way of advertising the services of lawyers and other experts keen to exploit the latent legal market. The holistic approach that self-help websites promote constitutes a very enterprising attempt at framing legal problems as requiring the consumption of a wide range of commodities (including, it seems, some fine wine from the wine store hyperlinked to Divorce-online.co.uk). Getting divorced, instead of just taking a couple of visits to a lawyer, now also requires a trip to the shops to acquire a new wardrobe as well as countless (real or virtual) visits to the stress counsellor, hairdresser and dating agencies to get one's life back on track, not to mention the many self-help products which users are encouraged to buy. The commodification of divorce represents an essential feature of the online self-help industry: it takes only a click of the mouse or a phone call to purchase the products promoted by different experts. Thus, to quote Giddens (1991: 198): 'To a greater or lesser degree, the project of the self becomes translated into one of the possession of desired goods and the pursuit of artificially framed styles of life.'

Notwithstanding the intense commodification, the validation of first-hand experience in sources of cyber-advice has an obvious emancipatory appeal: internet users are decentring the expert as the fount of all knowledge, providing what Harshman *et al.* (2005: 232) term 'a correction to the asymmetrical power relationship that often defines professional–lay interaction'. Bakardjieva (2003) notes how users of medical self-help message boards appear to be

> short-circuiting the medical establishment and the expert knowledge produced by it and [are] learning from each other. More accurately, they [are] collectively appropriating and using expert knowledge in ways they [have] found relevant and productive in their own unique situations of sufferers and victims.
>
> (Bakardjieva 2003: 303)

Rather than being satisfied with the old-fashioned label of client or patient, users see themselves as collaborators who are on an equal footing with the expert (see Parr 2002). If the expansion of expert systems involved a 'deskilling' and devaluing of lay knowledge, the user-turned-expert represents a reverse process of 'reskilling' and wrestling back of power from experts (Giddens 1991). While Giddens is not talking specifically about legal self-help here, his comments are an apt characterisation of the broader dynamics involved:

> As a result of processes of reappropriation, an indefinite number of spaces between lay belief and practice and the sphere of abstract systems are opened up. In any given situation, provided that the resources of time and other requisites are available, the individual has the possibility of a partial or full-blown reskilling in respect of specific decisions or contemplated courses of action.
>
> (Giddens 1991: 139)

It would be a specimen of technological determinism (and media centrism) to attribute such developments to the internet alone. I have argued that by profiling themselves online, professionals may in fact be expanding their market. Nevertheless, the internet may also turn out to be a decisive factor which has intensified an already strong challenge to professional monopolies, leaving us to ponder: 'If control over knowledge is lost, what happens to power?' (Boon *et al.* 2005: 474).

Conclusion

The topics under consideration in this chapter constitute a rich field of analysis that I have only been able to explore in a cursory manner. While media culture is often noted in academic and legal circles for its larger-than-life characteristics, legal self-help media are reassuringly grounded in the mundane universe of everyday legal problems. Their intervention consists of trying to promote the self-confidence and awareness needed to take the necessary steps towards resolving a legal problem. Media attempts to inform people of their basic rights and obligations require a strong collaboration with the legal profession, if only to give the information the seal of credibility. The resident expert is often a legal practitioner who uses advice pages to showcase and promote his or her skills, potentially generating considerable (free) publicity. Such communications also fulfil a public service function as they provide a convenient channel through which the legal profession can engage in some basic public education. The collaboration between the media and the legal profession has become arguably stronger over time as it witnessed the convergence of two key developments: the managerialisation of everyday life as expounded, for example, in the lifestyle magazine, and changes in legal policy which have meant that self-help is now fully recognised as a valid method for the delivery of legal services.

Divorce, with the many lifestyle choices that it throws up, is particularly suited to a strategy which repositions lawyers as lifestyle experts. Some family lawyers take this as far as rebranding themselves as 'divorce doctors' and relationship gurus, quietly playing down any association with the emotionless and uncaring world of the law. The validation of first-hand experiences of divorce creates a level playing field in which experts and recipients of advice can converse as equals. Online forums in particular are noteworthy for their blurring of the distinction between experts and users. It is not so much a case of the expert becoming obsolete; it is more a case of lay people aspiring to develop their own alternative expertise on the basis of their lived experience. The phenomenon of users counselling each other represents an important aspect of self-help culture which has been boosted by the internet.

Online legal self-help does not amount to an unequivocal empowerment of lay people: it confronts both users and policy makers with the problem of who to trust in a communicative environment in which there are few clues to distinguish the genuine expert (either the professional or the experiential expert) from the fraudster. Users may seek to reskill themselves and take charge of their own legal problems, but there are also recurring concerns as to whether law is a suitable self-help target. One might cite something as fundamental as illiteracy as a reason why some groups are excluded altogether from participating in legal self-help. However, a factor such as a lack of emotional distance has also been highlighted as a possible obstacle (Giddings and Robertson 2003), suggesting that the kind of close personal involvement which provides the foundation for self-expertise may also constitute a serious impediment which may only be surmountable with the help of a third party who is not personally involved.

That the overall media landscape has been drastically changed by new ICTs needs little further explanation. Castells sums this up in the following way:

> The new media system is not characterised by the one-way, undifferentiated messages through a limited number of channels that constituted the world of mass media. . . . Slowly but surely, this new media system is moving towards interactivity, particularly if we include CMC [computer mediated communication] networks, and their access to text, images, and sounds, that will eventually link up with the current media system.
>
> (Castells 2004a: 143)

Inevitably, the concept of the 'media user' as inherently active challenges any lingering notion that the audience is a silent and passive mass which simply absorbs what it sees or hears. This does not render the debate concerning the impact of media culture obsolete but it makes it even more complex and fascinating. As Livingstone (2003) suggests, it is perhaps for the first time in centuries – think of the Elizabethan era when theatregoers very vociferously showed what they thought – that the reactions of the audience-turned-user can be observed and recorded so easily. The consumer-sphinx, referred to in Chapter 2, has begun to reveal some of its secrets. If we are to learn more about the relationship between media culture and what people think and know about law, we cannot afford to ignore such significant developments.

Chapter 6

Law and the media: liberal and autopoietic perspectives

Introduction

I have argued in previous chapters that concerns about media influence are important in unravelling the uncomfortable relationship between law and the media but I have also outlined the shortcomings of a simple media effects model. This led me to explore various methods of conceptualising audiences and the meaning-making processes at work in everyday life, with both reality television and legal self-help media offering specific examples of the growing prominence of the active audience. In this chapter, I aim to demonstrate that tensions between media and the legal system do not just find an expression in concerns about media effects but also have an institutional basis in the media's 'self-chosen' (McQuail 1992: 3) role as guardians of the common good who critically and objectively monitor public life, giving the media a broad mandate for exposing wrongs and problems in the legal system. Viewed from this perspective, the uneasy relationship between law and media is not so much a problem as a healthy sign of a vibrant democracy which attracts measured yet significant legal protection, most crucially in the shape of press freedom. However, this quintessentially liberal doctrine has come under attack on several fronts. The criticism ranges from suspicions that the media are systematically biased in favour of dominant forces in society and are more interested in entertaining audiences than in empowering citizens with balanced and factual reporting, to deep misgivings about the relevance of the watchdog model in a mass democracy. Much of the criticism portrays the media's democratic aspirations as being constantly thwarted because of their own greed, their hunger for power and their inclination to pander to the lowest common denominator.

However, I want to question the orthodoxy that the media should in principle be capable of offering a more accurate portrayal of the legal system. This will take me down the path of exploring the theory of autopoiesis which throws into doubt the very possibility of a largely opaque legal discourse being translated without distortion. Autopoiesis, which holds that social systems are entirely self-generated and largely impenetrable to each other, focuses attention on the way in which the legal system and the media deploy very different criteria for validating and creating reality. In doing so, it puts a question mark over the ability of the media to jeopardise a closed and self-referential legal system in such a way as to force through reforms which run counter to the rule of law itself, for example a more punitive sentencing regime. In common with the liberal watchdog model, autopoietic theory envisages a strong degree of independence and friction between the media and the legal system but, unlike the liberal narrative, it arrives at the rather different conclusion that media discourse is necessarily and systemically at variance with truth claims validated by the legal system.

Liberal media doctrine

The glorious 'Fourth Estate'

A robust set of legal institutions, especially an independent judiciary willing and able to uphold the constitution, and a free press are considered to be the twin jewels in the crown of liberal democracy. Indeed, it has been suggested that press freedom cannot be sustained without the necessary constitutional and judicial guarantees and that these must therefore be ranked higher than the presence of favourable market conditions stimulating the unimpeded flow of ideas (see e.g. Mickiewicz 2000; Becker 2004). The idea that press freedom, and in modern times freedom of expression in electronic media, is a pre-requisite of democracy is a fixture in the contemporary liberal narrative (Curran 2002). Legal doctrine has duly acknowledged the centrality of media freedom, fleshing out the conditions that are conducive to its promotion. The US Supreme Court, watching over freedom of expression as embodied in the iconic First Amendment, has famously likened media pluralism to 'an uninhibited marketplace of ideas' (*Red Lion Broadcasting Co v FCC* 395 US 367 (1969) p 389) which ensues from free competition among media, emphasising the importance of an absence of state intervention. By contrast, in various European countries such as France and Sweden, there is a well-established tradition of state intervention in the form of press subsidies which are allocated on the basis that they help to promote a diversity of ideas which would not be able to survive in aggressive market conditions (McQuail 1992: 43). A strong public service model, imposing public service norms on broadcast media, is another feature of media policy in Europe where it often works in tandem with commercial radio and television (Varney 2004).[1]

Not surprisingly, freedom of expression figures prominently in human rights declarations. The European Court of Human Rights, providing a uniquely powerful enforcement mechanism for the European Convention on Human Rights (ECHR), has made it clear in its jurisprudence that media institutions occupy a special position in the promotion of the free flow of ideas in democracy which justifies an enhanced degree of protection for journalists and other information providers who contribute to the adequate monitoring of the state (see e.g. *The Observer and Guardian v UK* (1992) 14 EHRR 153; *Steel and Morris v UK* (2005) 41 EHRR 22). For example, restrictions of this freedom will only be considered 'necessary in a democratic society' in the case of a demonstrable 'pressing social need'. The corollary of these special legal safeguards, however, is the expectation that high journalistic standards will be maintained: Art 10(2) of the ECHR makes it clear that freedom of expression brings with it a set of responsibilities. The media's freedom of expression is not a privilege of the individual but an unmistakable public good,[2] something which has been repeatedly emphasised by the European Court through its insistence that the right of the press to disseminate information correlates with the right of the public to receive information, suggesting that the public interest is a weighty factor in assessing the way in which media actors exercise their freedom.

Both legal doctrine and political theory therefore support the idea that the media occupy a special position in the constitutional make-up of the liberal state. The epithet of 'Fourth Estate' reflects a belief in the media's unique and necessary contribution to monitoring the three (other) branches of government. News media in particular are the 'unofficial fourth branch of government' (Gordon *et al.* 1999: 33) which performs a public service by providing an additional form of checks and balances. Journalists preside over the court of public opinion, assisting citizens in the exercise of their right to democratic scrutiny and alerting them to any abuse of power which could betray the trust that they place in their elected representatives. A critical plank in the Fourth Estate argument is the assumption that an engaged citizenry weighs up the information it receives and uses the flow of ideas in the media as a basis for rational decision making which culminates in weighty and important choices at the ballot box (Lichtenberg 1990: 110).

This is evidently as much of an elegant legal fiction as it is a glossing over of the realities of democracy-in-action (see below), but it nevertheless accounts for the legal and ethical expectation that journalists perform their educating role conscious of the seriousness of the task entrusted to them. A commitment to truth, objectivity, neutrality, good faith and a meticulous vetting of sources, to name but a few, are important factors in judging whether journalists put their freedom of expression to good use. It is assumed that any abuse of the media's power over public opinion could have consequences of such gravity and importance that they could change the direction of the entire polity. Whether the media are capable of having such powerful effects is a moot point that has been discussed extensively in previous chapters. This need not detain us any further here; what matters most is that policy makers, media actors and members of the other branches of government orient their own practices in a way which is clearly predicated on the notion that media organisations have the potential of shaping people's perceptions of the wider political process.

One important consequence of the Fourth Estate doctrine is that the relationship between the media and any form of officialdom, be it legislative, executive or judicial, is infused with an inevitable degree of distrust. Journalists should by definition be wary of being fed information by government sources or other interested parties if they aspire to have the bite of a watchdog of power. The reporter's instinct is to be sceptical and aloof. Hence, in Pauly's (1999: 137) words, 'professional journalists . . . consider themselves unrepentant sceptics who constantly look for error and take pride in picking apart others' talk and behaviour'. This innate scepticism may sometimes be taken too far, creating the impression that confrontation is sought for confrontation's sake which could affect the reputation of both journalists and politicians. Commenting on the rise of the 'gladiatorial' political interview, McNair (2000: 94) points out that 'the style . . . may vary from the adversarial – in which the interviewer behaves like a lawyer in a court case – through the irreverently sceptical, to the overtly dismissive'. The parallel with court proceedings is especially eye-catching here, suggesting, as I discuss below, that both the legal system and journalism derive their legitimacy from their ability to establish the truth.

Jeremy Paxman, the BBC journalist whose trademark is his rather abrasive interviewing style, once said that 'the broadcaster's attitude towards politicians should display the same degree of respect which the dog reserves for the lamp-post' (cited in Franklin 1994: 3). The tabloid press is no less fierce, with criminal justice policy being a particularly noteworthy hobbyhorse (see Chapter 8). As a consequence, Franklin argues (1994: 15), 'conflicts between politicians and journalists remain not only possible but a routine feature of their relationship'. Such structural conflicts follow partly from the very different objectives that are pursued by politicians and journalists in their mutual contacts: according to Franklin, while politicians seek to persuade public opinion of the rightness of their cause, journalists are driven by a quest for objectivity. Whether objectivity is a workable criterion in assessing the quality of media reporting is something that I consider later in this chapter; suffice it to say here that the very different interpretative frames which journalists adopt readily set them on a collision course with the political classes.

The interdependence of legal institutions and journalism

It is crucial to the argument of this chapter that the monitoring role of the media also includes scrutiny of the legal system to allow ample scope for criticism of courts and the judiciary.[3] For the ideal of the Fourth Estate to make a wide impact, journalists must cast a watchful eye over officialdom in its entirety and maintain a critical distance towards every institution that is potentially vulnerable to an abuse of power. An element of scepticism and natural distrust is therefore part and parcel of the way in which the media are expected to perform their watchdog role in respect of the administration of justice.

However, it is also undeniably true that judges enjoy a much higher degree of protection from media criticism than do elected politicians. It would certainly appear that judges are entitled to greater respect and deference than that accorded to Jeremy Paxman's metaphorical lamp-post. It is worth noting, for example, that Art 10(2) of the ECHR explicitly mentions the importance of 'maintaining the authority and impartiality of the judiciary' as a possible restriction on freedom of expression which could be considered 'necessary in a democratic society'. The European Court of Human Rights has been called on several times to rule on the proportionality of sanctions against journalists who published materials that were extremely critical of individual judges. In *Prager and Oberschlick v Austria*, concerning the publication of an article containing serious allegations against judges in the Viennese criminal courts, the Court reiterated the importance of the media's watchdog role and emphasised that 'the system of justice' was a legitimate target for journalistic probing and criticism:

> The press is one of the means by which politicians and public opinion can verify that judges are discharging their heavy responsibilities in a manner that is in conformity with the aim which is the basis of the task entrusted to them.[4]
>
> (*Prager and Oberschlick v Austria* (1996) 21 EHRR 1 para 34)

However, the Court also believed that it could see an important difference between politicians and judges: it argued that, unlike the former, the latter are not in a position to reply openly to public criticism and therefore need to be protected from 'destructive attacks that are essentially unfounded' (para 34). Only then, the Court reasoned, would it be possible to maintain public confidence in the legal system. This view was also reiterated in the case of *De Haes and Gijsels v Belgium* (1998) 25 EHRR 1 which involved a series of magazine articles that were fiercely critical of senior judges in the Antwerp Court of Appeal. The argument that the judiciary needs particular protection from unsound media criticism because the nature of the institution precludes judicial office holders from tackling criticism head-on has arguably been weakened significantly by developments since the 1990s. As I discuss in the next chapter, judges in many jurisdictions today believe strongly in the potential of the media in strengthening public confidence, making them much more willing to be an active participant in media debates.[5]

Such active interventions may go some way to abating unfounded criticism and alleviating some of the pressures which excessive media attention is believed to exert on the administration of justice. However, this does not alter the fact that the relationship between media and legal institutions remains strained. The potential for tension is increased further by the legal system's function as ultimate arbiter of freedom of expression. Because of its constitutional significance, recourse to the judiciary is crucial to safeguard and set limits to media freedom (Ogbondah 2002). This can be briefly illustrated by looking at recent developments in Russia, which under Yeltsin enjoyed a reasonable degree of media freedom. However, one commentator observes that the situation under Putin has deteriorated significantly resulting in a 'neo-authoritarian media system' which combines privately owned media and open access with a remarkable level of self-censorship among journalists and the presence of almost arbitrary legal restrictions on freedom of expression (Becker 2004). One of the main reasons why freedom of speech in Russian media is curtailed despite the free market conditions concerns the concentration of power in the hands of the executive and the relatively weak position of the judiciary who are unable to adequately protect journalists and media owners against excessive government interference (Mickiewicz 2000). In other words, economic liberalisation, which has been especially successful as far as the Russian press is concerned, has in itself been insufficient to achieve the degree of freedom of expression required in a fully functioning liberal democracy.

Thus it seems that what liberal doctrine requires is an independent judiciary able to guarantee media freedom through the rule of law, but as my brief exploration of ECHR jurisprudence suggests, the rule of law also provides a legitimate basis for restricting media freedom of expression to protect the independence of the judiciary. The media owe both their freedom and restrictions to the strength of legal institutions: if the latter are vigorous, media freedom may thrive within judicially enforced boundaries, but conversely if they are weak, the media are left unprotected against excessive state interference. Lord Woolf, former Lord Chief Justice of England and Wales, offers a neat summary of the interdependence between media and the judiciary:

> Parliamentary democracy depends upon the existence of a free and independent media and a free and independent judiciary. What is more, it is possible that a free media depends upon the existence of a free judiciary, and a free judiciary depends in turn upon a free and independent media. While this may be true, the judiciary must be independent of the media and the media must be independent of the judiciary.
>
> (Woolf 2003: para 4)

Lord Woolf's speech has something of a rallying cry which seeks to unite judges and journalists. However, he paints what may be a deceptively harmonious picture of a relationship which is run through with fundamental tensions and even in some circumstances profound rivalry. The requirement that media and judiciary be independent of each other while in a position of mutual interdependence reveals a very delicate balance which is not just de facto hard to achieve but also remains conceptually difficult to envisage.

Bias and legitimacy

What judges and journalists have in common is that they both lack a direct political mandate and therefore need to gain public trust in a different way, namely by appearing to adhere to values such as objectivity, independence and impartiality. Journalists and judges routinely have to unpick conflicting accounts and contradictory evidence to produce by way of an end result something that comes closest to the truth. Any overt political leanings or partisan beliefs are likely to undermine the delicate manoeuvring which both journalists[6] and judges practise in this quest for objectivity. One of the worst accusations that can be made against journalistic reportage and the legal process is that they are biased. In law, it can be a ground for an appeal or a judicial review, while in journalism the suspicion of bias is a huge blemish on the professionalism of reporters.[7] What matters most in such truth-finding exercises is the deontology of the unclouded judgement and the willingness to confront events with an open mind. It is not the telling of an untruth, but intentional bias which appears to be the most serious violation of journalistic deontology. Gordon *et al.* (1999: 83) comment with cautious optimism: 'Rawls' veil of ignorance allows us to achieve objectivity – reporting without bias – more easily than achieving more complex ethical goals, such as truth.'

Such optimism, however, may not wash with those who regard the most insidious form of bias in the media to be of an ideological nature. There is an abundance of critical commentary (see Street 2001 for an overview) which is intent on demonstrating that media discourse amounts to little more than a collection of value judgements and partisan worldviews that are masquerading as a balanced and impartial picture of reality.[8] However, the accusation of ideological bias is less lethal than it may at times appear. As Street (2001: 31) explains, analyses of media bias have themselves been critiqued for their almost romantic belief that there is an independent and verifiable reality which is capable of being reported on objectively – a belief which it shares with the liberal narrative. Moreover, ideological bias may be too blunt a concept to explain why, despite both supposedly playing into the hands of dominant groups, the media and the legal system are capable of producing conflicting accounts.[9] If law and media are the product of the same hegemonic forces and feed off the same dominant ideology, it appears counter-intuitive for there to be such varying interpretations of reality. Moreover, it does not explain differences in media coverage. As Schudson (2002: 261) points out: 'The cultural knowledge that constitutes news judgment is too complex and too implicit to label simply "ideology". News judgment is not so unified, intentional, and functional a system as "ideology" suggests.'

The role of the media, news media in particular, as a stout watchdog of power makes it possible to explain tensions between media and legal institutions as a constitutive feature of the overall design of liberal democracy. However, an additional difficulty with this conception is not so much that the media fail to live up to these expectations because they are biased or skewed towards dominant interests but rather that the ideal itself no longer befits the conditions of contemporary democracy. Curran (2002: 217) succinctly summarises the problem: 'Many of the received ideas about the democratic role of the media derive from a frockcoated world where the "media" consisted principally of small-circulation, political publications and the state was still dominated by a landed elite.' In a similar way, media policy and legal doctrine tend to hark back to a rose-tinted and largely nostalgic reading of the media's facilitating role in democracy. The watchdog narrative may actually be inflating the importance of the media. As Street (2001: 16) points out, the emphasis on the media's contribution to democracy evidently assumes that there is a substantial role for them to play. The watchdog model may have worked well in a mythical era when, as in Habermas's (1992) portrayal of the historical public sphere, citizenship was the privilege of a handful of individuals who had the luxury of being able to spend time discussing public affairs in coffee houses and closely follow the minutiae of political debate in the newspapers, but it has limited appeal in the epoch of mass democracy (see Graber 2003). Schudson remarks:

> Many studies of media coverage of politics smuggle in the assumption that the news media should serve society by informing the general public in ways that arm them for vigilant citizenship. I am sympathetic to this as one of the goals of the news media in democracy, but it is not a good approximation of the role that the news media have historically played – anywhere.
>
> (Schudson 2002: 263)

It is also important not to underestimate the complex demands that are placed on contemporary media organisations. Whereas the liberal narrative sees free market conditions as a mere prop to sustain the political independence of the media, it is more likely for economic imperatives to direct editorial content. This does not mean that editors slavishly try to please media proprietors; the effects are much subtler. If journalists aim for neutrality in coverage of the news, this may have less to do with their awareness of their specific role in the grand design of democracy than with the desire not to alienate audiences (and see their market share shrink) through partisan or overtly biased reporting.[10] News selection is as inevitable as it is problematic: that it is simply impossible for a journalist to give a full account of events as they unravel in court or Parliament inevitably impinges on any assessment of the extent to which we can expect to find objectivity, accuracy and truth in reporting (Street 2001: 18). Even when cameras are present to record events, selectivity is still important, for example in the choice of camera angle or the subsequent editing of the footage. In fact, it could even be said that uninterrupted live coverage of an event even when there are few new developments and actual news is thin on the ground exposes the weaknesses of a 24-hour news culture desperate for the tiniest crumbs of information.

The watchdog model also jars with the mission of the media to bring stories that are above all entertaining. Pauly (1999: 147) comments: 'To say that reporters tell stories . . . makes journalism seem a less elevated calling than to say that they provide information crucial to democracy, but storytelling is just what they do.' Herein probably lies one of the main pressure points in the relationship between law and media: law offers a ready supply of narratives feeding the voracious appetite of a media machinery which is not interested in depicting law in an objective way but which cherry-picks the most entertaining aspects, displaying a cavalier attitude towards technical or procedural details. Compared to the interlocking geographies of contemporary politics and its confusing additives of spin and source control, the straightforward law-and-order story provides the elegant simplicity of clearly drawn distinctions between heroes and villains (see Sparks 1992). That journalists are drawn to such simple yet gripping narratives is not just a matter of ideological preference or bias, but is also the product of media selection processes which tend to favour stock characters, failsafe familiar narratives and other systematic patterns or frames (Gamson and Modigliani 1989).[11]

Law and media as autopoietic systems

Truth and autopoiesis

While tensions between law and media are inherent to the latter's watchdog function, I have also highlighted that, for a variety of reasons, the media may be less dedicated to this role than the liberal narrative suggests. In this section, I intend to examine the issue from a different angle, trying to explain why law and the media look at reality through a radically different lens and how this may account for their uneasy relationship. Truth may be elusive but it nevertheless orients the practices of actors in both media and the legal field. The problem, however, is that what counts as credible and truthful according to news-making criteria is not necessarily accurate in the legal sense, creating considerable scope for conflicting accounts.

We saw in Chapter 1 that concerns about the media's rather unrealistic and distorted depiction of legal issues are common. However, a question that is worth contemplating is how media discourse could ever be other than distorted. To expect that a journalist or scriptwriter observe the same standards as lawyers in their approach to law would show a profound a misunderstanding of the very different nature of their work. The media never set out to be a law school for the masses, although it is not inconsistent with the watchdog philosophy that media organisations should perform some educating role. Law in its modern-day guise is dense and complex, capable of confounding at times the most accomplished practitioner and, consequently, its undistorted portrayal is likely to elude the most conscientious reporter or editor. Nagging philosophical doubts concerning the very possibility of ascertaining truth by generally accepted criteria are undoubtedly capable of muddying the water even further (see e.g. Edgar 1992).

However, treating all truth claims as equally plausible or merely relative is also unsatisfactory in unravelling the problem of media distortion, especially as it could be seen as endorsing the same kind of postmodern relativism which some detect in cultural studies and related disciplines (see Chapter 4). It is very difficult to settle the question of who has ultimate purchase on the legal truth, but it is also clear that the truth as validated by law has a greater authority than does any other type of truth. This inevitably results in a hierarchy of knowledge regimes: media discourse projects and is in turn circumscribed by law's authority. If it is accepted that media actors are bound to judge truth claims by reference to criteria that are different but not arbitrary, the question arises as to whether discrepancies with a legally valid truth may ever be eradicated completely. Is law capable of being 'translated' in an undistorted way in media discourse or are the differences between media and law of such magnitude that they are in effect insurmountable?

A somewhat unorthodox perspective on this and other issues is offered by the theory of autopoiesis which its leading author, the late Niklas Luhmann, developed and applied extensively to both law and media (see Luhmann 1985; 2000). Autopoiesis has become a well established strand in the sociology of law, but as Couldry (2007) points out, it has yet to leave its mark on media studies. There can be no doubt that autopoiesis is a complex and at times controversial theory which is not helped by the density of Luhmann's writings. For example, autopoiesis's basic tenet that society is comprised of a range of specialised subsystems of communication, including law, which rather than interacting directly *with* each other, communicate *about* each other, making them closed and self-referential, has given rise to the impression that it promotes an extreme type of legal positivism (see e.g. Friedman 1989). Given this level of controversy, I want to attend first to two specific points of criticism before attempting to explain how autopoiesis may throw some light on the issue of media distortion.

Autopoiesis has been linked to a revival of functionalism, with Couldry (2004: 123) describing it as no less than 'embarrassing' that a functionalist perspective continues to inform some areas of media analysis. However, King and Thornhill (2003a) forcefully argue that autopoiesis is very different from functionalism in that it does not perceive systems to have been purposefully created to ensure the wellbeing and optimal working of society as a whole. Moreover, they also point out that the potential for crisis and disruption is engrained in the workings of various subsystems, which is another feature that distinguishes autopoiesis from functionalist perspectives stressing the harmonious state of the social totality. The focus in autopoiesis being entirely on the notion of communication, the theory is not concerned with the social benefits that flow from the activities of various subsystems. As I discuss below, this recognises inherent tensions between the legal system and the media as the inevitable consequence of their very different modes of communication.

Another controversial aspect of autopoiesis concerns the status it accords to human interaction (see e.g. Cotterrell 1993; Mingers 2002). Luhmann has claimed that human actors constitute separate systems which are part of the environment of social subsystems to which they only exist as communications, making autopoiesis vulnerable to the criticism that it represents a dehumanisation of the social: humans are 'psychic' or 'conscience' systems but they are not 'social' subsystems, which seems to exclude people as a proper concern for social analysis. King and Thornhill clarify the status of humans in autopoiesis as follows:

> People do exist in the form of 'the public', 'individuals', 'reasonable men', 'rational beings'. The subjects of experiments, clients, or patients form part of the environment of social subsystems, such as politics or law, science, economics, health or the mass media, but always as constructions of the system that is communicating about them.
>
> (King and Thornhill 2003b: 280)

In other words, people are treated as objects of social communication rather than being seen as direct participants in this process. Conversely, events (these being other systems' communications) occurring in the social system first need to trigger an observation at the level of individual conscience systems to generate a relevant communication in the human sphere. At first glance, this would appear to suggest that autopoiesis is ill equipped to unravel processes of media reception which figured prominently in previous chapters: media reception seems to be purely a matter of cognitive processing and translation by human beings, operations which, from an autopoietic perspective, fall outside the scope of the social system and the sociological enterprise. People may discuss the content of television programmes or internet websites with others but their conversations[12] can only become part of the network of social communications if they have been recognised as such by one or more of the various social subsystems. As King and Thornhill (2003a: 8) explain, for law, this could be in the form of evidence, for the media system this could take the shape of an analysis of TV ratings, for politics, it would be public opinion, and so on.

However, rather than dismissing this aspect of autopoietic theory as a specimen of dehumanisation, it could instead be seen as a recognition of the complex relationship between people and the systems to which they orient their everyday practices in the form of their own communications. For example, it may help us to appreciate that the discursive battles waged in the media arena in relation to politics or law are constructions of reality which do not automatically affect all individuals in equal measure. It is not because there is a media campaign to expose flaws in the legal system that people will be aware of this state of affairs or that it will significantly impact on their perceptions. What is portrayed as a crisis in the media is not necessarily read in such a way by audiences: as we know from Hall's encoding/decoding model (see Chapter 4), it is important to distinguish between the meaning(s) embedded in media texts and meanings produced by audiences.

Autopoiesis is a theory of contingency which acknowledges that there is always scope for misunderstanding in the communications between different systems because no interpretation can be seen as either necessary or impossible (King and Thornhill 2003a: 31). The same principle of contingency also characterises the relationship between law and media. Within each of these systems truth claims are not arbitrary: as I explain below, they flow from the self-referencing to previous communications through established forms of distinction. However, at an inter-systemic level, there can be no certainty that systems will generate the same interpretation of events occurring in their environment, which suggests that wide discrepancies cannot be ruled out.

The 'make-believe' worlds of law and the mass media

There can be little doubt that to Luhmann (1985; 2000) both law and the mass media are immensely important social subsystems. They are fully differentiated and each has a very different role to play in the process of social communication. Starting with law, the code which shapes its communications is the 'lawful/unlawful' and 'legal/illegal' binary divide: the way in which law processes events taken from its environment is based around these two sets of distinctions. The unique aim or function of this process is to stabilise normative expectations over time, which ensures other systems an element of certainty and predictability in what would otherwise be a world of communicative uncertainty. As Ziegert explains:

> a) Norms 'immunize' against the unpredictability of the future but cannot control the future, and b) the functional effect of norms is not the projection of an ideal future but the projection of a 'managed' alternative to an unpredictable future . . . Norms bind time and not people.
>
> (Ziegert 2002: 63)

The robustness of legal norms stems from their immutability in the face of repeated contravention: speeding does not invalidate the norm that it violates because only law itself can change its own norms, guaranteeing stability over time. Past experience is immaterial. As individuals we may be aware of the extent to which certain laws are not respected but we would be unwise to assume that such conduct is therefore lawful. Law itself is largely indifferent to the way in which its norms fare on the outside:

> If one takes a cynical perspective, law could well be seen as constructing a make-believe world which simplifies psychological, political, economic and other 'realities' to enable it to reject all knowledge which threatens to undermine the validity of its communications.
>
> (King and Thornhill 2003a: 54)

So too, of course, are the media very much in the business of (re)producing their own reality through the application of their unique code of 'information/ non-information'. Information for Luhmann (2000: 17) is the 'positive value' of the mass media system while 'non-information' is the 'reflexive' value providing the contrasting backdrop against which the media can distinguish themselves as a self-reproducing system. There is, in other words, a close relationship between old and new, or information which is no longer news because it has already been published (and is therefore 'non-information') and information which has current news value. 'Old' information (something of a contradiction in terms for autopoiesis for what is already known no longer has information value) is still important for framing the new in terms of what is familiar and came before. The dynamics of information and non-information underpin the entire media system, as Luhmann (2000: 20) explains: 'The system is constantly feeding its own output, that is, knowledge of certain facts, back into the system on the negative side of the code, as non-information; and in doing so it forces itself constantly to provide new information.' There is in other words a 'constant de-actualisation of information' (Luhmann 2000: 20) in the media which is most obvious in the continuing self-renewing cycle that is news, but entertainment genres too, as Luhmann (2000: 63) makes clear, are driven by a similar search for surprise and suspense resulting from what he describes as 'self-induced uncertainty'. The processing of information is evidently important to all social systems. Yet, for the mass media this process is at the centre of their activities, their communicative function consisting of the 'constant generation and processing of irritation – and neither in increasing knowledge nor in socialising or educating people in conformity to norms' (Luhmann 2000: 98).

The overarching role of the mass media is to give other social subsystems a present tense which they can take as 'given' for their own operations, using it to adapt themselves by anticipating future developments. Through the constant renewal and rendering obsolete of information, the media create a 'memory' for society, providing other systems with a stock of information which they can use for their own ends (Luhmann 2000: 65). Just as the legal system finds itself in a kind of 'make-believe' world through its own obliviousness to anything that goes on beyond what it constructs as its own environment, so too are the mass media wrapped up in their own reality, which as Luhmann (2000: 4) explains, can be defined as 'what *appears to them*, or *through them to others*, to be reality'. The notion of media distortion is flatly rejected by Luhmann:

The question is *not*: how do the mass media *distort* reality? For that would presuppose an ontological, available, objectively accessible reality that can be known without resort to construction; it would basically presuppose the old cosmos of essences. Scientists might indeed be of the opinion that they have a better knowledge of reality than the way in which it is represented in the mass media, committed as these are to 'popularization'. But that can only mean comparing one's own construction to another.

(Luhmann 2000: 7)

The question that is of most interest to my argument in this chapter is: how do the make-believe systems of law and the mass media relate to each other? As I have explained above, any direct interaction between social subsystems is ruled out by autopoietic theory. Instead, it relies on the notion of 'structural coupling' to describe partial overlaps in meaning between subsystems which occur when events act as irritants for each system concerned. A helpful definition of structural coupling is offered by King and Thornhill (2003a: 33): 'structural coupling . . . relates to the co-evolution of different systems (of whatever kind) whereby each includes the other in its environment, interpreting the outputs of the other in its own terms on a continuous basis.' Serious fraud, for example, represents a possible structural coupling between the economic and legal system as well as being a trigger to the media system because it has information value. When the matter is taken up by the legal system, resulting in a prosecution, further media coverage is likely to follow, leading to a further structural coupling between law and the media. For Luhmann, the strongest form of structural coupling occurs between the media and politics, leading to ample friction between them, but he seems to somewhat downplay law's relationship with the media by describing it as 'only relatively marginally affected' (Luhmann 2000: 68). Autopoiesis has nevertheless proved extremely useful to Nobles and Schiff (2000; 2004) in their work on media reporting of miscarriages of justice and the sense of crisis with which the media seem to engulf the legal system when high-profile cases of wrongful convictions occur.

The linchpin in their analysis, which is based on content analyses of newspaper reports, is the notion of 'stable misreading' whereby the media system consistently transforms legal truth into its own idiosyncratic reality. Any notion that the media could faithfully reproduce law in all its integrity violates the basic tenets of autopoiesis for it would mean that the media could no longer exist as a fully differentiated subsystem. For the media to copy law's communications would require that they forego encoding reality on the basis of their own 'information/non-information' principle, which would jeopardise their existence as an autopoietic system (Nobles and Schiff 2004: 226). As a result, the media's communications about law (and any other topic) involve a drastic degree of simplification and superficiality which are seen as unavoidable for a system that has to renew itself constantly to keep up its information production. To cover issues with the same depth as law and science do would mean a certain inertia for the media, which would result in a neglect of their information calling.

For Nobles and Schiff, the media's misreading of law takes on a specific form in the context of miscarriages of justice. When a defendant is convicted of an offence, the media tend to treat this as more or less absolute proof of guilt, whereas to the legal system such an outcome merely indicates 'a finding of guilt *following a fair trial*' (Nobles and Schiff 2000: 96; my emphasis). The requirement of fairness is likely to be omitted from media reports, this being taken as a given which holds very little news value. If the media found it worthwhile to report on the fairness of legal proceedings as a matter of course, it would suggest that unfairness is seen as the usual and not worth mentioning state of affairs, which in turn would reflect badly on the legal system. In other words, the legal system benefits from having its operations routinely misread by other systems. Nobles and Schiff suggest that it is a matter of convenience for the media not to delve too deeply into the background of a case: to question whether a conviction is safe would put an enormous burden on journalists who would have to gather their own 'evidence' and conduct their own enquiries to corroborate their story. This is of course the domain of investigative journalism, but it happens less frequently in run-of-the-mill reporting delivering next day's headlines.

When someone is acquitted, Nobles and Schiff believe that a similar pattern can be observed: acquittal is taken as a statement of innocence rather than as a failure to convict by prevailing standards of evidence. Both an acquittal and a conviction therefore give rise to stable misreadings of law, which, as the terms suggests, ensures a degree of stability in the relationship between law and other social subsystems. A particular problem arises, however, when a conviction is quashed on appeal: here too a misreading occurs in that this event is reported as a finding of innocence rather than being interpreted as an indication that the defendant did not receive a fair trial. This may lead the media to speak of 'a crisis in public confidence' flowing from the exposure of apparently serious flaws in the legal system, as has happened, for example, in recent years in England when the convictions of Sally Clarke and other women convicted of killing their babies were quashed on appeal (see Nobles and Schiff 2004). When this occurs, the stability of the structural coupling between law and media may appear to be in jeopardy.

However, considering that such a crisis is entirely of the media's own making – it is a media event in other words – and that interest is likely to wane after a while as the media go in search of new information and divert their attention elsewhere, Nobles and Schiff argue that the impact of such a crisis on the legal system is surprisingly minimal. Granted, public inquiries and reviews may ensue, but the end result is unlikely to be a radical reform of the criminal justice system. The argument goes that the news media simply cannot sustain their crisis narrative: they are too reliant on the information benefits that come with the 'normal' reporting of acquittals and convictions to maintain their criticism of the legal system. A return to a more stable set of interrelations with the legal system is therefore the most likely outcome of any periodical crises in public confidence. This does not mean that the legal system is incapable of change, but it does suggest that it changes only on its own terms through its usual way of processing events in its environment. The media's perception of what constitutes a serious problem or flaw does not necessarily coincide with the legal system's own definition of a mistake (Nobles and Schiff 2000: 167). In other words, media stories are not directly fed into the legal system to trigger a specific outcome. The legal system is likely to respond to its observations of its shortcomings through a further differentiation of its own operations as happened in 1997 when the Criminal Cases Review Commission (with jurisdiction over England, Wales and Northern Ireland) was set up in response to a series of miscarriages of justice. However, Nobles and Schiff (2000: 170) point out that 'the reform produced is, as a sceptic would anticipate, not root-and-branch reform, but changes intended to reassure the media of the legal system's ability to deal with its mistakes'.

Media threats to law's autonomy: dedifferentiation

Law's normative closure makes it exceptionally unreceptive to external pressures. While this helps it to fulfil its stabilising function, it should not be seen as a functional feature in the non-autopoietic sense: law may succeed in maintaining its own closure but it can nevertheless also be very much out of touch with other systems, including the human system. Nobles and Schiff's analysis suggests that even media exposure of serious problems can only have a limited effect on the actual working of the legal system. Such a closure is at once a strength and a shortcoming of autopoietic law. It also means that the extent to which the media are able to disrupt and even undermine the legal system should not be overstated. Even sustained periods of critical coverage only constitute an irritant to law which is likely to abate, failing to provoke the kind of upheaval which many practitioners and policy makers fear it could have.

The question is whether this means that autopoiesis under no circumstances envisages the possibility that the legal system may come under severe strain from the media. It certainly appears that there is an extreme scenario of 'dedifferentiation' which would severely compromise the autonomy of the legal system. As King and Thornhill explain:

> The single threat to law's effectiveness is that of *dedifferentiation*: that means the dissolution of law's boundaries so that its legal communications lose their distinctiveness and become corrupted through the

legal system's adoption of other ways of attributing meaning (perhaps economic, political, scientific, medical/therapeutic or religious).

(King and Thornhill 2003a: 40)

Law ceases to exist as a system when it no longer produces its own communications but replicates those of other systems. For example, if cases were thrown out of court after a while because they have lost their information value or if someone were convicted by a court of law solely on the basis of a media story, then we would be dealing with an instance of dedifferentiation. It is clear, however, that only extreme circumstances could produce a complete dedifferentiation. An occasional or isolated disruption is unlikely to have such dramatic effects. The dissolution of law's boundaries requires a form of drastic upheaval engulfing the entire social system, for example, a revolution leading to the creation of a theocracy which would put priests or clerics in charge of the administration of justice.

The concept of dedifferentiation makes it seem unlikely that media pressure alone is sufficient to threaten law's autonomy. Law, together with politics and science, is among the most powerful subsystems. Being the more authoritative subsystem capable of setting definitions of reality for the rest of society, autopoietic law has a tendency to dominate lesser systems. However, this does not mean that weaker systems are necessarily resigned to this particular distribution of meaning-making powers. As King points out:

It is always possible for the less prevalent systems to insist on their own self-reconstructions and indeed to reconstruct successful meaning systems according to their particular procedures and reality versions. The problem these weaker systems face, however, is to convince society, the world of social communications, to accept their versions of reality in preference to those of the more prevalent systems.

(King 1993: 231)

This particular vantage point is a very helpful tool in mapping out the battleground between law and the media. While it would be difficult to argue that the media are a particularly weak subsystem, it would certainly appear that as far as their relation with law is concerned, they are the weaker partner, as indeed Nobles and Schiff's analysis suggests. Much of the disquiet concerning the media's treatment and coverage of legal issues reveals concerns about the way in which this relationship is developing. Could it be that we are witnessing a shift in the balance of power whereby the media's misreadings of law are growing in stature and becoming increasingly successful in passing themselves off as generally accepted and authoritative statements of legal meaning? Are the boundaries between law and media 'vanishing' as Sherwin (2000) claims and will this ultimately bring about a scenario of dedifferentiation?

It could be argued in typical autopoietic fashion that law's own communications concerning the threat which media culture poses tend to take on a life of their own, acting as a catalyst for a further differentiation of its operations so as to safeguard law against pressure from media and public opinion. It seems logical (at least within the autopoietic framework) for the legal system to find internal solutions to the repeated and at times intense pressure which constitutes critical media coverage. As long as law can turn to its own unique processing method in dealing with such pressures, its existence as an autopoietic system seems more or less guaranteed. The idea that crises surrounding law are media induced tempers the hypothesis that the media have a strongly disruptive effect on law: the autopoietic legal system is seen as robust enough to rise to the challenge and handle media pressure. Although it is possible for autopoietic legal systems to retreat from some areas and relinquish these to other systems (King and Piper 1995: 35), it is of course law's (relative) closure that protects it from being too easily disturbed by events in its environment (as opposed to being merely 'perturbed', which is a naturally occurring autopoietic operation[13]).

Conclusion

Autopoiesis tells a story that is rather different from the liberal narrative which readily accepts that legal actors should submit to a healthy dose of media scrutiny and criticism. The relationship between law and the media is viewed as problematic only to the extent that the latter target legal institutions with criticism that is misguided, ill-informed, gratuitous and outright damaging to people's confidence in the legal system. For many observers, such an irresponsible use of media freedom happens all too often, resulting in inaccurate and unsatisfactory media portrayals. Underpinning such concerns is the idea that but for the media's shortcomings, the public would be much better acquainted with the inner workings of the legal system and less likely to be dissatisfied with the administration of justice. Nobles and Schiff's (2000: 99) rather surprising conclusion that 'the media's misreading of legal operations exhibits a tremendous commitment and deference to law and legal processes' gives a strong indication of how autopoiesis challenges some of the received wisdom in this area.

The main point which autopoiesis drives home is that the media's distortions can be attributed to their need to maintain themselves as a differentiated system which leads them to create their own reality in accordance with criteria that are necessarily at odds with those with which the legal system produces its own communications. Secondly, the inherent superficiality of the media, which to liberal doctrine prevents them from performing their watchdog role effectively, is seen – rather perversely perhaps – as something that contributes to safeguarding law's unassailability because crises in public confidence are mere ephemeral media constructs that are incapable of provoking profound changes in the legal system. Of course, such insights are very broadly framed, offering only a general overview of the law/media nexus which no doubt needs refining if we want to be able to distinguish between different media forms and ways in which different aspects of the legal system are depicted by various media.

Autopoiesis works best as a theory which considers meaning and communication to be the connective tissue of society. As I have explained, people in their capacity as individual conscience systems largely remain beyond the autopoietic gaze. The fact that humans are located outside social subsystems is not as incongruous as it may at first glance appear. As I have explained in Chapter 2, it is not inconceivable for people to feel detached from both law and the mass media despite these being institutions that pervade every facet of their lives. Systems such as law and the media 'imagine' people as clients, litigants, viewers, audience ratings and consumers just as they produce other aspects of their own reality. However, such imaginings do not necessarily correspond with how people experience – or construct – their own reality. Heated media debates and even deep crises of legitimacy, being a product of an intense coupling of events, may fail to register precisely because such communications take place in an autopoietic, self-reproducing and closed-off environment.

Chapter 7

Press judges and communication advisers in courts

Introduction

In the previous chapter, I have explored how journalists espousing the doctrine of the Fourth Estate consider it their professional duty to subject the legal system to constant vigilance and scrutiny, which means that they are inclined to adopt distrust and cynicism as their default position. However, it has also been observed that media reports may be seen as deferential in other respects: superficial and even distorted reporting may gloss over elements of legal procedure (for example, by taking the fairness of a trial as a given) which, if they were extensively commented on by the media, would testify to an even greater cynicism. This chapter seeks to examine how judges themselves respond to growing media criticism of their work which has become, to put it in the words of Mr Justice Kirby (1998), a justice in the High Court of Australia, 'a universal phenomenon'. Although his comments mainly concern common law jurisdictions, it is safe to assume that many judges in continental Europe would agree with his claim that media deference for judges has become a thing of the past.[1]

In an interview in 1995, Jean-Pierre Cochard (1995), an honorary magistrate with a 40-year career in the French judiciary, talked of the emergence of a media-driven parallel system of justice in France which he thought was capable of rivalling the judicial process, exerting potentially enormous pressures on judges in both civil and criminal cases. A complicating factor in many continental legal systems (including France) is undoubtedly the position of the public prosecutor's office constituting a branch of the judiciary which, in addition to a prosecution role, is also closely involved in the pre-trial phase (Hodgson 2001). This means that prosecutors may have to contend with considerable pre-trial media attention, which many consider could amount to a significant interference in the investigation of high-profile crimes.[2]

Whatever the differences in judicial organisation, growing and often intrusive media scrutiny is almost invariably seen throughout common law and civil law jurisdictions as something that calls for a robust response. For judges to remain passive in the face of ever-closer media interest and negative cover-age is today no longer considered an option. While silence and passivity may once have been seen as the most dignified response to media criticism as well as a necessary safeguard for judicial impartiality, many judicial systems today favour an altogether more proactive approach. In France, the idea that it is preferable to take the lead in information provision rather than passively undergoing its consequences has gained considerable currency among members of the judiciary, especially in the public prosecutor's office (Civard-Racinais 1997). John Doyle (1997), Chief Justice of South Australia, even goes so far as to suggest that judges should shoulder part of the blame for inaccurate media reporting if they fail to involve themselves actively in the way in which public information about courts is disseminated. Therefore, it is today common practice for press officers to be deployed to represent judges in the media and fulfil a more general public relations function, while judges themselves are also much more willing to debate their role publicly.

While in most jurisdictions these are relatively recent developments, in the Netherlands, the twin institutions of press magistrate and press judge, a judge combining a judicial role with a media liaison role,[3] have been part of the fabric of the court system for over 30 years, making Dutch courts pioneers in media liaison techniques. The Dutch approach will be extensively analysed in this chapter. The fieldwork for this study, one of the first of its kind to research the function of press judge through a qualitative methodology,[4] draws on ten in-depth interviews with five press judges and five communication advisers in nine different courts, including seven District Courts, one Appeal Court and one Special Appeals Tribunal.[5] A former national communication adviser to the judiciary was also interviewed.

In the first part of my discussion, I set out the thinking behind changing judicial attitudes to the media, focusing on recent changes in the British context. Secondly, I will explain the historical and legal background to court–media relations in the Netherlands, the argument being that the relative harmony existing between courts and media there reflects deeply entrenched Dutch values. The third part of this chapter will look at the way in which press judges and communication advisers put their media liaison role into practice. I will argue that their mission merely to act as neutral messengers on behalf of courts cannot be divorced from an inevitable desire to manage public perceptions of the judiciary. Finally, there will also be a reflection on how proactive communications strategies are impacting on the tense relationship between law and the media. My argument in the previous chapter has been that such tensions are to a large extent unavoidable, with the result that any attempt at trying to eradicate these may not just be futile but also undesirable. The public information efforts undertaken by press officers bring into focus a potential struggle for influence over the media's agenda which may in effect amount to an attempt by the legal system to strike back against the pressures brought to bear on it by increasingly inquisitive media. The notion of law's embattled empire bravely attempting but barely able to withstand media pressures will be contrasted with that of an empire on the offensive attempting to ward off the consequences of negative media coverage by vigorously protecting the integrity of its own message.

Judges under pressure: problems and solutions

In British media, there is increasing attention on the personal background of judges, including their political, moral and religious beliefs, a change which has been attributed to the Human Rights Act 1998 (HRA) and the shift in institutional power in favour of the judiciary (Woodhouse 2004). Moreover, the increased confidence with which senior judges post-HRA are asserting themselves vis-à-vis the Executive has proved capable of extending the constitutional battleground to the media. Broad-sweeping and often controversial reforms have afforded many an opportunity for public comment and criticism by judges in recent times. To give just one example, the former Lord Chief Justice, Lord Woolf, gave a high-profile interview on the BBC Radio Four *Today* programme, broadcast in a slot usually reserved for senior politicians, to voice his discontent concerning the ill-conceived cabinet reshuffle of June 2003 which aimed to abolish the office of Lord Chancellor.[6] Enhanced judicial independence has also generated a greater awareness of the need for transparency and accountability in judicial decision making. This has turned the spotlight on how judges might improve public understanding of the legal system by adopting a more accessible style of communication (Woodhouse 2004).

However, already in the 1990s, Lord Mackay, then Lord Chancellor, had sought to encourage a proactive media approach by the judiciary, ending the strict regime of silence which was instituted in 1955 by one of his predecessors, Lord Kilmuir, in a letter to the BBC (the so-called 'Kilmuir rules'). Lord Taylor, who was appointed Lord Chief Justice in 1992, proved a strong ally in promoting this new culture of openness. He was noted for his own media appearances and his strong belief that judges should be more visibly present in the public sphere (Malleson 1999). Most recently, as a result of the reforms implemented by the Constitutional Reform Act 2005, a separate Judicial Communications Office was created to speak on behalf of judges while courts have their own dedicated press office.[7] Whereas previously the judiciary would rely on the assistance of the press office of the Lord Chancellor's Department in its dealings with various media, the stronger separation of powers resulting from the Constitutional Reform Act meant that it was considered more appropriate for judges to have their own independent channel for communicating with the media and the general public (Woolf 2003). While Malleson, writing in 1999, pointed to the judiciary's lack of a coherent media approach, some decisive steps have recently been taken towards developing a more co-ordinated public relations strategy. In April 2006, the

Judicial Communications Office launched its own website[8] which enables it to communicate directly with the general public without depending on the vagaries of coverage in the mass media.

What is striking about the proactive media approach adopted today in Britain and elsewhere is that it is underpinned by a strong pedagogical ambition. The aim is to enlighten journalists and the general public so as to correct erroneous understandings and banish misconceptions concerning the nature and the role of the judiciary. If only the public were better informed, so the argument goes, people would be more appreciative of the work of judges and hold them in high(er) esteem. As I suggested in Chapter 6, talk of misreporting in the media relies on an implicit claim that there is a truthful way of portraying the work of judges. However, what exactly counts as a complete and legitimate understanding is much more difficult to determine. What is accurate from a legal viewpoint does not necessarily coincide with what journalists regard as essential ingredients of a truthful story. Both judges and journalists are inevitably selective in their reality claims. For example, what is inadmissible as evidence in court (for example, details of previous convictions) may well be of relevance to a journalistic account because it offers an important and newsworthy perspective on the background of a particular case, however objectionable the publication of such information is from the viewpoint of legal procedure.

Secondly, the media liaison effort of judges rests on the assumption that media portrayal of judges is, indirectly at least, a reliable barometer of public opinion: media distortion is treated as a firm indication of widespread public misunderstanding. As I highlighted in Chapter 1, gauging public opinion or even ascertaining its mere existence is notoriously difficult: indeed, Bourdieu (1973) once famously argued that public opinion did not exist. The notion that public esteem for the judiciary can be read off from the way in which the media report specific cases risks conflating a range of very different issues. It ignores, for example, the possibility that people can form an opinion of the judiciary which not only goes against a particular media portrayal (see Chapter 4) but which can also be developed independently from the media, for example, through personal contact with courts (see Chapter 2).[9] Similarly, public regard for courts and the judiciary as an organisational entity may need to be distinguished from the way in which people perceive specific issues such as sentencing.[10]

Finally, from an autopoietic perspective, the harmonisation of reality claims through direct information exchanges simply becomes impossible because each system operates with entirely unique codes (legal/illegal in law and information/non-information in the media) recursively derived from existing internal communications.[11] But even if we were to accept that media distortion could be remedied and tensions between the media and the legal system could be greatly reduced, this is not necessarily wholly advantageous from a classic watchdog perspective which, within limits, considers a strained relationship with officialdom a prerequisite for effective media scrutiny. Viewed from this angle, a proactive information policy which aims to provide journalists with bite-size stories, for example, in the shape of easily digestible press releases, is a cause for concern as it risks making journalists overly dependent on official sources and could even result in the stifling of legitimate criticism, further undermining the media's much-beleaguered watchdog role.

The emergence of the press judge in Dutch courts

While it took until the 1990s for the idea of a proactive public relations approach to take hold in other countries, by then it had already become well established in the Netherlands. The Dutch setup involves a division of labour whereby the public prosecutor's office relies on the services of designated magistrates in its dealings with the media, while press judges act as spokespersons on behalf of the courts. For a judge (for both press magistrates and press judges are technically members of the judiciary) to step into the limelight as a matter of course may seem highly unusual, even when taking account of the greater openness to have emerged recently in other jurisdictions.[12] For any judge to be discussing individual cases or points of law in the media may seem difficult to reconcile with the impartiality and independence that is expected of the office (Brants 1993). My focus here is on the role of press judges, mainly because their interventions in the media may indeed give rise to delicate issues of propriety. For a press magistrate to comment on a current investigation or prosecution is not irreconcilable with the nature or tasks of the public prosecutor's office, whereas for a court judge to make any statements about court proceedings even when these have been concluded requires a potentially difficult balancing exercise precisely because the appearance of impartiality has to be preserved at all costs.

The fact that courts in Belgium and, more recently, in Croatia (Netherlands Helsinki Committee 2004) have looked to the Dutch model for inspiration in handling their own media relations further underscores its significance. Yet, it took some considerable time for the press judge to mature into the institution that it has become today: court judges (also known as the 'sitting' judiciary) became only slowly convinced of the merits of a proactive media approach. This was in stark contrast with the situation in the public prosecutor's office which suffered most severely from the anti-establishment backlash during and after the social unrest of the 1960s. Brants and Brants (2002) locate the origins of the anti-establishment sentiments of that particular decade in the breakdown of the consensus model which had characterised the postwar Netherlands. Operating in a society in which conflicts were settled and accommodated by representatives of the various ideological, religious and philosophical 'pillars' to make up Dutch society (Lijphart 1968), the media until the late 1960s were part and parcel of this consociational model. Not only were the press and television run in accordance with this model, reporting on the working of the institutions was also characterised by the same consensus-driven spirit. Rather than being confrontational or inquiring, journalists discreetly turned a blind eye leaving issues of public concern to be addressed through consultation among elites representing the various pillars. The media interpreted their task as one of messenger for the pillars, passing on information rather than subjecting it to critical reporting (Brants 1993). Such an uncritical attitude also extended to the institutions, including courts and the judiciary. Information was handled in a spirit of co-operation and mutual consultation: for example, in the 1950s representatives of the criminal justice system reached an agreement with journalists that suspects should not be identified in press reports except by their initials (Brants and Brants 2002). In short, before the 1960s, there was very little evidence of a vibrant press willing to take on a monitoring role and fulfil the critical watchdog function which today the European Court of Human Rights recognises in its jurisprudence the media ought to play (Addo 2000).

The climate in the Netherlands changed radically in the late 1960s. There does not appear to have been a single cataclysmic event that can be identified as the trigger for this transformation. Instead, it appears that as new social movements (including feminism and environmentalism) gathered pace and resistance against the consociational model increased, the authority of the pillars began to be eroded (Thomassen and van Deth 1989; Lijphart 1989). The media, themselves affected by the decline of the consociational model, were increasingly willing to offer a platform to these new political forces. This also afforded an opportunity to bring into focus what were now perceived to be serious shortcomings in various institutions, which in relation to the court system and the judiciary involved their lack of transparency and openness resulting in insufficient accountability. Wishing to equip themselves against rising public criticism and adapting to a media climate which was markedly less deferential than at any other time in the post-war period, magistrates in the public prosecutor's office felt the need to become involved in a public information campaign aimed at better communication with a growingly critical and inquisitive press.[13] The first step towards such an information programme was taken in 1972 when a national communication adviser to the judiciary was appointed.[14] The information policy adopted by the judiciary was a response which was typical of the consensus model: rather than risking an escalation of tensions in court–media relations, the aim was to restore the culture of co-operation and goodwill (Brants 2001). The model of openness that was subsequently adopted was very much a controlled form of openness which was intended to give courts and their partner institutions (for example, the police) the upper hand in information provision.

Courts followed the example of the public prosecutor's office by appointing press judges in 1974, although this move was marked by considerable reticence. The idea initially received a lukewarm reception and the press judge in courts was very much an inactive institution until the late 1980s. A plausible explanation for this is that until that period, despite rising media criticism, the integrity of the judiciary was never at issue and competition between the media was limited, resulting in what can with hindsight be seen as rather sedate court reporting and moderate media interest in the administration of justice. The late 1980s saw the arrival of a deregulated media landscape which brought criminal justice to the top of the agenda because it was an important arena for media competing with each other for a share of the market. Whereas run-of-the-mill court reporting may have been in decline, there was growing media interest in high-profile 'scandalous' cases (for example, white collar crime) in which the focus was not only on key suspects but also on the ability of the judiciary (both prosecutors and court judges) to prosecute and punish such crimes (Brants and Brants 2002). In 1989, press judges decided to meet annually to discuss their experiences and consult each other on matters of media strategy, further evidence that it was not just press magistrates in the public prosecutor's office but also press judges in courts who now felt the need for a more concerted effort in the way in which they handled their relations with the media.

Since the late 1990s, there has been an increasingly professional approach to public relations in Dutch courts. In 1998, there was a campaign to recruit communication advisers to support press judges as well as to co-ordinate internal communication in courts. All District Courts, which act as courts of first instance and are comprised of several 'sectors' (including an administrative, a civil and a criminal sector), today employ one or more communication advisers who look after a wide range of organisational issues. They liaise with press judges, publish press statements, provide practical information to journalists (for example, dates and times of court hearings), write annual reports and organise court visits for the general public. What communication advisers are bringing to the equation are specific skills and expertise which press judges do not always possess, in spite of the media training which many of them receive. Moreover, communication advisers ease the workload of press judges whose role as media spokesperson is secondary to their judicial function.

However, significantly, press judges are nowadays formally credited for their media-related work, which is another indication that managing court–media relations is increasingly recognised as a core activity and is no longer seen as something peripheral that press judges can effortlessly combine with their normal workload. Further evidence of the move towards proper recognition for press judges came with the introduction in 2003 of a general function profile setting out the skills that candidates applying for the function of press judge must be able to demonstrate. Whereas previously presidents of courts would offer the job of press judge to any judge willing to take on the role, candidates are today subjected to a more stringent recruitment process, resulting in a greater formalisation and also undoubtedly in a better monitoring of judges' media-related work. Furthermore, since 2003, there is a national press directive setting out the rules and guidelines which courts adopt in their contacts with the media. It regulates media access and information provision. However, the directive has no binding force: individual courts and even individual judges are perfectly entitled to depart from it, for example by denying television cameras access to court in defiance of the directive. Judicial independence in the Netherlands is quite literally the independence of individual judges who are free to decide on the best way of conducting proceedings in the courtroom. In some cases, this undoubtedly requires press judges to engage in some diplomatic manoeuvring when trying to persuade more media-sceptic colleagues to authorise camera access or release the transcripts of their judgments so that journalists and news editors can be properly briefed or briefed in a timely fashion.

Judicial independence also explains why, with the exception of the recently introduced function profile and national directive, the regulatory framework in which press judges operate is very unspecific. Basic legal principles, such as the requirement that cases must be heard in public, that due consideration be given to the privacy of parties and the recognition that the media play a legitimate monitoring role vis-à-vis the judiciary, evidently apply. Such principles have also been enshrined in the Dutch constitution, penal code and privacy laws as well as in supra-national human rights declarations and relevant jurisprudence. These provisions, however, are not specifically tailored to the work of press judges and communication advisers and as such they provide very little guidance as to how court officials should conduct their relations with the media. Jurisprudence in this area is almost non-existent: to date, there has only been one ruling by the Ombudsman Division of the Supreme Court specifically considering the issue of whether for a press judge to give a joint press conference with a press magistrate on a *sub judice* case amounted to a violation of the appearance of judicial impartiality (Brants 1992).[15]

Sanctions against journalists who contravene the press directive or the basic principles that it seeks to protect are also virtually unknown. The Netherlands has no contempt of court laws and trial by jury is unknown. The only remedy for individual parties who have been aggrieved by intrusive media practices lies in civil action, which is of little use to judges or prosecutors seeking to safeguard the public interest against prejudicial media reporting (Brants 1993; Brants 2001). The press directive stipulates that journalists who break the rules may be barred from court, but one press judge whom I interviewed had strong doubts about the legality of imposing such a sanction. Moreover, barring journalists does little to promote the quality of court reporting, which is why there appears to be some considerable reluctance to resort to such extreme measures. Journalists have their own professional disciplinary body (the Dutch Council for Journalism) which regularly hears complaints against individual members (complaints which do not necessarily relate to court reporting). However, membership is not compulsory and the decisions of the Council are not binding, although they do carry significant moral weight (Brants 2001).

Despite this light-touch approach to the regulation of court–media relations, the consensus expressed by interviewees was that Dutch media generally conduct themselves with propriety. Frictions and misunderstandings were mentioned, but these were overwhelmingly treated as minor irritations that did not amount to any serious tensions. None of the interviewees argued that there should be tighter regulation for the media, with the exception of one press judge who thought that disciplinary measures against the media ought to be strengthened. His principal concern was the growing diversity of media outlets, mainly in the form of free door-to-door newspapers giving rise to a new breed of court reporters who are not members of the Council for Journalism and who are not necessarily committed to certain 'quality criteria' such as a regard for privacy and accuracy. Quite the opposite view was expressed by another press judge: there was no need in his view for formal sanctions against the media. By way of explanation, he referred to the consociational model 'which means that not everything has to be regulated by law. That generally works very well in this society.' This is very much consistent with Lijphart's (1989) assessment that the pillar model still has a strong presence in the Netherlands and, as my findings suggest, its ethos equally continues to permeate court–media relations. For example, the 1950s 'gentlemen's agreement' between courts and media that only a suspect's initials should be published is still to some extent being observed, despite the absence of legislation to buttress it and drastic changes in the media landscape. The Dutch consociational approach to court–media relations appears effective largely because it resonates with some enduring values in Dutch society.

A transmission or orientation role?

Although the function of press judges and communication advisers in the Netherlands is the product of a specific historic and social context, the day-to-day contact that they have with journalists raises issues which have a much wider resonance. For example, Woodhouse commenting on the relationship between the media and a future United Kingdom Supreme Court attaches great importance to ensuring transparency and public confidence through measures which would help the general public to form a better understanding of complex and controversial cases:

> To aid public understanding, judgments should be accompanied by a brief explanation of the case and the court's decision, written in plain English. They [the Supreme Court] could also appoint a press liaison or communications officer and provide journalists with facilities to read the judgments and write their reports. Such developments would have

resource implications but they are important in terms of transparency and public understanding of what the court does.

Woodhouse (2004: 149)

Not only are the specific suggestions made by Woodhouse strikingly similar to the media liaison arrangements of Dutch courts, but she also highlights what Dutch press judges and communication advisers see as their single most important challenge: the labour of translation (in Dutch 'vertaalslag') which requires them to simplify their message and render it accessible to a lay public while simultaneously conveying the doctrinal complexities and nuances of judicial rulings. Whether law is capable of undistorted translation by the media is a moot point, as I indicated in Chapter 6: autopoiesis evidently casts doubt on the prospect of any kind of successful translation of legal communications that would be compatible with the relevant codes of other systems. Nevertheless, the struggle to identify a suitable translation which satisfies the media's own criteria of newsworthiness yet also respects the integrity of a judgment was very much at the heart of interviewees' concerns.

However, it would be misleading to reduce the effort which press judges, or their counterparts elsewhere, undertake to improve judges' relationship with various media to an attempt at translation alone. In addition to the 'transmission' model, which involves media liaison personnel devoting energy to helping the media to decipher the most opaque aspects of judicial discourse through translation techniques, their efforts are also characterised by what I will call an 'orientation' model. In media studies, the transmission model is a familiar way of conceptualising the mass communication process by breaking it down into several key moments. The starting point is when a 'source' selects a message which is then transformed by a 'transmitter' into a 'signal' suitable for communication through a particular 'channel' to a 'receiver' which relays the signal to its eventual 'destination', with the possibility of a varying level of 'noise' disturbing the process and distorting the message relayed by the original source (Fiske 1990: 7). While not being the original 'source' of the message (for that would be the judge or judges making a ruling, granting a remedy or imposing a sentence[16]), interviewees overwhelmingly saw themselves as transmitters helping journalists, also acting as purveyors of the judicial message, to reduce the level of noise (or disturbance) and portray a court's decision through a set of signals which are most compatible with the original judgment. Noise reduction would be a good means of describing the way in which press judges and communication advisers define their own input, a job description which also enables them to interpret their role as that of facilitators – and not as manipulators – of information.

Nevertheless, the orientation model, which implies a degree of steering to give some direction to the raw information, is not irreconcilable with the transmission model but is logically entwined with it. The reduction of noise as a cybernetic aim in the transmission model implies a desire to exert control over the signal or central message and shape it in a way in which there is minimal variation between the message as conceived by the original source and as it is eventually received at the other end of the communication process (Fiske 1990). For the message to be received in all its 'authenticity', a degree of manipulation is therefore inescapable. The dilemma of transmission and orientation of information is vividly illustrated in the following interview excerpt:

> I don't stand there with the intention to influence. I stand there with the intention to give an account of what has happened. What the rest of the world makes of it is up to them. But my experience is that everything is reduced to a couple of sentences, that what you are actually saying [on television] does not accurately reflect what you wanted to say. So in that sense I'm becoming more and more aware that how I put it determines how they [journalists] will write it down. And then you find yourself thinking of a strategy and I don't feel comfortable with that. I only want to tell the truth in all its nuances.

The interviewee, a press judge, very strikingly and courageously acknowledges that manipulation of the media is the inexorable outcome of his wish to safeguard the integrity of the judicial message against media distortion and counteract the manipulation which information inevitably undergoes within the media system itself. To be honest and truthful he feels that he has to be sufficiently calculating so as to enable him to determine what form of presentation gives him the best chance of getting his message across in all its integrity.

Furthermore, image building, although it may appear to be of a different order altogether, is part and parcel of the orientation effort underpinning media liaison by Dutch courts.[17] The wish to be perceived as neutral transmitters of a particular message is pivotal to the image of impartiality which judges ultimately wish – and undoubtedly feel legally compelled – to convey of themselves. Paradoxically, this means that even when press judges speak in the most neutral of terms and steer clear of interpreting a judgment, they are still unwittingly engaging in image building. After all, creating the *appearance* of impartiality and detachment is a quintessential aspect of the performance of the judicial role. This is not a trite observation: it appeared to be a vexing issue for press judges who wanted to be able to draw a clear line between explaining and commenting on a judgment. This can engender a state of near paralysis. It is clear that some press judges, when confronted with questions from journalists, resort to simply quoting the original decision without offering any meaningful clarification for fear of compromising their neutrality or adding what could be perceived by the media to be a note of dissent to the original decision.[18] However, the distinction between transmitting a message in relation to a judgment and manipulating it either to reduce the noise level or to impress a certain image upon the public mind is difficult to maintain in practice. To use a Goffmanian term, impression management would appear to be an integral part of the media liaison function performed by press judges and communication advisers (Goffman 1959).

There are a number of factors which seem to belie the importance of image building in this context and these need to be addressed first. Interviewees insisted that they were simply messengers of the law as a system of rules applied in court, which seems to indicate that they act with absolute neutrality as to their own professional standing. For example, when confronted with critical questions from the media attacking a judicial decision, press judges will generally resist the temptation to offer any justification or come to the defence of colleagues whose decisions are under attack. Retractions are also rarely asked for. This effectively means that press judges often pass up the opportunity to defend their own corporate image. Moreover, it has to be said that, all things considered, the judiciary may not be in much need of a public relations exercise. Dutch judges are held in relatively high esteem by the public (de Keijser and Elffers 2004) and they have been unaffected by the type of scandals that have tarnished the image of the judiciary elsewhere, for example, across the border in Belgium (Gies 2003b). What the Dutch judiciary is dealing with is a mere decline in deference in the media so that, to use the words of one press judge, 'authority now has to be earned', but this does not amount to a wholesale attack on judges. It also appears that media interest in the private lives of individual judges is moderate, which means that judges on the whole are able to stay out of the spotlight. Some judges were said by interviewees to resist the presence of cameras in their courtrooms precisely because they feared that this could deprive them of their anonymity and ultimately also affect their right to privacy. One press judge said that, although he was happy for the media to use his surname and initials, he objected to them mentioning his first name because this was too personal a detail. A gradual growth in media interest in judges' personal background was most notably being observed in the Amsterdam District Court (the largest district in the Netherlands), giving rise to similar concerns.

While Dutch judges do not suffer from any significant deficit in public esteem and are generally able to keep their private lives out of the media spotlight, in many other ways their institutional image is difficult to disentangle from court–media relations, especially considering that they consciously step in to play a significant liaison role and make themselves more visible in this way. The aim of image building in this respect is not so much to undo any serious past damage as to reverse the trend of a gradual decline in public deference. We may even wonder whether the fact that the integrity of Dutch judges has not been seriously questioned in recent times may at least partly be attributed to the robust media liaison framework for which the groundwork was laid more than 30 years ago. There are several indications which support the argument that the image of the judiciary is a central, if often unconscious and by no means malicious, factor in media liaison. Firstly, this is apparent again from the way in which press judges handle their role as translators. In addition to those judges who feel unable to offer much by way of explanation because this would give the wrong impression of their own position and betray their *esprit de corps*, there are others who are much bolder in their approach, often to achieve a similar effect. Perhaps the boldest move taken by some is to suggest to a presiding judge ways of clarifying a judgment so that it would be easier to explain to the media. This seems to happen when the motivation of a judgment is obscure or insufficient. This is a very clear example of how media liaison is having a (benign) impact on the actual practices of judges, but it also amounts to another subtle example of image building: press judges believe that it would have dangerous implications for their role as neutral messengers if they themselves have to openly make up the missing parts of a judgment in front of journalists. It is even experienced as a professional embarrassment by press judges, who are after all assumed to be well acquainted with the judicial process, not to be able to properly explain a decision taken by another judge.[19]

The ramifications of such gaps in the motivation of a judgment are most keenly felt in relation to sentencing. The discomfort at having to explain to the media the rationale of sentencing was explicitly cited by three press judges who indicated that such a situation made them all too aware of the fact that the length of a sentence may ultimately be the individual and arbitrary decision of another judge.[20] However, they simultaneously felt that such a candid admission would be impossible to contemplate in their dealings with the media because it would not only expose the indeterminacy of a pivotal aspect of judicial decision making, but could also have disastrous consequences for public confidence in the judiciary. 'Judges are not magicians, they are artisans', proffered one press judge as observation, the implication being that judicial decision making was fallible but also perhaps that such vulnerability had to be concealed from the media and public opinion.

A second example which further emphasises the image-building aspects of public relations in Dutch courts is their policy concerning cameras. The presence of recording equipment in court is governed by relatively detailed provisions in the press directive. In principle, only the procession of judges and prosecutors as they arrive in the courtroom and the reading out of charges and the judgment may be recorded, although further recordings are again at the discretion of the presiding judge. The parts of the proceedings which can be filmed are undoubtedly those which can be most easily controlled by judges and prosecutors through advance preparation. Very little is left to coincidence. It is not unheard of for the procession of judges and prosecutors at the start of a hearing to be meticulously rehearsed in advance. Television images of a stumbling judge, a disorderly entrance or other mishaps would do little to convey the solemnity of the occasion. Moreover, in high-profile cases, communication advisers and press judges put together detailed scenarios (complete with stage directions) allowing them to carefully orchestrate the proceedings.[21] While these scenarios are not just intended to manage media interest (for example, they may also contain details of police security checks to be carried out prior to hearings), they do make specific provisions for journalists and contribute more generally to the orderly organisation of the hearings. They therefore assist in achieving the image that judges undoubtedly wish to project at moments when they are at the centre of exceptionally intense media attention.

Thirdly and finally, the importance of image building is also apparent from the very subtle tensions that exist between communication advisers and press judges. The division of labour ought to be clear in principle: communication advisers work behind the scenes while press judges step into the media limelight to explain matters of court policy and individual judgments. The rationale for this is that judges are thought to be ideally placed to phrase their message in such a way that it does not compromise the impartiality of the court or cause the public to doubt the legal soundness of a judgment. Moreover, there also seems to be a feeling that the wider public wants to hear the message from someone who stands in a very close professional relationship with the original decision makers. Journalists themselves clearly prefer to be given chapter and verse by press judges instead of having to make do with a communication adviser (Malsch 2004: 47). Judges lend authority to the message communicated to the media because of their status and professional expertise.[22] Once again, constructing the right image and reassuring the public seem to be a very relevant consideration.

However, one communication adviser quite openly challenged this approach, arguing that judges did not have the skills to communicate effectively with the media. In her view, spokespersons need to have a very specific and specialist understanding of the media in order to successfully negotiate the various pitfalls that can arise. She referred to an unfortunate incident involving a press magistrate: he had claimed that the defence argument in a drug trafficking case that luggage tags had been switched was improbable because such tags were absolutely tamper-proof. The press magistrate then unwisely agreed to give a demonstration on camera, only to find that the tag actually could be removed quite easily. According to my interviewee, this incident was a typical example of a mistake made by someone with insufficient knowledge of how the media operate. Considering that such ill-judged conduct could have disastrous consequences for the public image of the judiciary, she believed that it would be preferable if properly qualified and experienced communication officers handled particularly tricky and image-defining situations.

What we see being played out here is a (subtle) conflict over who is best placed to act as guardians of courts' and by extension the judiciary's relations with the media: a judge with specific legal expertise or a communication adviser with specific media expertise.[23] All interviewees resisted any suggestion that they were spin-doctors employed to manipulate the media, but they did describe their approach as consciously proactive. The message which is being transmitted by them is the product of careful reflection and conscious decision making and it is conceived with image-specific objectives in mind: ensuring public confidence by creating appearances which are consistent with impartiality, transparency, openness and ultimately also the rule of law. Yet, one cannot help noticing that the public relations effort is caught up in a web of tensions. The appearance of openness is in many ways just that: an appearance which is intended to conceal an element of opacity concerning the indeterminacy that underpins judicial decision making. Furthermore, the conscious effort of press judges not to justify a court's decision in the media serves as ultimate legitimation of the judicial process: to add any explanation or qualification would undermine the completeness and finality of a ruling. Finally, the careful balancing act between transmission and manipulation of information rests on a distinction which is in practice difficult to maintain. These dilemmas are consistent with a perception that the authority and legitimacy of institutions are no longer self-evident but require extensive explanation and justification in the public sphere. Judges now have to 'earn' respect and this is an increasingly laborious task, taking them onto unfamiliar territory. This potentially transforms their role but it does not necessarily curtail or undermine it.

Pre-emptive strikes and embattled empires

It was only comparatively recently that the institutional landscape in the United Kingdom evolved sufficiently for the judiciary to be given its own Communications Office. Whereas the Dutch have opted for a system of designated press judges and locally based communication advisers, the Judicial Communications Office in England and Wales provides centrally co-ordinated media assistance to all judicial office holders. Both systems nevertheless seem to support a similar division of labour between (senior) judges who have a visible presence in the media and communication professionals who work behind the scenes in an advisory and supportive capacity. In terms of what judges are prepared to discuss, there is a striking similarity in that Dutch press judges are in practice as reticent as many of their colleagues elsewhere to talk about the specifics of a case in a way which would create ambiguity and compromise their impartiality.

Leaving aside the specific socio-cultural factors that have shaped media liaison in Dutch courts, the doctrinal considerations underpinning the policy of controlled openness vis-à-vis the media are very recognisable. The Dutch policy is couched in a language of fundamental legal principles, the most important of which is the public character of court proceedings as a basic safeguard for the right to a fair hearing. An important rationale for media liaison provisions in Dutch courts is that contemporary media (for better or for worse) act as an extension of the public gallery and as such deserve the active co-operation of court personnel (Malsch and Hoekstra 1999; Malsch 2004). However, to describe the contributions made by press judges and communication advisers as something which merely assists in the achievement of a very worthy civil liberties cause would detract from the space of conflict which court–media relations often occupy. This struggle is somewhat blunted by the consociational philosophy characterising the situation in the Netherlands. Nevertheless, one only has to look at the historical reasons why press judges were introduced to realise that media liaison was a tool with which the judiciary wished to equip itself to fight back against increasingly critical media. Defending the judicial territory against media intrusion was a central concern. The human rights angle is another feature, encompassing considerations which only became more prominent at a later stage.[24]

Interpreting the growing importance attached to media liaison as a kind of defence mechanism inevitably means conjuring up the image of law's embattled empire. This is consistent with the idea, subjected to critical scrutiny throughout this book, that law is being trampled on by media riding roughshod over precious legal principles which are becoming indistinguishably mixed up with the entertainment values of popular culture. My findings do not lend much support for this thesis: the only tangible media impact that I have uncovered concerned press judges requesting that changes be made to the final draft of a judgment so that the motivation or reasoning would be clearer and easier to explain to the media, but this seems hardly evidence of negative media influence. Of course, one might say, the lack of any such influence is a fine example of how successful the Dutch defence barrier is.

The metaphor of a pre-emptive strike is perhaps a more appropriate way of characterising the balance of relations between judges and the media. It is undeniably true that better communication with various media is inspired by the noble aim of allowing judges to fend off baseless criticism and foster a greater understanding of their work, but by the same token it is also an example of the battle for supremacy between the 'make-believe' worlds of law and the media (see Chapter 6). One could argue that this is not so much a case of law going pop as a case of the media being subjected to the incursions of an institution which has gone from an isolationist position to taking a much more outward looking yet nevertheless controlling stance. The repression of judicial criticism may be a thing of the past in many jurisdictions and it has never been favoured in the Dutch context, but media liaison equally constitutes an attempt to impact on media reporting.

Court reporting is particularly susceptible to influence by official sources and news gathering in this context can be a very passive process.[25] This is capable of fostering an environment in which there is a high degree of dependency on the information which court officials (including prosecutors and parties' legal teams) decide to release. It should be acknowledged that this largely suits the news media's own agenda. Resources for more critical and investigative journalism may be mobilised by national – and even inter-national – media for the most high profile of cases, but run-of-the-mill court reporting is often under-resourced and, in the Netherlands for example, it is virtually the exclusive territory of a much smaller regional press. However, whether attempts at reorienting or steering media coverage in a particular direction are ultimately successful remains to be seen. It is one thing for the media to take advantage of the 'information subsidies' (Gandy 1982) on offer through press officers but quite another matter for this to result in more favourable coverage. In Chapter 6, I characterised divergences between media and legal discourse as something which is hardwired into their very different *modus operandi* and which prevents the complete harmonisation of their respective communications. This inbuilt capacity for misunderstanding may yet prove the ultimate safeguard of media independence as institutional efforts to manage information flows become ever more pronounced.

Chapter 8

Law and the media: in whose favour are the scales tipping?

Collapsing boundaries?

In March 2007, only weeks away from completing this book, I attend a lecture by Lord Phillips, Lord Chief Justice, at Birmingham University. The topic is murder. The lecture lasts for well over an hour during which Lord Phillips takes an attentive audience of mainly students and academics through some of the difficulties which make this area of law cry out for reform (Phillips 2007a). The following days, the knives in the media are out for the Lord Chief Justice. Predictably, his criticism of mandatory life sentences does not go down well with the tabloids. The gist of their commentary is that once again the senior judiciary is too lenient and out of touch. One remark in particular seems to have stuck with both broadsheets and tabloids, namely the Lord Chief Justice's (2007: 2) statement that 'in 30 years' time the prisons will be full of geriatric lifers'. The *Guardian* journalist Marcel Berlins (2007) rushes to the defence of Lord Phillips: 'I expect exaggerated, misleading and sometimes deliberately false responses to just about any comment the lord chief justice makes about sentencing policy. Successive home secretaries and certain newspapers can be relied on to react in Pavlovian fashion.' How are we to read this particular incident? Is it part of the drip, drip, drip effect of the media inexorably leading to the erosion of the authority and independence of key legal actors? Or is it business as usual, as indeed Berlins' comments suggest: a senior judge rocks the boat, politicians give him a slap on the wrist and the media spout their customary distortions, but before too long the storm dies down and everyone moves on?

In making up our mind about this issue, it is important to remember that law *is* the media's business, just as regulation of the media is law's business. Their mutual busy-bodying becomes problematic only if these two formidable players interfere to such an extent that they actually prevent the other from fulfilling its core tasks: for the media, these consist, among other things, of the monitoring of the exercise of institutional power, whereas the legal system has exclusive competence to administer justice. The aim of my analysis in this book has been to probe arguments about media harm and unravel the thinking behind the idea that media influence poses a serious risk to treasured legal values. We have seen how Sherwin (2000) claims that the boundaries between law and popular culture are vanishing: law has gone 'pop', which means that it is increasingly adopting a *modus operandi* which is essentially media-driven and wholly alien to its own reasoning methods. Thus he asserts that 'law cannot be and historically speaking never has been insulated from popular culture. Today, however, the influence is having a particularly pernicious effect' (Sherwin 2000: 37). The pernicious effect in question is a postmodernisation of law under the influence of visual media that have made law just another story or just another perspective on an ever-more elusive truth which is sapping law's authority and leads to widespread 'popular disenchantment' (Sherwin 2000: 245). Whatever enchantment there was previously, it seems, was part of an illusion which the media, aided and abetted by postmodernists, have cruelly destroyed. The discovery that legal truth is fragmented and contingent is not seen by Sherwin as part of the public's coming of age or its growing sophistication. On the contrary, he believes that it mainly fuels people's cynicism and disbelief. However, it is a finely balanced assessment: the claim is not that law has turned spectacular under the media's influence but that it is no longer telling its own stories and is content to simply imitate the media spectacle. Sherwin (2000: 241) lays the blame for this not just at the door of media actors but he also points the finger at (American) lawyers who have created a 'litigation public relations movement' involving the use of media publicity to influence the legal process.

The 'boundaries' or 'lines' which inform discourses of collapse of law into popular culture are of course only metaphorical boundaries which can be made to accommodate a rather different interpretation, one in which they are less vulnerable. In Chapter 6, I studied a counter-argument to the collapsing boundaries scenario, including Nobles and Schiff's (2000) argument that despite miscarriages of justice triggering regular episodes of 'crises' in confidence, it is very much business as usual during and after such acutely tense periods. The media continue to report on acquittals and convictions as evidence of innocence and guilt, and justice continues to be administered as before, except perhaps for some superficial changes intended to reassure media and public. Law's boundaries in Nobles and Schiff's analysis are of an autopoietic nature making law to a large extent immune to media pressures, which means that, while the media continue to peddle half-truths about the law, judges are still judging, the police are still policing, prosecutors are still prosecuting and lawyers are still practising the law. Moreover, on this interpretation, it is difficult to envisage that the media would do anything other than distort the law because theirs is a reality which is constructed according to entirely different criteria from those used to determine legal truth. For example, Lord Phillips's Birmingham lecture was quite predictably reduced to the 'geriatric lifers' soundbite. It is difficult to see how it could have been any different when an hour-long lecture delivered to students and scholars is compressed into a newspaper article intended for consumption by a generalist audience.

There is a very real temptation to regard the dissolution of law into media culture as a uniquely contemporary threat. However, any long-term or medium-term predictions as to whether media reporting is corrosive of law's autonomy would have to have sufficient regard to the historical aspects of the law/media nexus.[1] While it has not been the aim of this study to give a detailed historical account – that would conceivably be a topic for another book – Chapter 6 has focused on how liberal doctrine has traditionally lent strong support to the press's monitoring role, which explains at least in part why contemporary media consider it their rightful task to scrutinise the workings of the legal system. There is, in other words, a history to the tensions which we are today detecting in the interactions between the legal system and contemporary media. In Chapter 7, I briefly examined how the decline in deference for the judiciary in the Netherlands can be traced back to the changing socio-political climate and anti-establishment feelings of the late 1960s. This does not only belie any notion that the current problematic appeared overnight but it also suggests that to blame the media for being the chief instigator of a decline in public esteem risks overlooking other contributing factors. In Chapter 4, I highlighted the importance of adopting a non-mediacentric perspective precisely to avoid giving precedence to the media in explaining multifaceted and complex issues such as the extent to which different publics have trust in the institutions of justice. This is not just a matter of avoiding making scapegoats of the media ('The media are not the poisoners of the social', as Brown (2003: 194) puts it) but is also a matter of acknowledging that making the media change their ways (assuming that this were possible) may fail to provide an adequate solution to problems for which they are all too easily blamed.

Technological futures

The era of the mass media is drawing to a close. This development is not so much triggered by the decline or disappearance of the mass media as by their convergence with new technologies that are rapidly changing them beyond recognition. Whereas the mass media were once thought of as a 'primary source of definitions and images of social reality and the most ubiquitous expression of shared identity' (McQuail 2000: 4), the new media landscape is marked by fragmentation and dispersion, making shared definitions of reality ever more unattainable. Mass communication is no longer the preserve of resource-rich organisations but is now within the reach of ordinary citizens who, thanks to the internet and other relatively cheap technologies, are able to communicate with each other on a global scale. The following comments on blogging are particularly perceptive:

It's hard to underestimate what a big deal this is. For as long as journalism has existed writers of whatever kind have had one route to readers: they needed an editor and a publisher. Even in the most benign scenario, this process subtly distorts journalism. You find yourself almost unconsciously writing to please a handful of people . . . Blogging simply bypasses this ancient ritual.

(Sullivan quoted in Bird 2003: 183)

The American *Time Magazine* – ironically itself an old-fashioned form of mass communication which has merged with new technologies – declared that its 'person of the year' in 2006 were ordinary people who were busily blogging, camcording, podcasting and messaging to make their voices heard around the world. The point of the award is that it highlights that people are no longer just consuming media contents but are themselves involved in generating mass communications on an unprecedented scale, as *Time Magazine* put it, to 'seize the reins of the global media' (Grossman 2006: html), although evidently global capitalism is clearly very much at home in the new media environment. Predictions about the digital democracy may appear slightly too optimistic: after all, there are still large numbers of people who do not have the necessary skills or resources to stake their claim in the new media landscape. Moreover, it is by no means clear how much attention obscure blogs and home videos attract and how much of a political difference they are making. Nevertheless, the emerging trend is undeniably one of increased user involvement, heralding the decline of the intermediary function of institutionalised mass media which are no longer needed to the same extent to meet society's information needs.

This trend has significant implications for the future of law and media culture. It may prove that much of the thinking behind the idea that the mass media have the power to influence people with their distorted portrayals of law to such an extent as to harm public confidence is obsolete. As I indicated in Chapter 4, the model of the audience passively undergoing the influence of the mass media was discredited in the 1980s when cultural studies suggested that the audience was a fully-fledged – and by no means always compliant – partner in the mass communication process. Although the active audience model has over time attracted some fierce criticism of its own, current developments in the use of new ICTs may yet prove its ultimate vindication. A changing media culture is making it easier for users to go in search of the information they require and also crucially generate such information themselves. Legal self-help is a case in point. As I explained in Chapter 5, 'interactive' columns and programmes carrying legal information aiming to be responsive to audiences' problems and queries were an established feature of media culture long before ICTs became mainstream. However, the internet has given self-help culture the impetus it needed for it to become a potentially innovative way of approaching everyday legal problems.

At present, it is a matter of speculation as to whether this has indeed the makings of a phenomenon which could radically transform legal practice, but that is not the issue here. The point is that legal self-help is part of a much wider trend in the information society in which information about law – but also about health and other areas of professional expertise – is no longer exclusively being disseminated by traditional mass media but is increasingly being provided by users themselves or by qualified practitioners operating on the internet. The diminished importance of traditional mass media arguably means that they have less scope to influence and distort public perceptions. This creates challenges as well as opportunities. Very limited editorial control is being exercised on the internet and information can soon become misinformation or, even worse, blatant deception. The difficulties in verifying where the information comes from exacerbate what is essentially a problem of trust. However, at the same time it is also possible to compare and cross-check information in a way which would have been previously very difficult for mass media audiences. Moreover, a strong representation by various legal institutions on the internet means that they are able to bypass the mass media and, as I pointed out in Chapter 1, in some cases they are actually becoming media in their own right by communicating directly with their target audiences.

When Sherwin (2000: 252) argues that 'the public needs to be trained to decode the skewed meanings and distorted effects of mediatised legal representations', he echoes the familiar refrain that education is the only effective way to immunise the public against the effects of media distortion. However, it is worth bearing in mind that such a literacy is already largely present in mass media audiences (see e.g. Schrøder 2000) but also that these skills are increasingly being acquired by new media users who, by virtue of their own participation, are likely to have a better knowledge of the way in which media contents are produced (see e.g. Bird 2003).[2] Amidst all the optimism about the new media landscape, however, there is also scope for a cautionary note about the dangers of heaping too many expectations on technology. Schoenbach (2001: 367) warns against the optimism that seems to invariably accompany new technology and involves the belief that because a technology is creating new opportunities, people will actually seize these with both hands.

As I have argued in this book, audience or user indifference is one of the problems we need to grapple with if we are to make sense of how distorted media portrayals relate to public perceptions of the law. We simply cannot process all of the information which comes our way in a multimedia environment: instead we select, we forget and we probably ignore most of it (see Couldry 2000; Bird 2003). Stories about law – and it is essentially narrative which appeals most about law – no matter how great their magnitude or potential to shock, may not register with as wide a public as legal actors often fear and the memory of such stories may soon fade as the media move on to the next story. Take Lord Phillips's Birmingham lecture: it only made headlines for a day or two and while there were some outspoken reactions among readers responding on newspaper websites, on the whole the number of people taking the trouble of posting a message was rather modest. Resonance, as I argued in Chapter 2, is an important factor in explaining which stories are likely to leave a deep impression on which audiences. New ICTs which enable users to filter the information themselves are reinforcing the resonance factor to a point where, as Bird (2003: 185) suggests, it may even result in a 'retreat into an individualised world inhabited only by people who only think exactly as we do'. As online forums of legal self-help suggest, users' desire to converse with and receive information from like-minded people who are able to validate each other's experiences offers a glimpse of a future in which law's publics become increasingly fragmented. Consequently, it will become even more difficult to generalise the extent to which media representations are capable of influencing and mobilising people.

Everyday legal experience: from public confidence to public participation

Throughout this book, it has been clear that legal actors' concerns about the effects of distorted media portrayals of law stem from their perception that audiences are passive and at great risk of being duped by the media. The risk is judged even greater because of audiences' presumed lack of significant first-hand legal experience which is thought to make them highly dependent on media sources. This 'window on the world' argument (McQuail 2000: 66) suggests that we rely on the media to broaden our horizon and gain exposure to phenomena and ideas we rarely come into contact with in the unmediatised realm of our experiences. While it is unarguable that mediatised experience is an integral aspect of everyday life, it is, as I suggested in Chapter 2, much more problematic to claim that we rely *exclusively* on the media to gain exposure to law. How great a role law plays in everyday experience and to what extent we are aware of law's presence is a matter of both theoretical and empirical analysis.

The notion that law is constitutive of everyday experience has gained considerable currency in research on legal consciousness. Legal consciousness, as we have seen, can be defined as an individual awareness of law and legality which has a profound ideological effect on people's outlook on the world and their sense of self. Acknowledging the difficulties involved in trying to separate out mediatised legal experience from other forms of contact with the law, I have suggested that legal consciousness research raises two very important issues: firstly, it focuses attention on the way in which legal consciousness is mobilised by audiences to make sense of media contents and, secondly, it raises our awareness of the extent to which the media in turn act as a resource for audiences' legal consciousness.

By making legal consciousness our central research focus, it is possible, I believe, to move questions concerning the media on from a narrow concern with effects to an inquiry which is foremost about the broader cultural strategies and schemata informing people's experiences of law. This would in turn enable us to bring into focus the reception context shaping media consumption. As a framework of research, this would more adequately represent current thinking in both the socio-legal field and in media and cultural studies. For example, one specific benefit is that legal consciousness is much better suited as a concept to grappling with law's different publics and their different levels of engagement with law than is 'public opinion'. While public opinion tends to generalise by assuming that there is a certain uniformity to public perceptions, legal consciousness has an inbuilt capacity to capture individual patterns of thinking about and acting on law's presence in everyday life. The methodology is also radically different, public opinion research being more closely associated with quantitative methods whereas legal consciousness research mainly builds on ethnographic traditions, potentially delivering the kind of 'thick description' needed to unravel the relationship between media culture and everyday legal experience. Law is not just something that people either trust or distrust: it is something in which they actively participate. Attending to this participatory dimension is a way of making everyday practice central to our understanding of law's place in media culture.

Everyday legal experience figured prominently in this book not just because it is the relevant backdrop against which to consider people's reception of media representations of law but also because it is something which is increasingly significant as an object of media portrayal. The 'window on the world' metaphor belies the fact that media experience is as much about deepening and affirming audiences' sense of what is familiar as it is about exposing them to what is new and unfamiliar. Reality TV, as I argued in Chapter 3, has been noted for its recognition of the everyday and its celebration of the seemingly ordinary. Thus Biressi and Nunn (2004: 47) observe that: 'With Reality TV the aim is not so much to take viewers outside of their own experience but to present them with a fully recognisable and familiar realm of the ordinary and the everyday.' Reality TV capitalises on a desire for an escape not from but into reality, or to be more precise, a hyperreality which appears more real than any unmediatised reality.

For Sherwin, however, the ascendancy of the hyperreal signals a further deterioration in law's problematic relationship with pop culture. He considers it to be a further cause of the collapse of any remaining boundaries which protect law from becoming just another media story: everyone can stake a claim on reality, signalling a loss of authority and meaning for 'grand narratives' including law. There is, it seems, no longer a stable referent at the other side of the media window. Furthermore, Sherwin comments that:

> The virtues of judicial prudence and ordinary common sense are being corrupted. Artificially heightened passions and strategically manipulated representations of legal reality are converting the traditional virtues of

common sense into defects. Virtuality, fantasy, and the hyperreal inextricably intermingle with and unconsciously inform offscreen experience.

(Sherwin 2000: 243)

The implication appears to be that real life experience is bound to disappoint when compared with its mediatised hyperreal equivalent: people coming into contact with the legal system will feel cheated that law is not more like its portrayal on television or in the movies.

I have suggested that reality television has important implications for our understanding of media distortion: 'distortion' implies a failed attempt at faithfully representing an external and independently verifiable reality, whereas the hyperreal denies any notion that there is an external reality to be represented. This is clear from the way in which many reality shows bring to life a reality which without their interventions would not exist or at least not in the same form. However, reality television formats are refreshingly open about their hyperreal credentials. Audience research bears this out (Hill 2004): viewers on the whole do not perceive reality TV to be a faithful depiction of reality. The suggestion that lived experience, including real life off-screen contact with law, will disappoint because it will be seen by audiences as a poor version of the super-enhanced and technologically engineered reality of television must therefore be treated with the same caution as any other discourses about media effects. Here too media literacy is key,[3] and just as the internet is capable of promoting an unparalleled degree of user participation, so does reality TV appear to stimulate a much greater audience involvement which can be achieved through interactive programme features, by incorporating footage supplied by 'ordinary' members of the audience or even through their direct participation as main protagonists. Audiences are not dupes of the illusion of reality TV; they are its accomplices. Moreover, as the epithet of 'water-cooler TV' indicates, it is the ability to provoke and get viewers to think and talk about certain topics that most clearly represents reality TV's capacity for audience involvement (Hill 2004: 180).

The entwinement of law and the everyday in reality television is of clear relevance when trying to unravel law's uneasy relationship with the media. For one thing, it suggests that a narrow concern with the issue of public confidence does not do justice to the broader relevance of law both off-screen and on-screen. To go beneath the skin of a media culture which is saturated with representations of law (or simulacra, as the hyperreal school claims), we need to do so much more than study its distortions and mechanically measure its effects on public confidence in the administration of justice.[4] Obviously, the confidence question because of its direct political relevance is at the forefront of the debate, but it is also important that we try to address the enchantment issue raised by Sherwin. This is more fundamental than the question of whether people have confidence in any particular institution and calls for an ongoing and wide-ranging enquiry into the popular legal imagination.

(Inter)disciplinary futures

A final topic worth highlighting concerns the future of the study of law and popular culture. As a form of scholarship it is somewhat uncomfortably wedged between several disciplines, including media and cultural studies, criminology and socio-legal studies. Moreover, entrenched views about what kind of research is worth pursuing and reflects well on the reputation of a law school are an obstacle to the development of new research areas, including research into law and popular culture (Bradney 2006). This should obviously not detract from the exciting work being undertaken in this field. Popular culture has a great deal to offer to scholars wishing to approach the study of law from a contextual perspective, enabling them to shine a more critical light on their subject. However, there is still considerable scope for a much wider engagement with methods and epistemologies drawn from media and cultural studies. What is problematic is that cognate disciplines have yet to consider the analysis of law as something that is within their own remit. Black-letter law remains an intimidating edifice: its claim to autonomy and exclusive competence does not make for an inviting environment in which scholars from other disciplines are made to feel at home.

This book has attempted to envisage an interdisciplinary future for the study of law and the media that takes it beyond the literary critique of media texts and connects it with the sphere of policy making. As I have tried to demonstrate, the problem of how the media impact on public perceptions is already shaping policy, for example, in the form of more intense public relations efforts that aim to set the record straight and protect the machinery of justice by circulating doctrinally 'correct' information. It has been my contention that such policy efforts build on specific assumptions about media culture which are less straightforward than they at first glance appear: it is here that a multidisciplinary approach is most likely to come into its own and make an invaluable contribution. Moving beyond the critique of individual media texts, film texts in particular, to survey the much broader terrain of media culture is a bold and ambitious project. There is no question that the challenge is considerable because it means becoming well versed in a multitude of aspects to inform media culture. The pace of change within the media landscape and the endless difficulties of trying to capture even a snapshot of its many different users and audiences only add to the enormity of the challenge of mapping the juridico-entertainment complex.

The place of theory within the emerging field of law and popular culture deserves a specific mention. Greenfield *et al.*, commenting on the paucity of theory in law and film analysis, observe that:

> It is not that law and film studies is intellectually stunted, but rather that its major impetus has historically been within a professional context. Black letter film work has not tended to acknowledge any particular

epistemological standpoint . . . While life may be, in reality, a . . . kaleido-
scope of equally compelling, competing and conflicting understandings,
the law is unable to operate on such a basis.

(Greenfield *et al.* 2001: 196)

In other words, the neglect of theory is ascribed here to the doctrinal inability
to confront fragmentation and ambiguity. The theoretical framework explored
in Chapter 6 brought out such contradictions: while in the classic watchdog
model the pursuit of the undistorted truth ranks among the highest journalistic values, setting a very high standard of media performance, attaining a
shared definition of what is truthful across different social systems is a conceptual impossibility in the autopoietic model. Such theoretical conversations
are necessary if we want to address wider concerns about the direction in
which the law/media nexus is developing. Furthermore, the issue raised by
Greenfield and his colleagues points to the significance of using our explor-
ations of media culture as a way of learning more about law itself. The study
of literature and film has been promoted in the law curriculum for pedagogical reasons, more specifically the belief that it would encourage students
to look at law from a different angle and is more attuned to their intuitive
grasp of the subject. The impact of such analysis remains somewhat limited
if it is confined to the classroom alone and fails to make much of a difference
elsewhere, for example, in generating a reflexive understanding of the way in
which law is practised.

To what extent are legal actors prepared to acknowledge their indebtedness
to media culture? Sherwin's analysis is premised on the idea that lawyers play
a prominent part in the infiltration of popular culture in court because they
believe that frequent references to film and television narratives make it easier
for them to appeal to jurors. This suggests that lawyers' own media savvy
is key to unravelling the uneasy relationship between law and the media.
However, this can yield only limited insights if we continue to focus on lay
expectations as the principal reason why popular culture is prominently present in court. What of judges and lawyers? How does popular culture inform
their worldviews and knowledge of the society in which they live? The fact
that they are known to complain about media distortions suggests that they,
like everyone else, are exposed to media culture on a daily basis, but it is also
true that they are keen to assume the guise of critical observers who are
themselves detached from media culture. But how credible is such aloofness?
For example, Karpin has pointed to

the ways in which culture and popular culture specifically is taken by the
judiciary to express particular normative and hegemonic ways of knowing the world. These ways of knowing are, however, never identified as
such but instead they materialise in judicial pronouncement as social fact.

(Karpin 2002: 64)

Furthermore, her final assessment gives much to think about: 'It is questionable then what is the larger problem for law: the fantasies the media portrays about the law or the judicial fantasy of themselves as discerning unembedded consumer' (Karpin 2002: 65). The latter aspect, namely the concern of judges to paint a picture of themselves as unaffected by any extraneous influences fits the doctrinal image of judicial impartiality and independence seamlessly. The role of law and popular culture analysis is to go against the grain of such doctrinal posturing by bringing to the fore ways in which popular culture is enmeshed with legal truth, not to track down any 'pernicious effects' but to illuminate shared signifiers and overlapping meaning-making processes.

For all his misgivings about postmodernity, Sherwin acknowledges that the postmodern mantra, very much in evidence in media culture, that law's truth is fragmented and relative holds certain benefits: 'This development in law may be viewed as a valuable corrective with respect to certain modernist distortions concerning law's unitary, objectivist and acontextual authority' (Sherwin 2000: 39). However, documenting how media culture is interwoven with law and justice should not be about endorsing a collapsing boundaries scenario, but should be chiefly concerned with a point which Sherwin himself aptly makes: namely that the boundaries between law and popular culture have always been porous. Similarly, the autopoietic model, despite its reputation for being a theory of legal closure, recognises that what happens in the media and other ambient systems may constitute events in the legal environment to which law is receptive. The disciplinary future of law and popular culture scholarship is tied up with the conundrum of how law can still operate as *law*, that is as something we recognise as distinctly legal, while also taking its place in a rich cultural tapestry where its symbols readily spill over into many different spheres. How can it be that law is something we want to be entertained by when we know all too well that it is a serious business which shapes lives, our lives, for better and for worse? How can law both be just another story – here today, gone tomorrow – and the ineluctable backdrop to our day-to-day existence? Could it be that confidence in the law is ultimately a matter of confidence in our own judgement as moral agents living in a 'runaway world' (Giddens 1991: 16) in which truth is carved up between competing knowledge regimes? The tensions and contradictions which are at the heart of such questions suggest that the relationship between law and the media will probably always be a distinctly uneasy one.

Notes

1 Anatomy of a troubled relationship

1 For example, Nobles and Schiff (2000: 168) quote from a journalist's letter to *The Times* published in 1996: 'I plead guilty to the Lord Chief Justice's charges against those in the media who "do not shrink from substituting their assessments for those made by the Court". The difference is that my assessment is mere criticism; theirs put people in prison for life.'

2 An interesting parallel can be drawn here with the circumstances in which ministers are expected to resign in the United Kingdom. There are no hard rules governing ministerial resignations: media pressure can be a factor but so can declining support from the Prime Minister and the mood in the Parliamentary party (see Munro 1999: 85).

3 According to Couldry (2000: 2): 'Cultural studies began with a democratic critique of earlier elitist approaches to culture, recognising the fundamental importance of "popular culture": the experiences and pleasures of those outside the cultural elites. This step was absolutely essential in expanding the range of cultural production deemed worthy of academic study.'

4 See <http://www.judiciary.gov.uk> (accessed 10 March 2007).

5 Furthermore, this resonates with Habermas' (1992) thesis of 'refeudalisation' of the public sphere in which information management and public relations are suppressing critical public debate in favour of display and spectacle.

6 See also Lord Justice Moses' (2006: html) use of theatrical metaphors in his comments on recent constitutional reform initiatives in the United Kingdom: 'In the bustle to shed the cloaks and wigs of archaic practice of tradition and ritual, and don the mantle of constitutional progress, I fear we may have discarded one item of costume too many. We may have even lost the cloak-room ticket. It is the mask, the form through which the judges deliver their decisions.'

7 For example, Haltom and McCann (2004) note that US news media devote most of their energy to covering the pre-trial and post-trial aspects of tort proceedings but are generally speaking far less interested in the complexities of the actual process of litigation, which is subject to all sorts of vagaries characterising the adversarial encounter between parties in court.

8 This was amply illustrated in a recent study by Feilzer and Young (2006), which attempted to replicate in a natural setting the findings of an experiment by the Home Office (Chapman *et al.* 2002) which suggested that it was possible to foster more positive public attitudes towards crime and criminal justice by educating the public. The authors published a weekly column addressing different aspects of criminal justice in a local paper during a 26-week period but they found no

evidence in their subsequent field research that readers' knowledge of criminal justice had improved significantly as a result. Even more important perhaps is their suggestion that crime is not as salient an issue to the general public as is often assumed and that a lack of interest therefore possibly explained why their column failed to improve interviewees' knowledge of and attitudes towards criminal justice.

9 For example, judges who are concerned that negative media reporting undermines public confidence in their profession may be relieved to know – in so far as this could be relied on as an indicator of public opinion – that a recent MORI poll in the UK has revealed that theirs remains one of the most trusted professions, while journalists continue to be the least trusted. Perhaps somewhat surprisingly, the same poll revealed that newsreaders are much more trusted than journalists. See <http://www.ipsos-mori.com/polls/trends/truth.shtml> (accessed 10 March 2007).

10 I am indebted to Richard Nobles for this insight, which emerged from a discussion at the 'Justice, Media and Public' workshop (Keele University, 3 November 2006).

2 Media, everyday life and legal consciousness

1 'Everything is calculated here because everything is numbered: money, minutes, metres, kilogrammes, calories . . .' (Lefebvre 1984: 21).

2 See Poster (2004) for a discussion of resistive practices fuelled by recent digital technologies such as mp3 players and digital television recorders (which, for example, allow viewers to skip commercials).

3 Burkitt (2004) warns against the tendency to treat everyday life as a sphere of predominantly informal social interactions. 'Official ideas and ethics are part of the fabric of everyday life and, consequently, law in its formalised form is integral to the everyday. He argues that the 'official' in everyday life clearly impinges on the 'unofficial', citing the example of how family law sets out a clear policy framework defining family life, including limitations on the type of intimate relations that are considered worthy of receiving state recognition and protection (Burkitt 2004: 215).

4 However, Morley (1992: 261) qualifies this: 'Matters are, of course, not quite so simple as that. It is also a question of how different pre-existing cultural forma- tions of temporality determine how audiences relate to broadcast schedules.'

5 See for example Morley's (1992: 252) comments on the so-called 'narcotic' effects resulting from the flood of information to reach us through the media.

6 The campaign to bring the killers of Stephen Lawrence to justice enjoyed huge support from all mainstream media. The *Daily Mail* in particular, a tabloid paper, took the extraordinary step of publicly naming the five suspects in the case. As Yuval-Davis (1999) points out, public support for the case partly reflected a genu- ine shift in awareness of matters of race and multiculturalism. However, the middle-class background of the Lawrence family, in her view, also made the media particularly sensible to their plight. Other less 'deserving' groups may not be so fortunate, and their quest for visibility often has to do without the support of media and public opinion. See also Bridges (1999).

7 Significantly, the Stephen Lawrence case was also mentioned by ethnic minority participants in Genn's (1999: 243) survey of people's experiences and perceptions of the legal system.

3 Reality TV and the jurisprudence of *Wife Swap*

1 It is a familiar argument that narrativity in popular culture models itself closely on the drama of law: 'It would appear that a certain narrative economy, initiated by the breaking of a social boundary, law or taboo and moving through a series of conflicts towards a decisive act of retribution or restitution is common in many periods and cultures' (Sparks 1992: 37).

2 As fans of shows such as *The X-Factor* and *America's Next Top Model* will know, participants who 'talk back' to the 'experts' often attract opprobrium and risk elimination from the contest while a similar fate often befalls those who commit the heinous crime of concealing their real age because they are either too young or too old to take part in the talent contest.

3 The very word 'reality' is a misnomer as many seemingly unscripted reality programmes are often accused of being highly contrived and artificial (Couldry 2002). Truth and accuracy being the benchmarks against which audiences themselves judge reality television (Hill 2004), much of the entertainment value resides in the audience's ability to spot the deceit, although many programmes make little effort to conceal the extent to which events are staged (Tincknell and Raghuram 2004). Despite the 'reality label', any attempt at separating fact and fiction is doomed to failure as the distinctions between different media genres have virtually evaporated through their continual 'cross-dressing' (Brown 2003: 46).

4 Among the latter are 'surgico-entertainment' shows such as *Extreme Makeover, The Swan* and *Ten Years Younger* in which participants risk life and limb in search of the prevailing beauty ideal but also more responsible programmes which seek to create greater wellbeing by encouraging participants to change their lifestyle by eating more healthily, taking up physical exercise or simply cleaning their home.

5 One example is the Channel 4 programme *Faking It* in which participants pretending to be accomplished professionals face the challenge of tricking a panel of experts into believing that they are genuine cooks, musicians, hairdressers, etc.

6 The concept of 'lifestyle' is analysed in Chapter 5.

7 Although there is evidently a long history of newspapers, magazines and television shows soliciting audience input (Griffen-Foley 2004), the widespread availability of new interactive technologies has expanded the role of the audience.

8 It seems hardly coincidental that the encroachment of a law-and-order imagery in lifestyle programming should run parallel to policy initiatives such as anti-social behaviour orders in Britain which seek to curb socially undesirable conduct by casting the net of legal sanctions ever wider.

9 The following observation concerning celebrity culture seems particularly apt here: 'They are celebrities – they have fame – precisely *because* they have a public. It is the public that defines their status and provides them with the richest of gifts' (Friedman 1994: 117).

10 The hyperbolic realism of reality television is also reminiscent of theatrical exaggeration. See Aristodemou (2000: 33).

11 See Milovanovic (1992: 114): 'Doing law can be seen as a highly rationalised (secondary process) enterprise whereby affectively and sensory charged data are stripped of their intensities as the phenomenal experience (the "what happened?") undergoes translation into legal thought acceptable in a court of law. . . . Affect is repressed, but remains a residual source of energy (excitations) seeking expression, more often becoming a basis of yet further highly abstract rational thought. In short, a perpetual search for catharsis exists, but this endless and futile search for plenitude is precluded by the very internal dynamic by which thought is objectified into a verbal form acceptable by the courts. A reality is indeed constructed but one cleansed of Real world intensities.'

12 Online blogs give a good flavour of the opposing views. See for example: <http:// www.amandacraig.com/pages/journalism/features/wife_swap.htm>; <http:// www.stephennewton.com/2004/10/wife-swap-defying-snobs-on-good-tv.html> (accessed 1 June 2006); <http://www.tobyyoung.co.uk>; <http:// www.thefword.org.uk/reviews/2003/02/wife_swap> (all accessed 1 June 2006).

13 Threadgold (2002: 26) observes: 'Law is a discursive community embodied and formed in the practices of everyday life, but *qua* law habitually authorised to magically institute what it says as performative speech acts. These by their very generic nature as law then deny their intertextual and citational links to the body and the everyday. In many ways this distance from the body, this denial of the implication in the field of everyday life, is the greatest and dangerous fiction which law constructs.'

14 This trait has also been commented on by viewers contributing to Channel 4's online discussion forums. See <http://community.channel4.com/eve/forums/a/tpc/ f/2080012933/m/6890029554> (accessed 1 June 2006).

15 One notable exception is an episode of the first series of *Wife Swap USA* in which a lesbian couple swaps with a homophobic heterosexual couple.

16 For example, in episode 6 of the second series and episode 4 of the first series of *Wife Swap USA*.

17 In an episode of the second series, one of the wives was so worried that the other woman would seduce her partner during the swap that she promptly terminated the experiment.

18 Or indeed 'Class Swap' as one online message board suggested. See <http:// www.atforumz.com/archive/index.php/t–211900.html> (accessed 1 June 2006).

19 It has been suggested that the reason why the men are allowed to stay in their comfort zone has to do with the fact that 'men's lives are far too difficult and too important to be messed around like that' (Forrest 2003), the reasoning being that while wives are interchangeable and easily replaceable because of the very simple nature of their work in the home, men are unique and cannot be exchanged as if they were dispensable spare parts.

20 See <http://headlines.agapepress.org/archive/5/afa/212004g.asp> (accessed 1 June 2006).

21 The humiliation which flows from such revelations is an inherent part of the reality television format. See Mendible (2004).

22 A viewer sums it up nicely: 'So far, we have seen some horrors. We have had fish-wife women swapping with demure creatures; complete slobs swapping with the most awful control freaks; selfless swapping with the selfish. The nation passes judgement on who is the better wife and mother.' See <http://www.ciao.co.uk/ Wife_Swap_Channel_4__Review_5361914> (accessed 1 June 2006).

23 The transcript does not contain the full verbal exchange as some parts of the conversation are inaudible or drowned out by surrounding noise.

24 There have been reports that one episode was axed because the two couples were simply too friendly with each other, although this was strongly denied by RDF Media. See <http://news.bbc.co.uk/go/pr/fr/-/hi/entertainment/tv_and_radio/ 3239765.stm> (accessed 10 March 2007).

25 See <http://community.channel4.com/eve/forums/a/tpc/f/2080012933/m/ 9980028164> (accessed 1 June 2006).

26 See <http://www.ciao.co.uk/Wife_Swap_Channel_4__Review_5360193> (accessed 1 June 2006).

27 In the words of Stephen Lambert (2005), executive producer of RDF Media: 'The programme does not judge the parenting styles of the families who take part. It shows how exposure to alternative family values will often lead to reflection and

fundamental changes in the way parents treat their children. There may often be conflict in Wife Swap, but there is also frequently transformation.'

28 Description taken from <http://www.channel4.com/life/microsites/W/wife_swap_usa/families.html> (accessed 1 June 2006).

29 A similar sentiment is expressed in the following online review of the programme: 'It does have some sociological content but is presented in a quite sensationalist way. If by watching it we learn more about our own relationships and seek to improve them then that's fine. However I am more inclined to believe it shows an acceptance of certain forms of behaviour as a norm.' See <http://www.dooyoo.co.uk/tv-programs/wife-swap-channel-4/1007375/> (accessed 1 June 2006).

4 Method, audience and social practice

1 This is a concern which is shared by the Nuffield Inquiry on Empirical Research in Law. See <http://www.ucl.ac.uk/laws/socio-legal/empirical/> (accessed 10 March 2007).

2 This does not necessarily leave consumers completely disempowered. As the example of 'slash fiction' demonstrates, fans disagreeing with a specific storyline may decide to rewrite certain materials so that they are more in keeping with their own preferences (Jenkins 1992). In Chapter 5, I will also attend to the way in which the internet is enhancing users' choice and autonomy.

3 The issue is virtually identical in studies of legal consciousness. What benefits, one may ask, are there to be derived from an 'against the law' type of legal consciousness if there is no concomitant pressure to change the material conditions of people on benefits, ethnic minorities and other marginalised groups who are most likely to display a resistive awareness of law in their everyday lives?

4 For example, the main limitation of the encoding/decoding model is that it is still very much media centred, in the sense that a strong emphasis is placed on the way in which the media structure people's understanding of reality. Audiences respond to media texts, either to resist or to accommodate their dominant meanings, but the encoding/decoding model tells us little about the way in which people's constructions of reality encompass a wider catalogue of experiences in which the media are sometimes of little or no importance. Reception analysis, like research into media effects, is fairly narrowly focused on the interrelations between media and audiences, despite its attempt at incorporating everyday life as a central category in explaining this relationship.

5 Cultures of legal self-help

1 The present chapter complements the examination of the judiciary's use of the media for similar purposes in Chapter 7.

2 There is a growing literature analysing users' experiences of online medical self-help (see e.g. Parr 2002; Bakardjieva 2003), which is not yet mirrored by an equivalent body of research concerning online legal self-help.

3 Tesco promotes its legal services through its online legal store: <http://www.tescolegalstore.com/> (accessed 1 February 2007).

4 For example, the British women's weeklies *Take a Break* and *Bella* run a general advice page which also advertises a telelawyering helpline. *Yours* (aimed at the retirement market) features free telephone helplines run by charitable organisations like The Samaritans and Age Concern besides offering free publications, but it also sells its own booklets, such as the 'Your rights in retirement' booklet which readers can purchase for £4.50 (September 2001 issue).

5 See <http://www.accidentadvicehelpline.co.uk/esther/esther.htm> (accessed 1 February 2007).
6 Magazines such as *Bella* and *That's Life!* are mass-market magazines which target a less affluent readership than the classic glossy lifestyle magazine. However, as Giddens (1991: 6) argues, it would be a mistake to assume that only the more affluent make lifestyle choices: ' "lifestyle" refers also to decisions taken and courses of actions followed under conditions of severe material constraint; such lifestyle patterns may sometimes also involve the more or less deliberate rejection of more widely diffused forms of behaviour and consumption.'
7 It is not unusual for solicitors dispensing advice in a magazine to share a general problem page with other experts such as vets, fashion advisers, doctors, dieticians, antiques auctioneers and agony aunts.
8 Those who are familiar with the work of Alcoholics Anonymous, one of the most prominent proponents of self-help, will undoubtedly recognise the parallel with its 12-step recovery programme in *Vive*'s step-by-step guide to divorce.
9 See <http://www.hmcourts-service.gov.uk/> (accessed 1 February 2007).
10 The aim of reducing costs through a greater use of ICTs in legal practice is also an important rationale in current plans in England and Wales to allow external investors to participate in so-called 'alternative business structures' consisting of a mix of lawyers and non-lawyers. See Dow and Lapuerta (2005).
11 Or as Castells (2004b: 160) puts it laconically: 'The digital divide is not important in terms of access. . . . The issue is what you do with your cultural and educational resources once you are connected.'
12 This explains the 'quality mark' for reputable websites instituted by the Legal Services Commission for England and Wales (Legal Services Commission 2001).
13 This case illustrates a neglected concern which Simpson (2005) highlights: amidst worries that adults pose as children on the internet, it tends to be forgotten how easy it is for children to adopt the guise of an adult when online.
14 However, there is a legitimate question to be raised as to whether concerns about internet deception are disproportionate to the actual threat which it poses. As Pauwels (2005: 605) comments: 'There is . . . little reason to distrust an email message or information on a website more than a telephone conversation.'
15 <http://www.divorcemag.com/love/index.shtml> (accessed 1 February 2007).
16 <http://www.divorcemag.com/articles/Divorce_Lawyers/the_a_team.html> (accessed 1 February 2007).
17 <http://www.divorcemag.com/NY/> (accessed 1 February 2007).
18 <http://www.divorce-online.co.uk/> (accessed 1 February 2007).
19 The reasons as to why a makeover may be deemed desirable are manifold. As Asimow *et al.* (2005) observe, public satisfaction with lawyers' work has decreased noticeably in England and Wales in recent years, although public perceptions of lawyers in the US are still much worse. Furthermore, as Francis (2004) notes, there is also a growing fragmentation and internal competition within the legal profession which could explain why some firms feel the need to portray themselves in a way which sets them apart from their competitors.
20 <http://www.divorcesolicitors.com/index.html> (accessed 1 February 2007).
21 <http://www.divorcemag.com/articles/Divorce_Lawyers/the_a_team.html> (accessed 1 February 2007).

6 Law and the media: liberal and autopoietic perspectives

1 The contrast between an interventionist and a non-interventionist approach (absence of censorship or interference) corresponds with different interpretations

of what freedom of expression is ultimately about: a diversity of viewpoints or the ability to express ideas free from state interference. See Lichtenberg (1990: 107).

2 Another way of looking at it is to say that press freedom is an instrument which only warrants special protection if it achieves the aims for which it was designed. See Lichtenberg (1990: 104).

3 As Addo (2000: 23) points out: 'The question of whether the liberal constitutional requirement to maintain judicial independence can withstand criticism is easily answered: criticism is a central and unavoidable part of the democratic ideal. In relation to the judiciary, criticism is one clear way of ensuring public participation in, and scrutiny of, judges' work.'

4 This is consistent with the earlier decision in the case of *The Sunday Times v UK* (1979–80) 12 EHRR 245 in which the European Court stated the importance of the media's monitoring of the administration of justice: 'As the Court remarked in its Handyside judgment, freedom of expression constitutes one of the essential foundations of a democratic society; subject to paragraph 2 of Article 10 (art. 10–2), it is applicable not only to information or ideas that are favourably received or regarded as inoffensive or as a matter of indifference, but also to those that offend, shock or disturb the State or any sector of the population (p. 23, para. 49). These principles are of particular importance as far as the press is concerned. They are equally applicable to the field of the administration of justice, which serves the interests of the community at large and requires the co-operation of an enlightened public. There is general recognition of the fact that the courts cannot operate in a vacuum. While they are the forum for the settlement of disputes, this does not mean that there can be no prior discussion of disputes elsewhere, be it in specialised journals, in the general press or amongst the public at large. Furthermore, whilst the mass media must not overstep the bounds imposed in the interests of the proper administration of justice, it is incumbent on them to impart information and ideas concerning matters that come before the courts just as in other areas of public interest. Not only do the media have the task of imparting such information and ideas: the public also has a right to receive them' (para 65).

5 See also Addo (2000) for additional reasons as to why an enhanced protection for judges against public criticism can no longer be justified.

6 Evidently, a distinction has to be made here between media reportage and media commentary, with the latter allowing for the expression of political viewpoints and opinion leadership, most notably in the press.

7 For example, Harrison (1985) gives a vivid account of the shock and outrage which the 'Bad News' study, containing numerous allegations of bias by the Glasgow University Media Group (1976), caused among British television journalists.

8 The critical legal studies project is similarly driven to expose bias: its main target is not journalistic accounts of reality but the way in which law's apparent neutrality masks a narrow range of preferences, for example, in terms of gender, class and race (see Příbáň 2002). The politics of a deceptively objective and self-standing rule of law have been deconstructed to lay bare specific ideological orientations in law making and they draw attention to how law is skewed towards dominant interests.

9 For example, the famous notion that official sources within the criminal justice system act as 'primary definers' of news which journalists as 'secondary definers' transform into largely compliant accounts (see Hall *et al.* 1978) has been challenged in subsequent research (see Schlesinger and Tumber 1994).

10 For example, in their study of media coverage of personal injury cases in the US, Haltom and McCann (2004: 168) suggest that by first selecting information which

favours one particular party (mostly pro-claimant) and then providing the account with an apparently balanced commentary, media reports end up being both partial and impartial.

11 As Street (2001: 37) explains, frames, just as bias, are indicative of certain types of preferences in the construction of a story, but these preferences are not necessarily or exclusively of an ideological nature.

12 In autopoiesis, these exchanges constitute 'systems of interaction' but they are distinguishable from systems of communication (King and Thornhill 2003b: 281).

13 Subsystems respond to events in their environment through communication, but this will never lead to a fusion with other systems: autopoietic systems always maintain their distinct identity and structures in the process, which means that they act autonomously (see King 1993: 225; Mingers 2002: 293).

7   Press judges and communication advisers in Dutch courts

1 The causes of this change in attitude are beyond the scope of this chapter. Judges' heightened visibility in the media can be attributed to many different factors, ranging from increased judicial activism triggering more media interest and criticism to controversies such as miscarriages of justice which impact on the reputation of judges (see e.g. Malleson 1999; Nobles and Schiff 2000).

2 For an analysis of this problem in the French context, see for example Garapon (1996) and Civard-Racinais (1997). Echoes of such concerns can also be found in Dutch literature on the media and the judiciary. See, for example, Groenhuijsen (1997).

3 Any translation of the Dutch nomenclature is bound to be imperfect. The original term for the magistrate acting as media spokesperson in the public prosecutor's office is 'persofficier' while the press judge in court is a 'persrechter' (or 'persraadsheer' at appellate level). One press judge very kindly gave me his English business card, which reads 'judge acting as spokesman for the court'. I prefer the terms 'press magistrate' and 'press judge' to this rather wordy description.

4 See Malsch (2004) for a recent quantitative study of the same subject.

5 The following District Courts were included in the research: Alkmaar, Amsterdam, The Hague, Rotterdam, Hertogenbosch (Den Bosch), Zwolle and Zutphen. The Appeal Court is based in Leeuwarden. The Special Appeals Tribunal is the Trade and Industry Special Appeals Tribunal based in The Hague. This is a representative sample: there are 19 District Courts, five Appeal Courts and two Special Appeals Tribunals in the Netherlands.

6 The interview was broadcast on 7 November 2003 and is also available online: <http://www.bbc.co.uk/radio4/today/listenagain/zfriday_20031107.shtml> (accessed 1 February 2007).

7 See the DCA press release of 15 March 2005 at <http://www.gnn.gov.uk/environment/dca/> (accessed 10 March 2007).

8 See <http://www.judiciary.gov.uk> (accessed 10 March 2007).

9 It is worth noting that the press release announcing the creation of a press office for judges in England and Wales did mention the intention to 'expand [judges'] communication base more widely, from a relatively narrow focus on media relations to a more comprehensive information service for the public as whole'. Such a wider public relations effort can also be detected in the Dutch context as well as in other jurisdictions including Canada and the US. See for example Esterling (1998).

10 For an example in the Dutch context see de Keijser and Elffers (2004).

11 As Nobles and Schiff (2004: 226) explain: 'The media can communicate about law,

but they cannot communicate law, that is, make legal communications. Similarly, the law can communicate about the media (in libel or contempt cases, and so on) but its own communications are not media communications, within the media's meanings.'

12 For a comparison: Canadian judges interviewed by Ericson *et al.* (1989) indicated that they observed a strict policy of media silence except for general issues relating to courts and the administration of justice.

13 The Studiecentrum voor de Rechtspleging, a training college for judges which also acts as a think tank for the judiciary, appeared to have played a central role in the formation of this policy.

14 It should be noted that the Dutch state has a long tradition of employing public information officers (de Wijkerslooth and Simonis 2002).

15 The court ruled that it was not improper for a joint press conference to have taken place because the press judge in this particular case had informed attending journalists that his role was very different from that of the public prosecutor's office.

16 As a general rule, if a press judge hears a case, he or she will not take any questions from journalists or offer any explanation on camera. Another press judge will then be called upon to address journalists' queries, which explains why most courts have more than one press judge.

17 Ninety-five per cent of press judges and communication advisers recently surveyed said that increasing public confidence was an important function of media liaison while 81 per cent thought that the creation of a positive public image was important (Malsch 2004).

18 The publication of dissenting judgments is unknown in the Dutch legal system: the deliberations of judges are treated as strictly confidential and they are never revealed in the judgment.

19 The idea that judges as legal experts are per se more knowledgeable than journalists with no legal background may be flawed: two press judges indicated that often journalists would know much more about a case than they did because they themselves were only distant observers with no detailed knowledge of the dossier.

20 It is worth pointing out that a report into regional variations in sentencing caused considerable media controversy in the early 1990s (de Groot-van Leeuwen 2000).

21 One such case leading to the creation of a scenario was the trial of the suspect in the case of the murdered Dutch politician Pim Fortuyn.

22 One press judge made the comparison with doctors in hospitals, arguing that when the explanation required by the media concerns a disease or a surgical procedure, it is only natural for the message to be delivered by a clinician rather than by a medically unqualified public relations officer.

23 The latter belongs to the growing population of what McNair calls 'source professionals' who use their professional skills to exploit the media's dependency on external providers of newsworthy information (McNair 1998).

24 Anecdotal evidence suggests that several among the first generation of press judges firmly believed that their role was to keep the media out rather than to promote transparency. This came to the fore in my interview with the former national communication adviser to the judiciary and various other accounts of the emergence of press judges seem to support this. Human rights considerations were not at the forefront of the debate when the function of press judge was conceived in the early 1970s. See for example van de Pol (1986) and Brants and Brants (2002).

25 See Ericson, Baranek and Chan (1989: 61): 'The regular court reporter is bound to join with legal officials in reproducing the appearances of formal legal rationality even if he knows that the system works in terms of other criteria.' Schlesinger and

Tumber (1994) paint a picture of court coverage as a disengaged process in which it is rare for journalists to attend court for the full length of the proceedings.

8 Law and the media: in whose favour are the scales tipping?

1   To quote Brown (2003: 190): 'That crime is an entity separable from the media is an untenable proposition. The development of the popular press from its inception confirmed "crime" as a moveable feast in everyday life.'
2   Moreover, as Haltom and McCann (2004: 177) suggest, the problem is not so much that we are unaware that news and other conventional mass media contents offer a distorted picture of law, but that we continue to depend on these sources despite our doubts about their reliability. The explosion of sources on the internet may reduce such reliance but, as I suggested in Chapter 5, it also shifts the burden of responsibility onto users to determine what information to trust.
3   Hill (2004: 177) comments: 'Audiences are able to switch from appreciation of . . . ordinary people and their experiences, to awareness of the staged nature of their experiences created for television', while Biressi and Nunn (2004: 52) suggest that media literacy is an integral part of reality TV's mode of audience address: 'Across the board there is a shared assumption that the audience possesses the media-literate capabilities to judge the contestants/participants of the Reality TV show – even though the criteria of judgement are often unformulated and unspoken.'
4   Sparks (1992: 152) seems to concur: 'Larger explanatory and systematic questions about the great public problems of crime and law enforcement tend to crowd out reflection on the place they occupy in ordinary, private experience.'

References

Addo, M. K. (2000) 'Can the independence of the judiciary withstand criticism? An introduction to the criticism of judges in Europe', in M. K. Addo (ed.) *Freedom of Expression and the Criticism of Judges: A Comparative Study of European Legal Standards*. Aldershot: Ashgate.

Alasuutari, P. (1999) 'Introduction: Three phases of reception studies', in P. Alasuutari (ed.) *Rethinking the Media Audience*. London: Sage.

Allen, R. (2006) 'What works in changing public attitudes to prison: lessons from Rethinking Crime and Punishment', in P. Mason (ed.) *Captured by the Media: Prison Discourse in Popular Culture*. Cullompton: Willan Publishing.

Ang, I. (1991) *Desperately Seeking the Audience*. London: Routledge.

Ang, I. (1996) *Living Room Wars: Rethinking Media Audiences for a Postmodern World*. London: Routledge.

Ang, I. and Hermes, J. (1996) 'Gender and/in media consumption', in J. Curran and M. Gurevitch (eds) *Mass Media and Society*. London: Arnold (2nd edition).

Aristodemou, M. (2000) *Law & Literature: Journeys from Her to Eternity*. Oxford: Oxford University Press.

Asimow, M., Greenfield, S., Jorge, G., Machura, S., Osborn, G., Robson, P., Sharp, C. and Sockloskie, R. (2005) 'Perceptions of lawyers: A transnational study of student views on the image of law and lawyers', *International Journal of the Legal Profession*, 12 (3): 407–36.

Atwood, M. (1986) *The Handmaid's Tale*. London: Jonathan Cape.

Baetens, J. (2005) 'Cultural studies after the cultural studies paradigm', *Cultural Studies*, 19 (1): 1–13.

Bakardjieva, M. (2003) 'Virtual togetherness: an everyday-life perspective', *Media, Culture & Society*, 25 (3): 291–313.

Ballaster, R., Beetham, M., Frazer, E. and Hebron, S. (1991) *Women's Worlds: Ideology, Femininity and the Woman's Magazine*. London: Macmillan.

Banakar, R. (2000) 'Reflections on the methodological issues of the sociology of law', *Journal of Law and Society*, 27 (2): 273–95.

Baudrillard, J. (1983) *Simulations*. New York: Semiotext.

Beck, U., Bonns, W. and Lau, C. (2003) 'The theory of reflexive modernity: Problematic, hypotheses and research programmes', *Theory, Culture & Society*, 20 (2): 1–33.

Becker, J. (2004) 'Lessons from Russia: A neo-authoritarian media system', *European Journal of Communication*, 19 (2): 139–63.

Berlins, M. (2000) 'Two of our judges are missing', *Guardian* 30 October.

Berlins, M. (2004) *Lies, Media and Justice: Distorting the Criminal Justice System*. Available HTTP: <http://www.law.bham.ac.uk/research/issues-criminal-justice.htm> (accessed 10 March 2007).

Berlins, M. (2007) 'No. 10 attack on top judge is mindless nonsense', *Guardian* 12 March.

Bird, E. (2003) *The Audience in Everyday Life: Living in a Media World.* London: Routledge.

Biressi, A. and Nunn, H. (2004) 'The especially remarkable: Celebrity and social mobility in reality TV', *Mediactive*, 2: 44–58.

Blomley, N. and Clark, G. L. (1990) 'Law, theory, and geography', *Urban Geography*, 11 (5): 433–46.

Boon, A., Flood, J. and Webb, J. (2005) 'Postmodern professions? The fragmentation of legal education and the legal profession', *Journal of Law and Society*, 32 (2): 473–92.

Boorstin, D. (1961) *The Image, or, What Happened to the American Dream.* London: Weidenfeld.

Bourdieu, P. (1973) 'L'opinion public n'existe pas', *Les Temps Modernes*, 29: 1292–309.

Bourdieu, P. (1987) 'The force of law: toward a sociology of the juridical field, *Hastings Law Journal*, 38: 814–53.

Bourdieu, P. and Wacquant, L. (1999) 'On the cunning of imperialist reason', *Theory, Culture and Society*, 16 (1): 41–58.

Bradney, A. (2006) 'The case of Buffy the Vampire Slayer and the politics of legal education', in S. Greenfield and G. Osborn (eds) *Readings in Law and Popular Culture.* London: Routledge.

Brants, C. (1992) 'De persweeën van het recht', *Recht & Kritiek*, 18 (4): 360–75.

Brants, C. (1993) 'Justice done and seen to be done? The institutionalized relationship between the press and the criminal justice system in the Netherlands', *International Criminal Justice Review*, 3: 60–76.

Brants, C. (2001) 'Pers en poldermodel: de verhouding tussen media en justitie in Nederland', *Orde van de Dag: Criminaliteit en Samenleving*, 14: 67–76.

Brants, C. and Brants, K. (2002) 'Vertrouwen en achterdocht: de driehoeksverhouding justitie-media-burger', *Justitiële Verkenningen*, 28: 8–28.

Bridges, L. (1999) 'The Lawrence Inquiry: Incompetence, corruption, and institutional racism', *Journal of Law and Society*, 26 (3): 298–322.

Brown, M. E. (1994) *Soap Opera and Women's Talk.* London: Sage.

Brown, S. (2003) *Crime and Law in Media Culture.* Buckingham: Open University Press.

Burkitt, I. (2004) 'The time and space of everyday life', *Cultural Studies*, 18 (2/3): 211–27.

Cain, M. (1979) 'The general practice lawyer and the client: Towards a radical conception', *International Journal of the Sociology of Law*, 7: 331–54.

Castells, M. (2004a) 'An introduction to the information age', in F. Webster (ed.) *The Information Society Reader.* London: Routledge.

Castells, M. (2004b) 'The information city, the new economy, and the network society', in F. Webster (ed.) *The Information Society Reader.* London: Routledge.

Chaney, D. (2002) *Cultural Change and Everyday Life.* Basingstoke: Palgrave Macmillan.

Chapman, B., Mirrlees-Black, C. and Brawn, C. (2002) *Improving public attitudes to the criminal justice system: The impact of information. Home Office Research Study 245.* London: Home Office.

Chibnall, S. (1977) *Law-and-Order News: An Analysis of Crime Reporting in the British Press.* London: Tavistock.

Civard-Racinais, A. (1997) 'Les journalistes dans la stratégie médiatique des sources d'information judiciaire', *Médiaspouvoirs*, 1: 53–60.

Clancy, A., Aust, R. and Kershaw, C. (2001) *Crime, Policing and Justice: The Experience of Ethnic Minorities Findings from the 2000 British Crime Survey*. London: Home Office Research, Developments and Statistics Directorate.

Clementi, D. (2004) *Report of the Review of the Regulatory Framework for Legal Services in England and Wales*. Available HTTP: <http://www.legal-services-review.org.uk/content/report/index.htm> (accessed 10 March 2007).

Cochard, J.-P. (1995) 'La crise de la justice', *Géopolitique*, 49: 55–59.

Collier, R. (2006) 'Peter's choice: Issues of identity, lifestyle and consumption in changing representations of corporate lawyers and legal academics', in S. Greenfield and G. Osborn (eds) *Readings in Law and Popular Culture*. London: Routledge.

Cooper, D. (1995) 'Local government legal consciousness in the shadow of juridification', *Journal of Law and Society*, 22 (4): 506–26.

Corner, J. (1996) 'Reappraising reception: Aims, concepts and methods', in J. Curran and M. Gurevitch (eds) *Mass Media and Society*. London: Arnold.

Cotterrell, R. (1993) 'Sociological perspectives on legal closure', in A. Norrie (ed.) *Closure or Critique: New Directions in Legal Theory*. Edinburgh: Edinburgh University Press.

Cotterrell, R. (2002) 'Subverting orthodoxy, making law central: A view of socio-legal studies', *Journal of Law and Society*, 29 (4): 632–44.

Couldry, N. (2000) *Inside Culture: Re-imagining the Method of Cultural Studies*. London: Sage.

Couldry, N. (2002) 'Playing for celebrity: Big Brother as ritual event', *Television and New Media*, 3 (3): 283–93.

Couldry, N. (2004) 'Theorising media as practice', *Social Semiotics*, 14 (2): 115–32.

Couldry, N. (2007) *Transvaluing Media Studies: Or, Beyond the Myth of the Mediated Centre*. Available HTTP: <http://www.lse.ac.uk/collections/media@lse/pdf/Couldry_TransvaluingMediaStudies.pdf> (accessed 10 March 2007).

Cowan, D. (2004) 'Legal consciousness: Some observations', *Modern Law Review*, 67 (6): 928–58.

Curran, J. (1996) 'Rethinking mass communications', in J. Curran, D. Morley and V. Walkerdine (eds) *Cultural Studies and Communications*. London: Arnold.

Curran, J. (2002) *Media and Power*. London: Routledge.

Currie, D. (2001) ' "Dear Abby": Advice pages as a site for the operation of power', *Feminist Theory*, 2: 259–81.

de Certeau, M. (1988) *The Practice of Everyday Life*. Berkeley: University of California Press.

de Groot-van Leeuwen, L. E. (2000) 'Criticizing Judges in the Netherlands', in M. K. Addo (ed.) *Freedom of Expression and the Criticism of Judges: A Comparative Study of European Legal Standards*. Aldershot: Ashgate.

de Keijser, J. W. and Elffers, H. (2004) *Het maatschappelijke oordeel van de strafrechter*. Den Haag: Boom Juridische Uitgevers.

de Wijkerslooth, J. L. and Simonis, J. (2002) 'Voorlichters, communicatieadviseurs en media-managers: de etaleurs van de overheid?', *Justitiële Verkenningen*, 28: 52–62.

Deacon, D. (2003) 'Holism, communion and conversion: Integrating media consumption and production research', *Media, Culture & Society*, 25 (2): 209–31.

Dow, J. and Lapuerta, C. (2005) *The Benefits of Multiple Ownership Models in Law Services*. Available HTTP: <http://www.dca.gov.uk/legalsys/dow-lapuerta.pdf> (accessed 10 March 2007).

Dowler, K. (2002) 'Media influence on citizen attitudes toward police effectiveness', *Policing and Society*, 12 (3): 227–38.

Doyle, J. (1997) 'The well-tuned cymbal', in H. Cunningham (ed.) *Fragile Bastion:*

Judicial Independence in the Nineties and Beyond. Judicial Commission of New South Wales.

Edgar, A. (1992) 'Objectivity, bias and truth', in A. Belsey and R. Chadwick (eds) *Ethical Issues in Journalism and the Media.* London: Routledge.

Ehrenreich, B. and English, D. (1979) *For Her Own Good: 150 Years of the Experts' Advice to Women.* Pluto: London.

Engel, D. (1998) 'How does law matter in the constitution of legal consciousness?', in B. G. Garth and A. Sarat (eds) *How does Law matter?* Illinois: Northwestern University Press.

Ericson, R. V., Baranek, P. M. and Chan, J. L. B. (1989) *Negotiating Control: A Study of News Sources.* Milton Keynes: Open University Press.

Esterling, K. M. (1998) 'Public outreach: The cornerstone of judicial independence', *Judicature*, 82 (3): 112–17.

Ewick, P. and Silbey, S. S. (1995) 'Subversive stories and hegemonic tales: Toward a sociology of narrative', *Law & Society Review*, 29 (2): 197–226.

Ewick, P. and Silbey, S. S. (1998) *The Common Place of Law: Stories from Everyday Life.* Chicago: University of Chicago Press.

Fairclough, K. (2004) 'Women's work? *Wife Swap* and the reality problem', *Feminist Media Studies*, 4 (3): 344–47.

Falconer, L. (2006) *The role of Judges in a Modern Democracy.* Available HTTP: <http://www.dca.gov.uk/speeches/2006/sp060913.htm> (accessed 24 October 2006).

Featherstone, M. (1992) 'The heroic life and everyday life', *Theory, Culture & Society*, 9 (1): 159–82.

Feilzer, M. and Young, R. (2006) *'Crime Scene' Oxford: The impact of a factual newspaper column on readers of a local newspaper.* Final Report to the Nuffield Foundation.

Felski, R. (1999) 'The invention of everyday life', *New Formations*, 39: 15–31.

Fiske, J. (1984) *Media Matters: Everyday Culture and Political Change.* Minneapolis: Minneapolis University Press.

Fiske, J. (1990) *Introduction to Communication Studies.* London: Routledge (2nd edition).

Fiske, J. (1992) 'Cultural studies and the culture of everyday life', in L. Grossberg, C. Nelson and P. Treichler (eds) *Cultural Studies.* London: Routledge.

Forrest, N. (2003) *Wife Swap.* Available HTTP: <http://www.thefword.org.uk/reviews/2003/02/wife_swap> (accessed 1 June 2006).

Francis, A. (2004) 'Out of touch and out of time: lawyers, their leaders and collective mobility within the profession', *Legal Studies*, 24 (3): 322–48.

Franklin, B. (1994) *Packaging Politics: Political Communications in Britain's Media Democracy.* London: Arnold.

Friedman, L. (1994) *The Republic of Choice: Law, Authority and Culture.* Cambridge, MA: Harvard University Press.

Friedman, L. M. (1989) 'Law, lawyers and popular culture', *Yale Law Journal*, 98 (8): 1579–606.

Gamson, W. A. and Modigliani, A. (1989) 'Media discourse and public opinion on nuclear power: A constructionist approach', *American Journal of Sociology*, 95 (1): 1–37.

Gandy, O. H. (1982) *Beyond Agenda Setting: Information Subsidies and Public Policy.* Norwood: N. J. Ablex.

Garapon, A. (1996) 'Justice out of court: The dangers of trial by media', in D. Nelken (ed.) *Law as Communication.* Aldershot: Dartmouth.

Gardiner, M. E. (2000) *Critiques of Everyday Life.* London: Routledge.

Gauntlett, D. (1995) *Moving Experiences.* London: John Libbey.

Genn, H. (1999) *Paths to Justice: What People Do and Think about Going to Law*. Oxford: Hart Publishing.

Geraghty, C. (1991) *Women and Soap Opera*. Oxford: Polity.

Gerbner, G. (1996) 'The hidden side of television viewing', in G. Gerbner, H. Mowlana and H. I. Schiller (eds) *Invisible Crises: What Conglomerate Control of the Media Means for America and the World*. Oxford: Westview Press.

Gerbner, G. and Gross, L. (1976) 'The scary world of TV's heavy viewer', *Psychology Today*, April: 89–91.

Giddens, A. (1990) *The Consequences of Modernity*. Cambridge: Polity.

Giddens, A. (1991) *Modernity and Self-Identity: Self and Society in Late Modern Age*. Cambridge: Polity.

Giddings, J. and Robertson, M. (2003) 'Large-scale map or A-Z? The place of self-help services in Legal Aid', *Journal of Law and Society*, 30 (1): 102–19.

Gies, L. (2003a) 'Explaining the absence of the media in stories of law and legal consciousness', *Entertainment Law*, 2 (1): 19–54.

Gies, L. (2003b) 'Up, close and personal: The discursive transformation of judicial politics in post-Dutroux Belgium', *International Journal for the Semiotics of Law*, 16: 49–74.

Glasgow University Media Group (1976) *Bad News*, vol. 1. London: Routledge.

Goffman, E. (1959) *The Presentation of Self in Everyday Life*. London: Penguin.

Goffman, E. (1963) *Behavior in Public Places*. New York: Free Press.

Golding, P. and Murdock, M. (1996) 'Culture, communications, and political economy', in J. Curran and M. Gurevitch (eds) *Mass Media and Society*. London: Arnold.

Goodrich, P. (1990) *Languages of Law: From Logics of Memory to Nomadic Masks*. London: Weidenfeld and Nicolson.

Gordon, A. D., Kittros, J. M. with Merrill, J. C. and Reuss, C. (1999) *Controversies in Media Ethics*. New York: Longman (2nd edition).

Graber, D. (2003) 'The media and democracy: Beyond myths and stereotypes', *Annual Review of Political Science*, 6: 139–60.

Gray, A. (1999) 'Audience and reception research in retrospect: The trouble with audiences', in P. Alasuutari (ed.) *Rethinking the Media Audience: The New Agenda*. London: Sage.

Gray, A. (2003) *Research Practice for Cultural Studies: Ethnographic Methods and Lived Cultures*. London: Sage.

Greenfield, S., Osborn, G. and Robson, P. (2001) *Film and the Law*. London: Cavendish.

Griffen-Foley, B. (2004) 'From *Tit-Bits* to *Big Brother*: A century of audience participation in the media', *Media, Culture & Society*, 26 (4): 533–48.

Groenhuijsen, M. S. (1997) 'Openbaarheid en publiciteit in strafzaken', *Delikt en Delinkwent*, 27 (5): 417–22.

Gross, H. and Pattison, H. (2001) 'Pregnancy and working: A critical reading of advice and information on pregnancy and employment', *Feminism and Psychology*, 11: 511–25.

Grossman, L. (2006) 'Time's person of the year: You', *Time Magazine*, December. Available HTTP: <http://www.time.com/time/magazine/article/0,9171,1569514,00.html> (accessed 9 January 2007).

Habermas, J. (1984) *Theory of Communicative Action, vol. 1*. Cambridge: Polity.

Habermas, J. (1986) 'Law as medium and law as institution', in G. Teubner (ed.) *Dilemmas of Law in the Welfare State*. Berlin: Walter de Gruyter.

Habermas, J. (1992) *The Structural Transformation of the Public Sphere: An Inquiry into a Category of Bourgeois Society*. Cambridge: Polity.

Hall, S. (1980) 'Encoding/decoding', in S. Hall, D. Hobson, A. Lowe and P. Willis (eds) *Culture, Media, Language*. London: Hutchinson.

Hall, S., Critcher, C., Jefferson, T., Clarke, J. and Robert, B. (1978) *Policing the Crisis: Mugging, the State and Law-and-Order*. Basingstoke: Macmillan.

Haltom, W. and McCann, M. (2004) *Distorting the Law: Politics, Media, and the Litigation Crisis*. Chicago: University of Chicago Press.

Hancock, P. and Tyler, M. (2004) ' "MOT your life": Critical management studies and the management of everyday life', *Human Relations*, 57 (5): 619–45.

Hanlon, G. (1999) *Lawyers, the State and the Market: Professionalism Revisited*. Basingstoke: Macmillan.

Hardey, M. (2002) 'Life beyond the screen: embodiment and identity through the Internet', *Sociological Review*, 50 (4): 570–85.

Harrison, M. (1985) *TV News Whose Bias? A Casebook Analysis of Strikes, Television and Media Studies*. Hermitage: Policy Journals.

Harshman, E. M., Gilsinan, J. F., Fisher, J. E. and Yeager, F. C. (2005) 'Professional ethics in a virtual world: The impact of the Internet on traditional notions of professionalism', *Journal of Business Ethics*, 58: 227–36.

Heins, M. and Bertin, J. E. (2003) 'The St. Louis Court brief: Debating audience "effects" in public', *P@rticipations*, 1: 1. Available HTTP: <http://www.participations. org/volume%201/issue%201/1_01_contents.htm> (accessed 10 March 2007).

Hermes, J. (1995) *Reading Women's Magazines*. Cambridge: Polity.

Highmore, B. (2002) *Everyday Life and Cultural Theory*. London: Routledge.

Hill, A. (2000) 'Crime and crisis: British reality TV in action', in E. Buscombe (ed.) *British Television: A Reader*. Oxford: Clarendon Press.

Hill, A. (2004) *Reality TV: Audiences and Popular Factual Television*. London: Routledge.

Hillyard, P. (2002) 'Invoking indignation: Reflections on future directions of socio-legal studies', *Journal of Law and Society*, 29 (4): 645–56.

Hirsch, S. F. (1992) 'Subjects in spite of themselves: Legal consciousness among working-class New Englanders', *Law and Social Inquiry*, 17 (4): 839–57.

Hodgson, J. (2001) 'The police, the prosecutor and the juge d'instruction', *British Journal of Criminology*, 41: 342–61.

Holmes, S. and Jermyn, D. (2004) 'Introduction: understanding Reality TV', in S. Holmes and D. Jermyn (eds) *Understanding Reality Television*. London: Routledge.

Jansson, A. (2001) *Image Culture: Media, Consumption and Everyday Life in Reflexive Modernity*. Göteborg: JMG.

Jenkins, H. (1992) *Textual Poachers: Television Fans and Participatory Culture*. London: Routledge.

Jermyn, D. (2004) ' "This is about real people!": Video technologies, actuality and affect in the television crime appeal', in S. Holmes and D. Jermyn (eds) *Understanding Reality Television*. London: Routledge.

Jewkes, Y. (2004) *Media and Crime*. London: Sage.

Judge, L. J. (2004) *Keynote Speech 'Law for Journalists' Conference*. Available HTTP: <http://www.judiciary.gov.uk/publications_media/speeches/2004/ljj261104.htm> (accessed 10 March 2007).

Karpin, I. (2002) 'She's watching the judges: Media feedback loops and what judges notice', in M. Thornton (ed.) *Romancing the Tomes: Popular Culture, Law and Feminism*. London: Cavendish.

Kellner, D. (2003) *Media Spectacle*. London: Routledge.

King, M. (1993) 'The "truth" about autopoiesis', *Journal of Law and Society*, 20 (2): 218–36.

King, M. and Piper, C. (1995) *How the Law Thinks about Children*. Aldershot: Arena.
King, M. and Thornhill, C. (2003a) *Niklas Luhmann's Theory of Politics and Law*. Basingstoke: Palgrave.
King, M. and Thornhill, C. (2003b) ' "Will the real Niklas Luhmann stand up, please". A reply to John Mingers', *The Sociological Review*, 51(2): 277–85.
Kirby, M. (1998) 'Attacks on judges a universal phenomenon', *Judicature*, 81: 238–43.
Koskela, H. (2004) 'Webcams, TV shows and mobile phones: Empowering exhibitionism', *Surveillance and Society*, 2 (2/3): 199–215.
Lambert, S. (2005) 'Uptight about Wife Swap parents', *Guardian* 7 March.
Lanctot, C. (1999) 'Attorney–client relationships in cyberspace: The peril and the promise', *Duke Law Journal*, 49: 147–259.
Langbauer, L. (1992) 'Cultural studies and the politics of the everyday', *Diacritics*, 22 (1): 47–65.
Lee, H. (2006) 'Privacy, publicity, and accountability of self-presentation in an on-line discussion group', *Sociological Inquiry*, 76 (1): 1–22.
Lefebvre, H. (1984) *Everyday Life in the Modern World*. New Brunswick: Transaction Publishers.
Legal Services Commission (2001) *The Quality Mark Standard for Websites*. London: Legal Services Commission.
Leman, J. (1980) ' "The advice of a real friend" Codes of intimacy and oppression in women's magazines 1937–1955', *Women Studies International Quarterly*, 3: 63–78.
Lichtenberg, J. (1990) 'Foundations and limits of freedom of the press', in J. Lichtenberg (ed.) *Democracy and the Mass Media: A Collection of Essays*. Cambridge: Cambridge University Press.
Liebes, T. and Katz, E. (1993) *The Export of Meaning: Cross-Cultural Readings of Dallas*. Cambridge: Polity (2nd edition).
Lijphart, A. (1968) *The Politics of Accommodation: Pluralism and Democracy in the Netherlands*. Berkeley: University of California Press.
Lijphart, A. (1989) 'From politics of accommodation to adversarial politics in the Netherlands: A reassessment', in H. Daalder and G. A. Irwin (eds) *Politics in the Netherlands: How Much Change?* London: Cass.
Livingstone, S. (1996) 'On the continuing problem of media effects', in J. Curran and M. Gurevitch (eds) *Mass Media and Society*. London: Arnold (2nd edition).
Livingstone, S. (2003) 'The changing nature of audiences: From the mass audience to the interactive media user', in A. Valdivia (ed.) *Companion to Media Studies*. Oxford: Blackwell. Available HTTP: <http://eprints.lse.ac.uk/archive/00000417/01/Chapter_in_Valdivia_Blackwell_volume_2003.pdf> (accessed 10 March 2007).
Livingstone, Sonia (1999) 'New media, new audiences?', *New media and society*, 1 (1): 59–66. Available HTTP: <http://eprints.lse.ac.uk/archive/00000391/> (accessed 10 March 2007).
Lloyd Platt, V. (2001) *Secrets of Relationships Success*. London: Vermilion.
Luhmann, N. (1985) *A Sociological Theory of Law*. London: Routledge.
Luhmann, N. (2000) *The Reality of the Mass Media*. Cambridge: Polity.
Macaulay, S. (1987) 'Images of law in everyday life: The lessons of school, entertainment and spectator sports', *Law & Society Review*, 21 (2): 185–218.
Machura, S. (2004) 'Procedural fairness in real and film trials: Why do audiences understand stories placed in foreign legal systems?', *Current Legal Issues* 7: 148–59.
Machura, S. and Ulbrich, S. (2001) 'Law in film: Globalizing the Hollywood courtroom drama', *Journal of Law and Society*, 28 (1): 117–32.
MacKinnon, C. A. (1995) Reflections on law in the everyday life of women', in A. Sarat and T. R. Kearns (eds) *Law in Everyday Life*. Ann Arbor: University of Michigan Press.

Malleson, K. (1999) *The New Judiciary: The Effects of Expansion and Activism*. Aldershot: Ashgate.

Malsch, M. (2004) 'Persvoorlichting en rechtbankverslaggeving', *Rechtstreeks*, 2: 35–71.

Malsch, M. and Hoekstra, R. (1999) 'De publieke tribune: controlemiddel voor de rechtspraak of opvangruimte voor daklozen?', *Delikt & Delinkwent*, 29 (8): 737–54.

Mason, P. (2000) 'Watching the invisible: Television portrayal of the British prison 1980–1990', *International Journal of the Sociology of Law*, 28: 33–44.

Mawby, R. (1999) 'Visibility, transparency and the police media relations', *Policing and Society*, 9: 263–86.

McGuigan, J. (1992) *Cultural Populism*. London: Routledge.

McNair, B. (1998) *The Sociology of Journalism*. London: Arnold.

McNair, B. (2000) *Journalism and Democracy: An Evaluation of the Political Public Sphere*. London: Routledge.

McQuail, D. (1992) *Media Performance: Mass Communication and the Public Interest*. London: Sage.

McQuail, D. (2000) *McQuail's Mass Communication Theory*. London: Sage (4th edition).

McRobbie, A. (1991) *Feminism and Youth Culture: From Jackie to Just Seventeen*. London: Macmillan.

Mendible, M. (2004) 'Humiliation, Subjectivity and Reality TV', *Feminist Media Studies*, 4 (3): 335–38.

Merry, S. E. (1986), 'Everyday understandings of law in working-class America', *American Ethnologist*, 13: 253–70.

Mickiewicz, E. (2000) 'Institutional incapacity, the attentive public, and media pluralism in Russia', in R. Gunther and A. Mugan (eds) *Democracy and the Media: A Comparative Perspective*. Cambridge: Cambridge University Press.

Milovanovic, D. (1989) *Weberian and Marxian Analysis of Law*. Aldershot: Avebury.

Milovanovic, D. (1992) *Postmodern Law and Disorder: Psychoanalytic Semiotics, Chaos and Juridic Exegeses*. Liverpool: Deborah Charles Publications.

Mingers, J. (2002) 'Can social systems be autopoietic? Assessing Luhmann's social theory', *The Sociological Review*, 50 (2): 278–99.

Moores, S. (2000) *Media and Everyday Life in Modern Society*. Edinburgh: Edinburgh University Press.

Moores, S. (2004) 'The doubling of space: Electronic media, time–space arrangements and social relationships', in N. Couldry and A. McCarthy (eds) *Mediaspace: Place, Scale and Culture in a Media Age*. London: Routledge.

Moorhead, R. and Pleasence, P. (2003) 'Access to justice after universalism: An introduction', *Journal of Law and Society*, 30 (1): 1–10.

Morley, D. (1980) *The 'Nationwide' Audience: Structure and Decoding*. London: BFI.

Morley, D. (1992) *Television, Audiences and Cultural Studies*. London: Routledge.

Morley, D. (1996) 'Populism, revisionism, and the "new" audience research', in J. Curran, D. Morley and V. Walkerdine (eds) *Cultural Studies and Communications*. London: Arnold.

Moses, L. J. (2006) *The Mask and the Judge*. Available HTTP: <http://www.judiciary.gov.uk/publications_media/speeches/2006/index.htm> (accessed 10 March 2007).

Mountain, D. (2001) 'Could new technologies cause great law firms to fail?', *Journal of Information, Law and Technology (JILT)*. Available HTTP: <http://elj.warwick.ac.uk/jilt/01–1/mountain.html> (accessed 17 January 2007).

Munro, C. R. (1999) *Studies in Constitutional Law*. London: Butterworths (2nd edition).

Netherlands Helsinki Committee (2004) *Strengthening the Legal Culture in Croatia: Improvement of the Relations between the Judiciary and the Media*, Second Progress Report.

Nielsen, L. B. (2000) 'Situating legal consciousness: Experiences and attitudes of ordinary citizens about law and street harassment', *Law & Society Review*, 34 (4): 1055–90.

Nobles, R. and Schiff, D. (2000) *Understanding Miscarriages of Justice: Law, the Media, and the Inevitability of Crisis*. Oxford: Oxford University Press.

Nobles, R. and Schiff, D. (2004) 'A story of miscarriage: Law in the media', *Journal of Law and Society*, 31 (2): 221–44.

O'Connell, M., Invernizzi, F. and Fuller, R. (1998) 'Newspaper readership and the perception of crime: Testing an assumed relationship through a triangulation of methods', *Legal and Criminal Psychology*, 3: 29–57.

Ogbondah, C. W. (2002) 'Media laws in political transition', in F. Hyden, M. Leslie and F. F. Ogundimu (eds) *Media and Democracy in Africa*. Uppsala: Nordiska Afrikainstitutet.

Orgad, S. (2004) 'Help yourself: The World Wide Web as a self-help agora', in D. Gauntlett and R. Horsley (eds) *WebStudies: Rewiring Media Studies for the Digital Age*. London: Arnold (2nd edition).

Palmer, S. (2006) *Toxic Childhood: How The Modern World Is Damaging Our Children And What We Can Do About It*. London: Orion Press.

Parr, H. (2002) 'New body-geographies: the embodied spaces of health and medical information on the Internet', *Environment and Planning D: Society and Space*, 20: 73–95.

Pateman, C. (1988) *The Sexual Contract*. Cambridge: Polity.

Pauly, J. J. (1999) 'Journalism and the sociology of public life', in T. L. Glasser (ed.) *The Idea of Public Journalism*. London: Guildford Press.

Pauwels, L. (2005) 'Websites as visual and multinodal cultural expressions: opportunities and issues of online hybrid media research', *Media, Culture & Society*, 27 (4): 604–13.

Petley, J. (2001) 'Us and them' in M. Barker and J. Petley (eds) *Ill Effects: The Media/ Violence Debate*. London: Routledge (2nd edition).

Phillips, LCJ (2006a) 'Foreword', Annual Report 2005/06 Sentencing Guidelines Council Sentencing Advisory Panel.

Phillips, LCJ (2007a) *Issues in Criminal Justice: Murder*. Available HTTP: <http://www.judiciary.gov.uk/publications_media/index.htm> (accessed 10 March 2007).

Phillips, LCJ (2006b) *Speech given at the Lord Mayor's dinner for judges*. Available HTTP: <http://www.judiciary.gov.uk/publications_media/speeches/2006/sp180706.htm> (accessed 10 March 2007).

Phillips, LCJ (2007b) *The Role of the Judge*. Available HTTP: <http://www.judiciary.gov.uk/publications_media/speeches/index.htm> (accessed 10 March 2007).

Philo, G. and Miller, D. (1997) *Cultural Compliance Dead Ends of Media/Cultural Studies and Social Science*. Glasgow: Glasgow Media Group.

Pleasence, P., Genn, H., Balmer, N. J., Buck, A. and O'Grady, A. (2003) 'Causes of action: First findings of the LSRC periodic survey', *Journal of Law and Society*, 30 (1): 11–30.

Poster, M. (2004) 'Consumption and digital commodities in the everyday', *Cultural Studies*, 18 (2/3): 409–23.

Postman, N. (1982) *The Disappearance of Childhood*. London: W. H. Allen.

Postman, N. (1986) *Amusing Ourselves to Death: Public Discourse in the Age of Show Business*. London: Methuen.

Přibáň, J. (2002) 'Sharing the paradigms? Critical legal studies and the sociology of law', in R. Banakar and M. Travers (eds) *An Introduction to Law and Social Theory*. Oxford: Hart Publishing.

Radway, J. (1984) *Reading the Romance*. Chapel Hill NC: University of North Carolina Press.

Redhead, S. (1995) *Unpopular Cultures: The Birth of Law and Popular Culture*. Manchester: Manchester University Press.

Robson, P. (2004) 'Law and film studies: Autonomy and theory', *Current Legal Issues*, 7: 21–46.

Sarat, A. (1990) 'The law is all over: Power, resistance and the legal consciousness of the welfare poor', *Yale Journal of Law and Humanities*, 2: 343–79.

Sarat, A. and Kearns, T. R. (1995a), 'Beyond the great divide: Forms of legal scholarship and everyday life', in A. Sarat and T. R. Kearns (eds) *Law in Everyday Life*. Ann Arbor: University of Michigan Press.

Sarat, A. and Kearns, T. R. (1995b), 'Editorial introduction', in A. Sarat and T. R. Kearns (eds) *Law in Everyday Life*. Ann Arbor: University of Michigan Press.

Sarat, A. and Simon, J. (2003) 'Cultural analysis, cultural studies, and the situation of legal scholarship', in A. Sarat and J. Simon (eds) *Cultural Analysis, Cultural Studies and the Law: Moving Beyond Legal Realism*. London: Duke University Press.

Sasson, T. (1995) *Crime Talk: How Citizens Construct a Social Problem*. New York: Aldine de Gruyter.

Scannell, P. (1996) *Radio. Television and Modern Life: A Phenomenological Approach*. Oxford: Blackwell Publishers.

Schlesinger, P. and Tumber, H. (1994) *Reporting Crime: The Media Politics of Criminal Justice*. Oxford: Clarendon Press.

Schoenbach, K. (2001) 'Myths of media and audiences', *European Journal of Communication*, 16 (3): 361–76.

Schrøder, K. C. (1999) 'The best of both worlds? Media audience research between rival paradigms', in P. Alasuutari (ed.) *Rethinking the Media Audience*. London: Sage.

Schrøder, K. C. (2000) 'Making sense of audience discourses', *European Journal of Cultural Studies*, 3 (2): 233–58.

Schudson, M. (2002) 'The news media as political institutions', *Annual Review of Political Science*, 5: 249–69.

Seale, C. (2002) *Media & Health*. London: Sage.

Seigworth, G. J. and Gardiner, M. E. (2004) 'Rethinking everyday life: And then nothing turns itself inside out', *Cultural Studies*, 18 (2/3): 139–59.

Severgnini, B. (2005) *La Testa degli Italiani: Una Visita Guidata*. Rome: Rizzoli.

Sherwin, R. K. (2000) *When Law Goes Pop: The Vanishing Lines Between Law and Popular Culture*. Chicago: University of Chicago Press.

Silbey, J. (2001) 'Patterns of courtroom justice', *Journal of Law and Society*, 28 (1): 97–116.

Silverstone, R. (1994) *Television and Everyday Life*. London: Routledge.

Silverstone, R. (1999) *Why Study the Media?* London: Sage.

Simpson, B. (2005) 'Identity manipulation in cyberspace as a leisure option: Play and the exploration of self', *Information and Communications Technology Law*, 14 (2): 115–31.

Sparks, R. (1992) *Television and the Drama of Crime: Moral Tales and the Place of Crime in Public Life*. Buckingham: Open University Press.

Stachenfeld, A. J. and Nicholson, C. M. (1996) 'Blurred boundaries: An analysis of the close relationship between popular culture and the practice of law', *University of San Francisco Law Review*, 30 (4): 903–16.

Stevenson, N. (1995) *Understanding Media Cultures: Social Theory and Mass Communication*. London: Sage.

Stevenson, N., Jackson, P. and Brooks, K. (2000) 'The politics of "new" men's lifestyle magazines', *European Journal of Cultural Studies*, 3 (3): 366–85.

Street, J. (2001) *Mass Media, Politics and Democracy*. Basingstoke: Palgrave Macmillan.

Surette, R. (1998) 'Prologue: Some unpopular thoughts about popular culture', in F. Y. Bailey and D. C. Hale (eds) *Popular Culture, Crime and Justice*. London: West/Wadsworth Publishing.

Susskind, R. (1996) *The Future of Law: Facing the Challenges of Information Technology*. Oxford: Clarendon Press.

Sutter, G. (2000) ' "Nothing new under the sun": Old fears and new media', *International Journal of Law and Information Technology*, 8 (3): 338–78.

Thomassen, J. J. A. and van Deth, J. W. (1989) 'How new is Dutch politics?', in H. Daalder and G. A. Irwin (eds) *Politics in the Netherlands: How Much Change?* London: Cass.

Thompson, J. B. (1995) *The Media and Modernity: A Social Theory of the Media*. Cambridge: Polity.

Thornton, M. (2002) 'Law and popular culture: Engendering legal vertigo', in M. Thornton (ed.) *Romancing the Tomes: Popular Culture, Law and Feminism*. London: Cavendish.

Threadgold, T. (2002) 'Lawyers reading law/lore as popular culture: Conflicting paradigms of representation', in M. Thornton (ed.) *Romancing the Tomes: Popular Culture, Law and Feminism*. London: Cavendish

Tincknell, E. and Raghuram, P. (2004) '*Big Brother*: Reconfiguring the "active" audience of cultural studies?', in S. Holmes and D. Jermyn (eds) *Understanding Reality Television*. London: Routledge.

Trubek, D. M. (1984) 'Where the action is: Critical legal studies and empiricism', *Stanford Law Review*, 36: 575–622.

van de Pol, U. (1986) *Openbaar Terecht: Onderzoek van het Openbaarheidsbeginsel in de Strafrechtspleging*. Arnhem: Gouda Quint.

Van Zoonen, L. (1994) *Feminist Media Studies*. London: Sage.

Van Zoonen, L. (2001) 'Desire and resistance: *Big Brother* and the recognition of everyday life', *Media, Culture & Society*, 23 (5): 669–77.

Varney, M. (2004) 'European controls on Member State promotion and regulation of public service broadcasting and broadcasting standards', *European Public Law*, 10 (3): 503–30.

Vine, I. (1997) 'The dangerous psycho-logic of media "effects" ', in M. Barker and J. Petley (eds) *Ill Effects: The Media/Violence debate*. London: Routledge.

Wall, LJ (2006) *Opening up the Family Courts: A Personal View*. Available HTTP: <http://www.judiciary.gov.uk/publications_media/speeches/2006/index.htm> (accessed 10 March 2007).

Weber, M. (1954) *Max Weber on Law in Economy and Society*, M. Rheinstein (ed.). Cambridge, MA: Harvard University Press.

Webster, F. (2004) 'Cultural studies and sociology at, and after, the closure of the Birmingham School', *Cultural Studies*, 18 (6): 847–62.

Widdison, R. (2003) 'Electronic Paths to Justice', *Journal of Information, Law and Technology (JILT)*. Available HTTP: <http://www2.warwick.ac.uk/fac/soc/law/elj/jilt/2003_2/widdison/> (accessed 10 March 2007).

Williams, R. (1974) *Television: Technology and Cultural Form*. London: Fontana.

Winship, J. (1987) *Inside Women's Magazines*. London: Pandora.

Winship, J. (1992) 'The impossibility of *Best*: Enterprise meets domesticity in the practical women's magazines of the 1980s', in D. Strinati and S. Wagg (eds) *Come On Down?: Popular Media Culture*. London: Routledge.

Woodhouse, D. (2004) 'The constitutional and political implications of a United Kingdom Supreme Court', *Legal Studies*, 24 (1/2): 134–55.

Woolf, LCJ (2003) *Should the Media and the Judiciary be on Speaking Terms?* Available HTTP: <http://www.judiciary.gov.uk/publications_media/speeches/pre_2004/lcj221003.htm> (accessed 10 March 2007).

Yngvesson, B. (1989) 'Inventing law in local settings: Rethinking popular legal culture', *Yale Law Journal*, 98 (8): 1689–708.

Yuval-Davis, Y. (1999) 'Institutional racism, cultural diversity and citizenship: Some reflections on reading the Stephen Lawrence Inquiry report', *Sociological Research Online* 12. Available HTTP: <http://ideas.repec.org/a/sro/srosro/1999–17–1.html> (accessed 10 March 2007).

Ziegert, K. A. (2002) 'The thick description of law: An introduction to Niklas Luhmann's theory', in R. Banakar and M. Travers (eds) *An Introduction to Law and Social Theory*. Oxford: Hart Publishing.

Index